WINNING

A Training and Showing Guide for Hunter Seat Riders

WINNING

A Training and Showing Guide for Hunter Seat Riders

by

ANNA JANE WHITE-MULLIN

Photography by A.O. White, Jr.
Computer Art by Cathia Mooney Strickland

Trafalgar Square Publishing

NORTH POMFRET, VERMONT

Published by Trafalgar Square Publishing
North Pomfret, Vermont 05053

Library of Congress Cataloging-in-Publication Data
White-Mullin, Anna Jane

    Winning: a training and showing guide for hunter seat riders / by
Anna Jane White-Mullin : photography by A.O. White, Jr. : computer art by Cathia Mooney
Strickland.
     p.   cm.
    Includes index.
    ISBN 0-9443955-51-3 (Hardcover) : $24.95
    1. Hunter classes. 2. Hunter seat equitation division. 3. Hunter seat equitation.
4. Hunter (Horses) — Training. I. Title.
SF296.H86W47 1992
708.2'4 — dc20   91-30951
                                                          CIP

ISBN: 0-943955-51-3
Printed in the United States of America
10 9 8 7 6   5 4 3 2 1

Designed by Mark Gabor

Acknowledgments

Special thanks to those who read portions of the text and offered their valuable opinions:

George Morris (flatwork)
Bertalan de Nemethy (gymnastics)
Christina Schlusemeyer (pony distances)
Major General J. R. Burton (dressage movements)
Dr. Webb Sledge (nutrition)

And to those who contributed to the making of this book in other ways:

Dr. Ron Blackwell
Fiona Baan
Cathy Cawthon
Nancy Lee Comer
Leo Conroy
Charles Dennehy, Jr.
Kathy Fallon
Joe Fargis
Charlotte Fitz
Gabor Foltenyi
Mark Gabor
Julie Gibbs
Steve Hawkins
Frank Helderman, Jr.

Conrad Homfeld
Madelyn Larsen
Maryanne and Alican Majerik
Eva Marie Morris
Sam Register
Caroline Robbins
John Rush, III
Julie Saye
Christine Jones Tauber
Greg Thompson
Marty Tyndal
Arlene K. Walters
Peter Winants

My deepest thanks to my family for thoroughly supporting me during this lengthy project. I am especially grateful to my husband, Neil, for his loving attention to our two small children during evenings and on weekends for the past two years so that I could work on the book. I am also appreciative of my father's extraordinary efforts in helping me with the photography at several locations, as well as for his financial support.

There have also been friends who have contributed in significant ways, including Dr. Robert Watkins, who did the initial editing of the book and lent his dark bay horse "Just Jackson" for the project; Fran Dilworth, who proofread the final version of the manuscript and who lent her chestnut horse "Nicholas," as well as assisting in the photography sessions at her farm; Barbara and Jenny Macon, who took time in the midst of an exhausting show schedule to help me photograph two horses; and Shelia Ellison and Barbara White, who moved fences in weather well over 100 degrees in preparation for one of the photographic shoots.

I hope you find this book to be a worthy reflection of our combined efforts.

Contents

With Love
I Dedicate This Book
to

George H. Morris

For Setting Such a Fine Example
As a Horseman, Teacher, Writer and Friend

Foreword

In a day and age when the horse business is growing in numbers, expense, and hectic pace, it is not easy to find the time for other things. Anna Jane White-Mullin has managed admirably to write a second book. Her first book was *Judging Hunters and Hunter Seat Equitation* and now her latest book *Winning: A Training and Showing Guide For Hunter Seat Riders* must be added to her accomplishments. I feel that they are both great books as well as much needed contributions to our horse community. Anna has a wonderful background in the horse business, having grown up with horses, going on to pursue competition on a national level, and then becoming an AHSA recognized judge. All of this thorough background has given her the necessary experience to write a book on training and instructing.

Being a teacher and trainer myself, I would want to have this book in my own horse library. I think it is very important for riders and trainers to look for new ways to keep their approach fresh and interesting. Anna has provided a unique tool to assist us all in keeping our systems innovative. Even a quick glance at the text, photos, and diagrams shows you that she has not allowed herself to fall victim to the same syndrome to which many of her peers have succumbed — becoming overly systematic and redundant.

Anna has been a friend and fellow professional to many of the leading horsemen in our country. I personally appreciate knowing her as a friend. I also respect her for writing this new book. Through her wonderful writing, I hope you, too, can get to know her.

Frank I. Madden
One of America's leading train-ers of hunters, jumpers, and equi-tation riders

Author's Note

Throughout the text, italicized words indicate that a definition is included at that point. A glossary is also provided in the back of the book. It includes definitions of both the italicized words and any equestrian idioms which appear in quotation marks within the text.

1

The Elements of Flatwork

Flatwork: The Cutting Edge of Success

Flatwork is the adaptation of the schooling movements and principles of dressage to the needs of hunters, equitation horses, and jumpers. While dressage encompasses difficult maneuvers such as the passage and piaffe, in which the horse's steps have a tremendous amount of suspension, these movements have no reasonable application for horses being shown in the hunter, jumper, or equitation divisions. For this reason, hunter seat riders must choose the dressage exercises which are the most beneficial and disregard those that are not helpful in achieving their goals.

In the discussion of flatwork, some terminology may be unfamiliar to you, so I will begin with a brief description of important terms. The basic elements of flatwork are pace, bending, and transitions. *Pace* is the speed at which a horse travels in each gait. *Bending* refers to the horse's body being positioned on a curve to either the left or right. *Transitions* are the brief periods of change between one gait and another and are categorized as either *upward transitions* , which are changes to a faster gait, or *downward transitions* , which are changes to a slower gait.

Advanced concepts of flatwork are impulsion, collection, and lengthening. *Impulsion* is the degree of thrust, or power, a horse has as it moves. *Collection* is the increased engagement of the horse's quarters for the benefit of lightness and mobility in the forehand. *Lengthening* is the forward swing of the horse's limbs in free and moderately extended steps, demonstrating impulsion from the hindquarters.

Although the word "flatwork" has been used in the United States for decades, prior to the 1960's it referred only to the most basic training exercises that would enable the rider to start, stop, turn, and regulate the pace of his horse. When I was a child riding in the early 1960's, only a few coaches talked about bending, and anyone who suggested the use of collection for a hunter became the center of controversy. Critics believed that collecting the animal would be detrimental to the natural beauty of its way of moving and would make the horse more excitable, while advocates of collection found that it provided greater and more subtle control of the horse. The debate finally waned when riders who practiced the more advanced concepts of flatwork were regularly winning, not only in the equitation and jumper divisions, but also in the hunter division.

By 1970, bending had become well established as a necessity in the show ring, and collection was generally recognized as part of the training regimen for equitation horses, jumpers, and hunters. When it became apparent that more collection was needed to perform precision work in the equitation division than to accomplish the basic tasks of the hunter division, some riders chose to use different horses for each. The horse that tends to be an "equitation type" has natural elevation in its forehand because of its conformation, a medium length of stride that normally covers about 12 feet but can be readily extended to 13 feet, a fairly flat jumping style, smooth-riding gaits, and an absolutely calm temperament. These elements make it easier for the rider to perform precision movements on the flat, control the horse within the lines of a complicated course, and stay in a fixed position over fences and on the flat. In contrast, an exceedingly long natural stride, a keen temperament, a powerful thrust over the fences, or gaits that are bumpy to sit on make it difficult for a rider to be competitive in the equitation division.

Of course, the ideal horse can do it all. One that has a medium-length flowing stride, good jumping form, a quiet temperament, and naturally good balance can make the adjustments necessary to be successful in both divisions. Throughout the book, however, I will refer to "hunters" and "equitation horses" separately, not only as acknowledgment that some riders continue to use different horses for each division, but also to clarify which exercises are appropriate for a horse according to the division in which it competes.

The 1980's further stressed the importance of flatwork, and this emphasis has continued to increase to the present. Now, a rider simply isn't going to get a ribbon on the flat or over fences in the equitation division at a large show unless he has a strong background on the flat. The tougher the competition, the more precise flatwork is required. Medal, Maclay, and USET classes all require it, and it is often the deciding factor in placing the riders.

I have heard riders say that they were not interested in the equitation division because they did not enjoy flatwork. However, when you look at who ends up each year with the Horse of the Year Awards in the various hunter divisions or examine the list of the top jumper riders in the country, it will not take long to realize that a rider who is poor in flatwork generally can't keep up in any division with those who do it well.

Work on the flat can be physically difficult, confusing, and frustrating to learn. This is because good flatwork requires precise coordination of your legs, hands, and weight. Once you are proficient on the flat, however, daily exercises will be enjoyable and fulfilling as your horse progresses. You will then view flatwork as a logical process which enhances the horse's abilities and minimizes its weaknesses, allowing your animal to be the best athlete it can be. Best of all, you will no longer consider flatwork boring, but appreciate it for what it is: the cutting edge of success that puts your horse's performance before others when the pressure is really on.

The Components of Flatwork

Frame: Collection and Lengthening

The horse's *frame* is the length of the animal's body as controlled by the rider. When a rider shortens his horse's body and length of step, he is collecting the horse into a "shorter frame"; when he elongates the body and length of step, he is lengthening the horse into a "longer frame."

A horse traveling on loose reins has "no frame." Its neck stretches forward to the point that its chin protrudes outward; its hocks move back and forth in sloppy movements; its topline appears flat and stiff; and it travels with most of its weight on the forehand (fig. 1-1).

Long Frame

If a rider establishes contact with the horse's mouth, but does not shorten the length of the horse's frame, hunter riders refer to the horse as being in a "long frame." A long frame can be beneficial in certain circumstances. For example, in an under saddle class, a horse with an excitable, "hot" temperament, may be shown to its best advantage in a long frame. Making hardly any demand on the horse to accept the weight of the hands, the rider can minimize the animal's nervous appearance (fig. 1-2 A & B).

1-1. Loose reins make it obvious that the horse is not in a frame. According to the AHSA Rulebook, in under saddle classes, "Light contact with the horse's mouth is required." Consequently, drooping reins are unacceptable in under saddle classes as well as in equitation classes. Notice that the horse is strung out, traveling heavily on its forehand and moving with weak, sloppy motions in its haunches.

1-2 A & B. When the rider attempts to shorten the frame of the horse, it grinds its teeth, pins its ears, and resists moving forward freely (A). By lightening the pressure on the reins and pressing with her legs, she encourages it to stretch its neck down and out, into a longer frame that allows it to travel more relaxed (B).

A long frame can also be used to de-emphasize the unattractive appearance of a horse with a short neck. Usually, a short-necked horse will move better when its neck is stretched down and out. As it reaches for the ground with its nose, its toes follow with a longer and lower step (fig. 1-3 A & B).

A long frame may also be used to minimize the high-headed appearance of a horse whose neck is attached too far up its shoulder. By driving the horse forward with your legs, you can cause the

1-3 A & B. The conformation flaw of a short, thick neck is accentuated when this mare is collected (A). To make the horse look its best in an under saddle class, the rider minimizes the flaw by allowing the animal to travel in a long frame (B).

animal to drop its head down and out into a better head carriage (fig. 1-4 A & B).

The long frame is appropriate in beginner equitation classes and for under saddle classes in the circumstances described above. Of course, judges realize when a rider is using a long frame to hide a problem, but the performance may beat that of someone else who has not been so clever in minimizing his horse's weaknesses.

1-4 A & B. This horse carries its head high from the slightest contact on the reins. Notice the muscular development on the underside of the neck, from the throat to the chest, which indicates chronic high head carriage (A). By lightening contact on the reins and pressing the horse forward with her legs, the rider encourages the horse to stretch its neck down and out, minimizing the problem (B).

Medium Frame

Many horses are shown to their best advantage in a "medium frame" in under saddle classes. For example, a horse that is long in its body will often appear sloppy if it is allowed to travel in a long frame (fig. 1-5 A & B). The medium frame results in slightly shorter steps at each gait, but what is lost in length of step is usually outweighed by the positive results of a better balanced horse. In a medium frame, the animal's hocks lose less energy backward in the posterior phase of each step than when the horse is in a long frame. The energy that would normally be lost backward is trapped by the rider's legs and cast forward, providing greater power in the anterior phase of each step and enabling the hocks to support some of the forehand weight.

1-5 A & B. The rider has established steady contact with the mouth of this long-bodied animal, but has not collected the horse at all. In a long frame, this horse inverts its topline and does not look athletic (A). When collected into a medium frame, the horse appears better balanced and more physically capable. It exhibits a competitive flair, generally referred to as "presence" (B).

To collect the horse into a medium frame, you not only restrict the backward movement of the hocks with your legs, but also the forward movement of the head and neck with your hands. In response to the coordinated action of your legs and hands, the animal will raise and arch its neck slightly, making its shoulder carriage higher, lightening its forehand, and causing its head to come in closer to the vertical (fig. 1-6).

The medium frame retains much of the natural flow of horizontal energy, while channeling a portion of that energy upward, providing lightness and balance in the horse, as well as greater control and comfort for the rider. When a horse is stationary, the vertical line running through its center of gravity is located just in front of the place where a hunter rider sits. As the horse's pace increases, the center of gravity is shifted increasingly forward. Through collection, the center of gravity can be shifted backward, enabling the rider to be closer to it and producing a smoother ride (fig. 1-7).

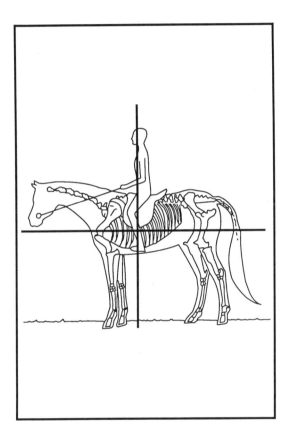

1-6. Notice the difference between the horse in a long frame, indicated by the shaded area, and the horse in a medium frame. When collected into a medium frame, the horse's steps are shorter, its head is brought closer to the vertical, its neck is arched slightly more, and its hocks move within a more restricted area—that is, remaining engaged and not trailing as far behind the animal each step.

1-7. The stationary horse's center of gravity is located at the intersection of a vertical line falling just behind the withers and a horizontal line running from the point of the shoulder to the buttocks. A rider's center of gravity is located in the middle of his pelvis, so the closer you sit to the pommel, the more nearly you will be in balance with your horse. It is also important to note that the animal's center of gravity shifts forward with increased speed, but can be made to shift backward through the use of collection.

If you watch an under saddle class, you will usually see riders on horses in a long frame rising out of the saddle at the canter. On a tense horse, a rider may be trying to avoid contact with the animal's back; but even if the horse does not have a nervous disposition, the rider will usually rise out of the saddle to avoid the bumpy motion caused by the horse's center of gravity being shifted forward. He literally cannot sit on his horse, for he is just far enough behind the center of gravity to make the ride very uncomfortable.

Not only is collecting the horse into a medium frame beneficial for making the rider more comfortable and for balancing a long, sloppy-looking animal, but it is also useful for giving an already good or excellent mover a little panache. The lighter forehand creates a slight degree of suspension in each step, making the good mover appear to be a much better mover than it really is and giving the gifted horse an even flashier, floating appearance as it moves (fig. 1-8).

The only substantial drawback of the medium frame is that nervous or sensitive horses may not appear as relaxed as when they're ridden with less pressure from the rider's hands, legs, and seat. If the horse plays with the bit a great deal, tilts its head from side to side, opens its mouth, pins its ears, or twists its tail in resistance to your signals when being collected into a medium frame, then the longer frame might be a preferable alternative in an under saddle class. The medium frame is not only appropriate for under saddle classes, but also for intermediate and advanced equitation classes.

1-8. An excellent mover skims over the ground with its toes as it travels in a medium frame. It moves with plenty of impulsion, but does not show any tenseness, achieving the ideal picture of balance and freedom of movement.

Short Frame

The short frame substantially restricts the backward flow of energy from the horse's hocks and channels it upward, so that the motion of the hocks appears to be circular. The animal's neck rises and arches to a greater degree than at the medium frame, and the head moves to a position only a few degrees in front of the vertical (fig. 1-9). The forehand becomes quite light, and the horse's steps are shortened as the animal's body is collected from a medium to a short frame.

The short frame is used to achieve maximum control of the horse during equitation tests of precision, such as the counter canter or changes of lead down the centerline of the arena. It is also used in training jumpers, enabling the rider to employ upper-level schooling movements on the flat to supple his horse (fig. 1-10).

1-9. The horse is traveling in a short frame, with its hocks engaged and forehand light. Notice that the neck is arched higher than in the previous pictures demonstrating a long or medium frame. It is the combination of the engaged hocks carrying some of the forehand weight and the higher neck carriage lightening the weight of the forehand that results in a horse's center of gravity being shifted backward as a result of collection. This backward shift of the center of gravity and the shorter steps that accompany a short frame enable the horse to perform precise movements easier than when in a medium or long frame.

1-10. When collected from a long or medium frame into a short frame, the horse's steps become shorter, its neck arches more, and the front plane of its face draws closer to the vertical. There is less energy lost backwards in the posterior phase of each step as more power is added to the anterior phase.

Flatwork vs. Dressage

In order to understand flatwork, it is helpful to know how and why it differs from dressage. One of the main differences pertains to the categories of length of frame. In dressage, the "long frame" for hunters still would be considered "no frame"; the "medium frame" for hunters would be a "long frame"; and the "short frame" for hunters would be a "medium frame." What then is a "short frame" to a dressage rider?

A short frame in dressage refers to the utmost engagement of the hocks and elevation of the forehand. In this frame, the horse can perform such difficult movements as the passage, in which the trot has as much vertical as forward motion, and the piaffe, in which the horse maintains the sequence of the trot in place (fig. 1-11). These movements go well beyond the requirements for hunters, equitation horses, and jumpers in terms of vertical motion on the flat.

1-11. The horse is performing the "passage," an upper-level dressage movement in which the animal trots with prolonged suspension at each step while maintaining regularity in the cadence. To perform this difficult movement, the animal must be collected into a very short frame. Photo: Ronald B. Blackwell, D.V.M.

Lower-level and Upper-level Movements

Daily practice of lower-level dressage movements, such as the circle, half-turn, halt, and shoulder-in, promote suppleness in the horse and obedience to the rider's commands. The lower-level movements are essential to the training of all hunters, equitation horses, and jumpers.

Since a greater degree of precision is required in advanced equitation classes and jumper classes, the rider must prepare for these by incorporating upper-level dressage movements into his daily routine. Some of the movements, such as the turn on the haunches, flying change of lead, and counter-canter, are included in AHSA "Tests 1-19," the official tests used in hunter seat equitation classes. Other upper-level movements, such as the travers (haunches-in), renvers (haunches-out), half-pass (two-track), and pirouette (the turn on the haunches at the canter), are only used for schooling advanced equitation horses and jumpers, since the performance of these tests is not required in the show ring.

Some basic criteria for distinguishing lower-level movements from upper-level movements:

- Lower-level movements require a moderate degree of rider manipulation of the horse's horizontal energy into vertical energy, while upper-level movements demand a much greater degree of vertical thrust of the horse's momentum.
- Lower-level movements that require the horse to move sideways while bent to the left or right (such as the leg-yield, shoulder-in, and basic turn on the forehand) are based on the principle of the horse moving away from the direction in which it is bent; while the upper-level movements performed with the horse in a bent position (such as the haunches-in, haunches-out, advanced turn on the forehand, turn on the haunches, half-pass, and modified pirouette) require the horse to move toward the direction in which it is bent.

(Note: The counter canter and flying change are two tests that do not meet both of the criteria stated above, but are considered upper-level tests because of their degree of difficulty.)

The Rider's Aids

The rider's *aids* are both his natural and artificial means of communicating with the horse. The *natural aids* are the rider's legs, hands, weight, and, on rare occasion, voice. The *artificial aids* are the spurs, stick (also called "crop" or "whip"), bit, martingale, or any other type of equipment that reinforces the rider's body commands.

The word "aid" is not only used to describe the means of communication, but also the position of the rider's body when giving a command. For example, a teacher might ask his student, "What are the aids for the canter?"

The student would reply, "The aids for the canter are the inside leg positioned at the girth, the outside leg behind the girth, and the hands positioned in an inside indirect rein."

There are two basic leg positions used in flatwork. The first, referred to as *at the girth*, is the placement of the rider's calf against the horse's flesh just behind the back edge of the girth. This position is used both to bend the horse and drive it forward (fig. 1-12). The second leg position is referred to as *behind the girth*, which is about four inches farther back than the first. This position affects the lateral, or sideways, movement of the horse's haunches and is also used to drive the horse forward (fig. 1-13).

The word, "lateral," defined by Webster as "per-

1-12. The at-the-girth position enables the rider to bend his horse and drive it forward. It is extremely important for this position to be correct in placement and secure on the horse's side, since it places the rider's calf over the horse's stationary center of gravity and is thus closer to the horse's center of gravity in motion (which moves forward as speed increases) than is the behind-the-girth position. When viewed from the side, the front of the rider's knee and the toe of the boot should be on the same vertical line. The stirrup leather should be framed on each side by the girth, with the iron perpendicular to the girth.

1-13. The behind-the-girth position is used to control the haunches. It signals the horse to use the proper hind leg to start the canter depart (in this example, the counter canter); it keeps the haunches from drifting outward on bending movements, such as circling or bending around the corners of the ring; and it initiates and maintains sideways motion during movements such as the leg-yield, half-pass, and turn on the haunches.

taining to the side," has two applications in hunter seat riding. *Lateral aids* refers to the use of the rider's aids on the same side of the horse, such as the right leg and right hand. This is opposed to *diagonal aids*, which are applied on opposite sides of the horse, such as the right leg and left hand.

Lateral movements, however, refers to any suppling exercises which are used to lessen the horse's stiffness from side to side. They range from the simple circle to more difficult movements such as the modified pirouette or half-pass. Even bending a horse around the corners of a ring can be said to be a lateral exercise, for it affects the animal's suppleness from side to side.

The rider's hands complement the legs by directing the horse and controlling the amount of energy that is allowed to flow forward in horizontal motion with each step. The hands perform these tasks

through the use of five reins aids and a technique called the "half-halt." The five reins aids and their functions are as follows (fig. 1-14 A, B, C, D, E):

1) the *direct rein* maintains straightness
2) the *indirect rein* bends the horse to the left or right
3) the *leading rein* (also known as an "opening rein") leads a horse to the left or right
4) the *neck rein* (also known as a "bearing rein") exerts pressure on one side of the horse's neck, causing the animal to move in the opposite direction
5) the *pulley rein* provides extreme force in an upward and backward action against the horse's mouth to stop the animal in emergency situations.

1-14 A, B, C, D, E. The direct rein maintains straightness in the horse's head and neck, with no evidence of bending to the right or left. It affects the horse's balance from forehand to haunches (A). The indirect rein causes the horse's head and neck to be bent slightly to the right or left. Pictured is a right indirect rein, in which the rider's right hand is placed above the withers and the left hand moves outward and forward to allow the horse to bend to the right. (If the right hand is placed in front of the withers, as

shown, the indirect rein displaces the horse's weight from the right shoulder to the left shoulder; and if the indirect rein is placed behind the withers, the horse's weight is displaced from the right shoulder to the left haunch. The behind-the-withers position is useful in controlling the haunches in lateral movements that require the horse to move toward the direction it is bent.) The indirect rein affects the horse's balance from side to side (B).

The opening or leading rein are different in degree, but are categorized together because they work through the same principle. Both are directional aids which guide the horse to one side or the other. The opening rein is more subtle, with the rider's hand moving away from the horse only five or six inches; while the leading rein opens as far as two feet to one side to literally lead the horse in the desired direction. Pictured is the action of the opening rein (C).

The neck rein, or bearing rein, requires both of the rider's hands to shift in one direction so that one rein acts as an opening rein to guide the horse, while the other presses against the horse's neck to push the animal away. In the photograph, the rider's left hand is in opening rein position, while the right hand is over and in front of the withers, causing the right rein to make contact with the horse's neck—that is, to bear against the neck. The neck rein enables the rider to restrict the horse's drift to the outside of a turn (D).

The pulley rein is an emergency rein aid. With one hand fixed in the dip just in front of the horse's withers and the other hand pulling back and up, the rider is able to exert extreme force against the horse's mouth when the animal refuses to respond to normal hand pressure. If the pulley rein is applied while the horse is traveling near the railing, pull back with the hand nearest the rail. This way, if the horse begins to turn toward the active hand, the railing will help you stop the animal (E).

Half-halts

The *half-halt* is a technique that consists of a sustaining leg aid and a two-phase movement of the hands. As your legs maintain the engagement of the hocks, your hands close slightly to add pressure to the horse's mouth, which is phase one of the hand movement. The simultaneous application of the driving and restricting aids momentarily traps the horse at both ends, so that the animal seeks the logical escape route, which is upward, by raising its shoulder, neck, and head, making its forehand lighter. At the moment the horse becomes lighter in front, ease the pressure on the reins to reward the horse for the proper response. This is phase two of the hand movement (fig. 1-15 A & B).

The basic give-and-take motion of the hands should be instilled in a rider starting with his earliest lessons. He should not be allowed to take an unrelenting hold on a horse's mouth to slow it down, but should learn to take back slightly, then ease off as the horse slows down, so that the animal receives the reward of a giving hand. This is necessary to reinforce correct behavior. The next step of coordinating the supporting leg with the flexible hand will be much easier for the rider to learn if he is already in the habit of keeping his hand mobile, rather than fixed, during a downward transition.

1-15 A & B. At the working trot sitting, the rider maintains impulsion with her legs while bracing with her back and squeezing her hands to ask the horse to half-halt (A). In response the horse collects, shortening the length of its frame by further engaging its hocks and raising its neck upward and its head inward toward its body, resulting in its forehand being lighter than before. When the horse collects, the rider relaxes her back and hands to reward the animal (B).

The half-halt can be used for any of these three functions: (1) to balance and slow the horse while maintaining the same gait; (2) to balance and slow the horse during the change from an upper gait to a lower one; or (3) to shorten the horse's frame while maintaining the same gait. At the lower levels of riding, the half-halt is used to balance the horse when going into turns, regulate the speed of the gaits, and help in accomplishing smooth transitions from upper gaits to lower ones. As the rider's education progresses, he also uses the half-halt to alter the horse's frame when needed, for it enables him to collect the horse and lighten its forehand for precision work. To alter the frame through the use of the half-halt, you must support the horse's rhythm with your legs, so that the animal collects without slowing down and breaking into a lower gait.

Half-halts vary greatly in their length and weight. A single half-halt might last one second on a well-trained, agreeable animal or five seconds on a horse that leans against the bit. (Generally speaking, if the half-halt lasts longer than five seconds, you're not really half-halting, but have gotten into a pulling match with your horse.) The half-halt might require only a squeeze of the hands with supporting legs, or it might take a well-anchored seat to reinforce arms briefly fixed against a strong animal. The amount of pressure needed to accomplish the half-halt, then, will depend entirely upon the horse's response to the aids (fig. 1-16).

Between half-halts, maintain a light, but steady feel of the horse's mouth. If the animal tries to avoid rein contact by raising its head or bringing it in toward its chest, press the horse forward with your legs. In reaction to your driving aid, it will attempt to lengthen its stride, which will shift its center of gravity forward and cause it to stretch its head and neck outward, creating more weight on the bit.

Added weight on the bit provides a firmer feel of the horse's forward movement. Men generally feel comfortable with more weight than women do, since many women find it to be a little intimidating. Although a woman may prefer less weight in her hands, she should not be content with the feeling

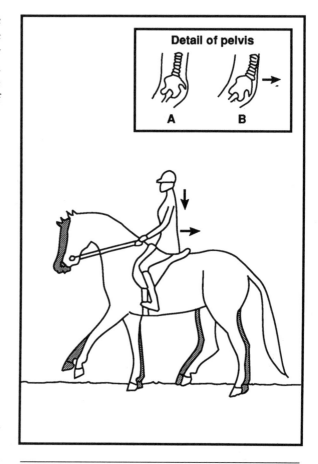

1-16. The detail of the pelvis shows the rider's lower back in normal position (A) and braced during the half-halt, when more pressure is needed on the horse's mouth than the hands alone can provide (B). Notice in the drawing of horse and rider that the rider's shoulders exert pressure downward, causing the muscles in her back to be flexed. The combination of flexed back muscles and the backward tilt of the pelvis enables the rider to use her upper-body weight to reinforce her hands during the half-halt.

1-17. This is an obvious example of the rider carrying the reins, rather than establishing steady contact with the horse's mouth. Notice the animal's unattractive concave topline and compare it with the pictures of the same horse in figs. 1-15 A & B.

1-18. The diagram demonstrates the proper function of the rider's arm. The upper arm should move freely, as though it were loosely hung from a hook at the shoulder. The elbow should allow continuous horizontal freedom of movement as it follows the back-and-forth motion of the horse's head and neck.

that she is "carrying the reins" without feeling any weight from the horse's mouth, for this means the horse is not properly moving onto the bit in response to her legs (fig. 1-17).

There should be the steady feeling of the reins lying with a slight heaviness against the base of the fingers. If the horse is relaxed, the muscles in its neck and jaw will create this feeling of relaxed weight on the reins. To sustain this steady contact, you must be relaxed from the shoulder to the hand, so that as the horse moves, your arms follow the motion of its head and neck (fig. 1-18). You can then adjust the weight on the bit by half-halting if the horse becomes too heavy during work or by driving the horse to the bit with your legs if the contact becomes too light.

Half-halts should be used liberally throughout all of your flatwork. In the span of a 20-minute work session, a good rider uses endless numbers of them to balance the horse, regulate its pace, or change its frame. They are used in closest succession during downward transitions and should be progressively lighter as the pace of the horse lessens, rewarding the animal for the proper response.

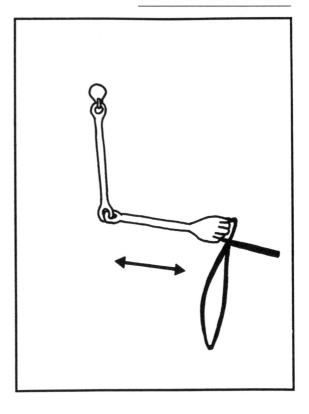

Pace

Pace is the speed at which a horse travels in each gait. The *working walk,* used for both equitation classes on the flat and under saddle classes, is a four-beat gait in which the horse travels approximately four miles per hour, or 352 feet per minute. Since the walk involves little pace, your upper body must be only a couple of degrees in front of the vertical to be with the motion at this gait (fig. 1-19).

In all gaits, the sequence of the feet is considered to start with a hind foot because the haunches are the horse's source of power. However, the sequence at the walk actually starts with one of the horse's forefeet. If the horse were asked to walk from the halt and began with its left forefoot, the sequence of footfalls would follow as right hind, right fore, left hind, left fore, and so on.

The feet are placed in rapid succession at the walk, so that at different moments in the sequence the horse's weight is supported by a diagonal pair of legs, a lateral pair of legs, or three legs. In the moments when the horse's body is supported only by a lateral pair of legs — that is, two legs on the same side — its balance is unstable. It moves its head and neck upward and inward to maintain its balance until the other legs are placed to help support its weight, at which moment the horse's head and neck drop and move forward again. These backward and forward motions of the head should be followed by your hands when the horse is in a long or medium frame at the walk. When the animal is collected into a short frame, the elevation of the its shoulders, head, and neck help it to keep its balance during the moments of potential instability, and there is very little back and forth motion of the head.

The *working trot rising* (also called the *posting trot*) is a two-beat gait, with a speed of approximately eight miles per hour, or 704 feet per minute. The feet strike the ground in diagonal pairs at the trot, with the right hind and left fore striking together and the left hind and right fore striking together. Your hands remain steady because the alternating diagonal pairs of feet provide stability for the animal as it moves.

1-19. At the walk, the rider's upper body is slightly in front of the vertical, just enough to be with the motion of the horse at this relatively slow, four-beat gait.

When the horse is moving clockwise at the posting trot, rise when its left foreleg goes forward and sit when it strikes the ground. Moving counterclockwise, rise when the horse's right foreleg goes forward and sit when it strikes the ground (fig. 1-20 A & B).

By freeing the horse's outside foreleg, posting allows the animal to remain balanced on turns. If you rise and sit in the incorrect rhythm, you are "posting on the wrong diagonal." On corners, this error causes your weight to land on the horse's back just as the animal is reaching with its outside foreleg, which must cover more ground each step than the inside foreleg does on a turn. The result is loss of balance for the horse, creating an awkward feeling for you and often making the horse appear lame.

1-20 A & B. At the posting trot, you should rise as the horse's outside foreleg moves forward (A). During the sitting phase of the posting trot, your upper body should be approximately 20 degrees in front of the vertical when the horse is traveling in a medium frame (B).

1-21. At the working trot sitting, your upper body should be in the same position as at the walk, just a couple of degrees in front of the vertical.

At the working trot rising, close your hip angle forward to allow your torso to follow the horizontal motion of the horse. When the horse is in a medium frame, your upper body should be inclined about 20 degrees in front of the vertical at the posting trot. The degree of inclination will vary somewhat if you change the horse's frame. For example, if a horse is put into a shorter frame for upper-level flatwork exercises, your upper body should reflect the vertical channeling of energy by straightening to a slightly more vertical position; and if the horse is traveling in a longer frame, your upper body should be inclined forward a little more.

The *working trot sitting* is performed at the same tempo as the working trot rising. During the working trot sitting, the upper body is only a couple of degrees in front of the vertical (fig. 1-21). This nearly upright position allows your weight to sink into the horse's back, so that you are firmly glued on and able to follow the motion with your seat and lower back.

The *working trot with a lengthening of stride* is executed at about ten miles per hour, or 880 feet per minute. To lengthen the stride, increase the pressure of your calves until the horse begins to take longer steps. As it stretches its head and neck forward during lengthening, follow this movement with your hands; but be sure to keep a steady feel of the reins, for even a small amount of slack will encourage a break into the canter. It is very important to maintain a steady tempo during lengthening, since loss of regularity is another cause of the horse breaking into an upper gait.

When the lengthening of stride is performed at the posting trot, your upper body should be inclined no more than ten degrees in front of the vertical. This enables you to use your weight as an additional driving aid and promotes lightness in the horse's forehand by shifting your upper-body weight more toward the haunches than at the normal working trot rising (fig. 1-22).

When the lengthening of stride is performed at the sitting trot, open your upper body to the vertical. From this upright position, you can use your weight as a driving aid; but be careful not to lean behind the vertical, for this is an unneccesarily severe position (fig. 1-23).

1-22. Captured during the sitting phase of the working trot rising with a lengthening of stride, the rider has opened her body to a more erect position than she had at the normal posting trot (see fig. 1-20 B). This allows her to subtly use her weight as a driving aid.

1-23. The rider's upper body is incorrectly positioned behind the vertical during the sitting trot with a lengthening of stride. In reaction to the severity of the rider's seat as a driving aid, the horse has unhappily pinned its ears back. The combination of an overly active seat and a braced, behind-the-motion upper body forces the horse to overflex at the poll, causing its head to be pulled behind the vertical.

On the corners of the ring, you can steady the horse slightly. It is not necessary to shorten the frame, for the ends of a hunter arena are usually wide enough to accommodate a sustained lengthening. It will be helpful in competition, however, to collect the horse into a slightly shorter frame for a few steps at the end of the corner preceding the pass in front of the judge, so that the horse will be in the process of lengthening as it makes the pass, giving it a flashy appearance. This is also good insurance, for there is less chance of a horse breaking gait early in the lengthening process than when it has been moving on an extended stride for a long period of time.

The *working canter* is a three-beat gait ranging between ten and twelve miles per hour, or 880 feet to 1056 feet per minute. At the working canter, your body should be positioned just in front of the vertical, to match the upward motion of this gait.

The sequence of the horse's feet at the canter establishes what is referred to as the "lead." When starting in proper sequence moving in a counterclockwise direction, the horse's right hind leg is the first to strike. It is followed by the diagonal pair of the left hind and right fore striking together. Finally, the left fore strikes, completing the sequence of the "left lead." When moving in a clockwise direction, the sequence is reversed, beginning with the left hind leg, followed by the right hind and left fore striking together, and ending with the right foreleg. This sequence is known as the "right lead" (fig. 1-24 A,B,C).

As a point of interest, when the horse is started into the canter from a halt, it will usually put one foreleg forward to support its forehand before it starts the canter sequence with the diagonally positioned hind leg. The exception to this is when the horse is in a very collected frame, in which case it is well-balanced enough to start the canter beginning with its hind leg.

At the moments during the canter sequence in which one hind leg or one foreleg is supporting the weight of the horse, the animal is unstable. Its head and neck move back and forth during the changes from stability to instability, providing it with a means of catching its balance. Your arms should follow this movement backward slightly as the horse begins the sequence with its outside hind leg, then move forward as its leading leg strikes the

1-24 A, B, C. Traveling clockwise, the horse picks up the correct (right) lead by striking the first beat of the sequence with its outside hind foot, which lifts the other three legs (A). The second beat of the canter involves the diagonal set of legs—inside hind and outside fore—striking simultaneously. The forward thrust of the inside leg at this stage in the sequence makes it appear to be the leading leg. Thus, the horse is said to be on the "right lead" (B). The third and final beat is struck by the inside foreleg (C).

ground with each stride. Again, collection will help the horse keep its balance and minimize the back-and-forth movement of its head and neck.

The *working canter with a lengthening of stride* is performed at about fourteen miles per hour, or 1232 feet per minute, with the difference between this movement and the basic working canter being length of stride, rather than a change of tempo. When lengthening the stride at the canter, sit in *three-point position* with your two legs and seat forming three points of contact with the horse. Your upper body should be erect, so that your weight can act as an additional driving aid; but your torso should not drop behind the vertical (fig. 1-25).

Prepare for the working canter with a lengthening of stride by collecting the horse into a short frame at the canter. Then press with your legs, easing off the reins slightly as the horse responds by lengthening. The animal should be steadied in the corners of the ring, but not brought back into a shorter frame unless the size of the ring is prohibitive. Again, during competition, a slight shortening of the frame just before the pass will set up the horse so that it will be balanced and in the process of lengthening as it passes the judge, giving the performance a little flair.

Both the working trot rising with a lengthening of stride and the working canter showing a lengthening of stride are required in the flat phase of the USET Junior/Young Rider Medal Class. The lengthening of stride at the trot can be a particularly brilliant movement and give you the edge you need to win the class. Though the lengthening at the canter is not as visually impressive, it is important to perform it well, making a clear distinction between lengthening and the working canter.

The *hand gallop* is used for jumping fences and is also one of the AHSA's Tests 1-19. It is performed at between fourteen and sixteen miles per hour, or 1232 feet to 1408 feet per minute, and should appear controlled and at a speed appropriate for the size of the arena. At the hand gallop, the horse's footfalls strike in the same three-beat sequence as at the canter. This distinguishes the hand gallop from the faster racing gallop, which through extension of the horse's limbs causes the feet to fall in four separate beats.

You should be in *two-point position* for the hand gallop, with only your two legs making contact with the horse, and your usual third point of contact, your seat, being raised above the animal's back. The lack of weight makes it easier for the horse to carry

1-25. The head position of the horse is incorrectly behind the vertical, but the lengthening of stride is very good. To correct the horse's head, the rider should raise both hands simultaneously with a very slight jab, encouraging the horse to lift its head into the proper position.

1-26. At the hand-gallop, the rider is in two-point position to clear her weight from the horse's back. The animal is exhibiting impulsion, balance, and relaxation as it hand-gallops down the long side of the arena.

you at greater speed and enables it to jump less encumbered.

Your torso should be inclined forward at the hand gallop, "with the motion" of the horse. The angulation will vary somewhat as the horse's stride is shortened or lengthened. For example, when the horse is hand-galloping down the long side of the arena, your hip angle should be closed about 30 degrees in front of the vertical to be with the motion (fig. 1-26). Just before the short side of the arena, you should open the angle to a slightly more erect position, so that your upper-body weight can aid your arms in collecting the horse to balance it for the corner.

In conclusion, pace is the foundation upon which all else is built. If an animal is too slow or too fast, every other aspect of performance will be affected. In a class over fences, a horse moving too slowly may add unnecessary strides between obstacles, refuse to jump, or even plop into the middle of a fence in slow motion. Conversely, the overly fast horse

may leave out a stride and dive into a fence, stop abruptly and sling the rider into an obstacle, or run out at a fence and race off. In riding, teaching, and judging, safety should be the first consideration. You must never lose sight of the importance of proper pace in achieving a safe performance that both the rider and onlookers can enjoy.

Evenness of pace is another important consideration, for it is the regularity of the horse's footfalls that makes the animal's performance pleasing to the observer. Whether on the flat or over fences, erratic pace robs the performance of its smoothness and points out the rider's and horse's lack of sophistication as a team.

Impulsion

Impulsion is the power a horse has in every step. Although impulsion and pace are related, they are not one and the same. The difference is that pace equals speed, while impulsion equals thrust.

1-27 A & B. On course, the horse is pulling against the rider at the hand-gallop and elongating its frame. As a result, it travels heavily on its forehand (A). When the animal is collected into a shorter frame, you can see how much lighter the forehand is at the same moment in the sequence of footfalls (B).

It is true that a galloping horse on light rein contact has a tremendous amount of natural impulsion, but this type of impulsion is horizontal energy, which is difficult to control on turns or within obstacles set so that they require the horse to take short strides. For beginner riders, impulsion that comes from pace will suffice for a straightforward hunter or equitation course. But when a rider progresses to more complicated courses, he must learn how to use his hands and legs properly to translate the raw energy of pace into the more sophisticated energy of impulsion (fig. 1-27 A & B).

Bending

Bending is directing the horse through the use of your hands and legs into a position in which the animal's body is curved to the left or right from head to tail. (Note: In some exercises, only the neck is bent. When applicable, this will be indicated in the text.) To position the horse in a bend, use the following aids: your hand toward the inside of the curve moves to a point just over and slightly in front of the withers; simultaneously, the outside hand moves away from the horse and forward to allow the animal to bend its neck, with the release of pressure being equal to the amount of pressure added by the inside hand; your leg toward the inside of the bend is positioned at the girth; and the outside leg is positioned behind the girth (fig. 1-28 A, B, C, D).

1-28 A, B, C. When traveling counterclockwise on a curve, bend the horse to the left with a left indirect rein, using your left leg at the girth to control the horse's left hind leg and your right leg behind the girth to control the horse's right hind leg (A). When traveling on a straightaway, the horse should be positioned straight with a direct rein and both of your legs at the girth (B). When traveling clockwise on a curve, bend the horse to the right with a right indirect rein, your right leg at the girth, and your left leg behind the girth (C).

1-28 D. When bending a horse, your shoulders should be parallel to the horse's shoulders (white bars), while your hips remain parallel to the horse's haunches (broken lines). A commom error committed by riders is to keep both the shoulders and hips parallel to the horse's haunches, which creates stiffness and lack of balance in the rider.

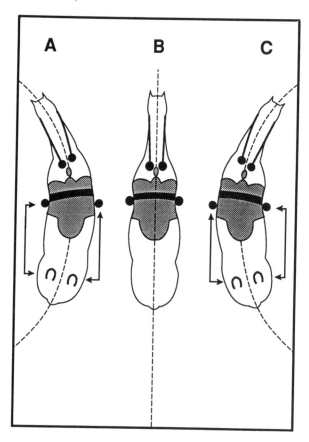

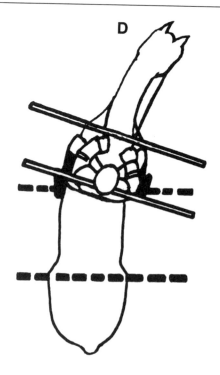

When viewed from above, as in figure 1-28 A,B,C, the horse's bend should match the curve along which the animal is traveling. According to current veterinary studies, the horse's spine is not flexible enough to adhere to an acute curve because the rib cage prevents the portion of the spine between the shoulder and hip from bending much at all. However, the connective tissues at the horse's shoulder and hip stretch to allow the animal's rib cage to be displaced to the outside of the curve, so that from a top view the horse appears to be evenly bent from head to tail. For practical purposes, then, the proper bend is described as being uniform from head to tail (fig. 1-29 A, B, C).

The basic purpose of bending is to allow the horse to stay balanced on curves. Instead of letting the animal drift toward the rail or cut into the center of the ring on turns, both of which are common errors, you must use your aids to keep its weight distributed equally on both sides of its body. Bending requires the horse to yield with its inside hind leg, so that the inside hind foot is placed laterally farther underneath the animal's body on a curve than when the horse is traveling on a straight line. Consequently, bending exercises can be useful in breaking up resistances in the haunches, for the movements require the horse to submit with its inside hind leg, blocking it from rigidly resisting with that leg.

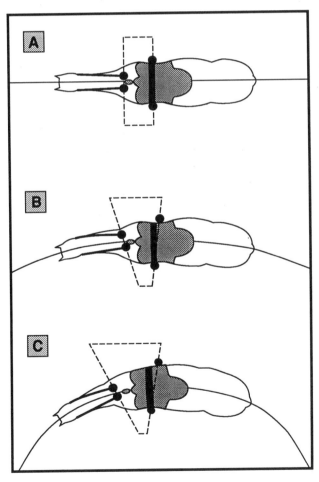

1-29 A, B, C. The greater the degree of bend, the more your outside hand must move forward to allow the horse to bend its neck and the farther back your outside leg must be positioned to hold the horse's haunches on the curve. The dotted lines show the difference between the position of the rider's aids during straightness (A), a slight bend to the left (B), and a tight turn to the left (C).

An untrained horse that is unaccustomed to your aids may resist your inside leg as you attempt to push its body into a bent position. It may press its rib cage back against you, giving you much the same feeling against your leg as you feel against your arm when you try to tighten the girth on a horse that "blows up" its stomach (fig. 1-30 A & B).

This is where tact comes in. The worst thing you can do is wallop the horse in the side with your heel, for the animal is responding naturally to an unfamiliar and somewhat uncomfortable pressure against its side. It is the horse's way of saying, "Hey, don't push me around." Instead of reacting by adding more force with your leg, try easing off the rein on the opposing side, moving your hand forward and outward in a leading-rein position. This gives the horse a sense of direction, an "open door" through which it can travel (fig. 1-31).

If you are an inexperienced rider, it will be easiest for you to learn how to bend your horse if you practice placing your aids correctly at the halt, then apply them at the walk in each direction, before you attempt bending at faster gaits. The principle of restricting pace when practicing new techniques holds true in most exercises for the horse or rider. The reason is that the greater the pace, the more the rider is at a disadvantage, since the horse can go

1-30 A & B. The feeling of a horse leaning into you as you try to tighten the girth will be familiar if you have worked with a number of horses. Notice how the horse has transferred weight to its left foreleg, leaving hardly any weight on its right foreleg, as indicated by the slightly bent right knee (A). A young or untrained horse may resist in precisely the same way, thrusting its rib cage toward the rider's active leg. As you can see, the horse is shifting its weight into, rather than away from, the rider's left leg aid (B).

farther astray in a shorter time, causing its mistakes to be exaggerated and the rider to become frustrated.

Once you are able to bend the horse properly each direction at the walk, attempt it at the trot, then at the canter. You should not only mold the horse's body to fit the curves at the end of the arena, but also practice circles, which require more refined coordination of your aids because you do not have the advantage of outside support from the railing.

Eventually, you can incorporate other lateral exercises into your daily work that will make flatwork sessions more interesting for you and your horse. Half-turns, half-turns in reverse, figure eights, serpentines, and changes through the circle are simple figures which will offer variety in your basic routine (fig. 1-32 A, B, C, D, E). They are more effective than a circle for suppling a horse because they involve a change in the direction of the bend within the figure. This change breaks up resistances on both sides of the animal, whereas a circle encourages suppleness on the inside of the curve, but allows resistances to build on the outside of the curve, often without your realizing that the horse is becoming stiff to one side.

1-31. To encourage the horse to displace its weight away from her left leg, the rider moves her right hand outward into a leading rein position. This gives the horse an "open door" through which it can easily travel, making it much more difficult for the horse to lean inward toward the rider's left leg than to take the more convenient option to the right. (Notice that the rider's eyes are down, which is an error. You should never watch your hands at work, but should always look ahead.)

1-32. Half-turn (A), half-turn in reverse (B), figure eight (C), change through the circle (D), three-loop serpentine (E).

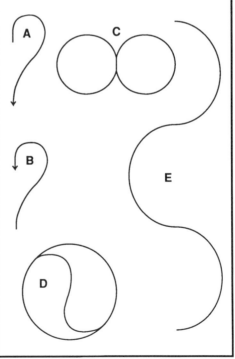

Your calves break up resistances by preventing the horse from bracing with its hind legs and stiffening its muscles. Think of the horse's rib cage as pliable material and your legs as the walls of a supporting corridor. Mold the horse's barrel into the desired configuration—either a left or right bend, or absolute straightness—by increasing or decreasing the pressure in each of your calves.

The hands come into play, too, as they allow or restrict lateral movement. If you increase pressure with your left leg, the horse will move to the right, unless your right hand does not relax enough and clashes with the left leg, preventing the horse from moving over (fig. 1-33 A & B). I believe the most common mistake riders make in attempting bending is not relaxing the outside aids as the inside aids are applied. A rider with a weak position or poor coordination will tend to flex all of his muscles or relax all of them, rather than being able to flex some

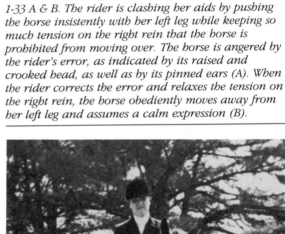

1-33 A & B. The rider is clashing her aids by pushing the horse insistently with her left leg while keeping so much tension on the right rein that the horse is prohibited from moving over. The horse is angered by the rider's error, as indicated by its raised and crooked head, as well as by its pinned ears (A). When the rider corrects the error and relaxes the tension on the right rein, the horse obediently moves away from her left leg and assumes a calm expression (B).

while relaxing others. You must be acutely aware of how your aids work independently, yet interdependently, before you can master bending or, for that matter, flatwork in general. It is the delicate coordination between your hands and legs that will allow you to mold the horse's body smoothly into a bend then back again to straight as the animal moves around the corners and straight sides of the arena (fig. 1-34).

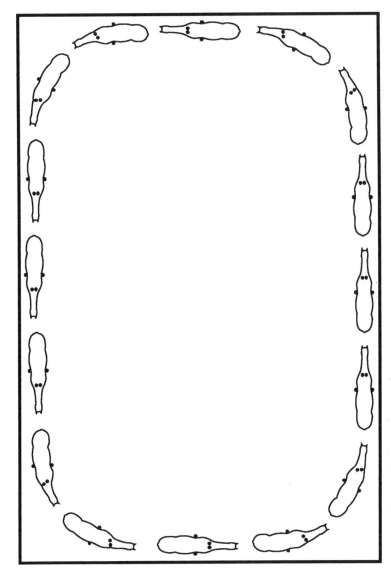

1-34. From this top view, you can see the rider's aids for traveling counterclockwise around an arena at the walk or trot. A direct rein and both legs positioned at the girth are used on the straightways. An indirect rein, the inside leg at the girth, and the outside leg behind the girth are used on the corners of the arena. (At the canter, the hand position and inside leg aid are the same, but the outside leg remains in a behind-the-girth position even on the straightaways, poised to add pressure to maintain the canter sequence if the horse tries to break to a lower gait.)

A

B

1-35 A, B, C. During a good transition from the canter to the halt, the horse remains collected, straight, calm (A & B). The downward transition culminates in the animal standing squarely, ready to perform further tests (C).

C

Transitions

Transitions are the periods of change between one gait and another. For instance, when your horse is walking (four beats) and you want it to canter (three beats), you apply your aids and the horse strikes out in a new sequence of its feet as it makes a transition between the walk and canter. There are *upward transitions* (halt to walk, halt to trot, halt to canter, walk to trot, walk to canter, and trot to canter) and *downward transitions* (canter

A

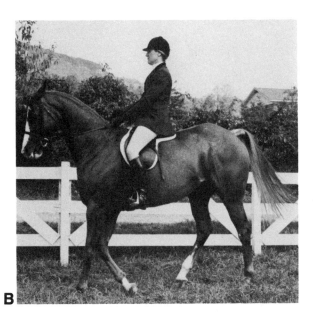

B

1-36 A, B, C. During a bad transition from the canter to the halt, the rider roughly pulls against the horse's mouth (A). Her upper body is behind the vertical in a severe, braced position. The horse responds to her aids with anger and tension (B). At the halt, the horse fidgets and moves its haunch to one side rather than standing squarely (C).

C

to trot, canter to walk, canter to halt, trot to walk, trot to halt, and walk to halt).

A good transition is smooth, with the horse's hocks remaining engaged, the tempo changing gradually as the animal moves into the new gait, and the frame being stable (fig. 1-35 A, B, C). A bad transition is abrupt, with the hocks dropping behind, the tempo changing radically from one gait to another, and the horse "falling out of frame" (fig. 1-36 A, B, C).

The hocks must remain engaged throughout the upward and downward transitions in order for the horse's frame to be stable. The following simulation demonstrates the way in which engagement and disengagement of the hocks affect the horse's frame. Start with your hands and knees on the floor, so that your weight is distributed on four supports, representing the stance of a horse. Then, raise your buttocks upward and stretch your head backward toward your seat. From this position, try to lower your head. You will find it difficult to put your head and neck down when the rest of your spine is curved upward (fig. 1-37 A & B). Now try the reverse. Curve your bottom underneath and drop your head so that your entire back is round. Then try to raise your head. You will find it equally difficult to do this (fig. 1-38 A & B).

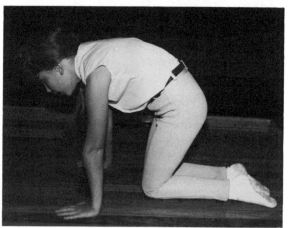

1-37 A & B. When you begin with your spine concave, so that your buttocks and head are up (A), you will find it difficult to put your head down (B). This represents the difficulty a horse has lowering its head when its hindquarters are not engaged.

1-38 A & B. If you begin with your spine convex, which represents the engagement of the horse's hocks (A), you will find it difficult to raise your head (B). This is why a horse that moves with its hocks engaged will keep its head in an acceptably low position, rather than being forced to lower its head.

It is the same with a horse. If you can keep the animal's hocks engaged, its hips will be lowered and its loins will be curved slightly upward, so that the horse's neck will be most comfortable following the downward curve. The horse will then remain in a stable, collected frame throughout the transitions (fig. 1-39 A & B).

Although half-halts used during downward transitions shift the center of gravity backward, causing the horse to have a lighter forehand, the lightness of the front end will not encourage the horse to raise its nose skyward. As explained above, the curve of the spine when the hocks are properly engaged makes it uncomfortable for the horse to travel with its head up. The forehand, then, can be lightened when necessary without adversely affecting head carriage.

Transitions are important at all levels of riding, for they demonstrate the degree of the horse's obedience and, consequently, are a means of assessing the rider's safety. If the horse is not willing to slow down when you ask for a downward transition on the flat, the problem will be magnified when the animal is traveling at a much greater pace around a course of fences.

In general, problems on the flat greatly increase in severity when the horse is ridden over fences. It is essential, then, to view flatwork in relation to jumping if you are to understand the benefits of its use for hunters and equitation horses. Unlike dressage, we are not concerned with suppleness, balance, and obedience in and of themselves as an art form. Rather, our primary concern is for control of the horse on course, which is much more likely to occur when the animal has first been trained properly on the flat.

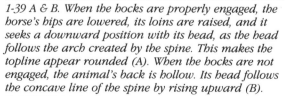

1-39 A & B. When the hocks are properly engaged, the horse's hips are lowered, its loins are raised, and it seeks a downward position with its head, as the head follows the arch created by the spine. This makes the topline appear rounded (A). When the hocks are not engaged, the animal's back is hollow. Its head follows the concave line of the spine by rising upward (B).

Punishment and Reward

From the horse's point of view, *punishment* is the application of the rider's natural and artificial aids, and *reward* is the lessening or absence of their use. If you want the horse to move forward a little faster, punish it with a squeeze of your legs. If this does not produce a response, use your spurs to reinforce the leg aid. If the horse is still unresponsive, apply your stick on its flank, just behind your calf, using only the degree of force necessary to motivate the animal. Once the horse is at the proper pace, relax the pressure of your calves to reward it.

Punishment from the hands depends upon the amount of pressure you have against the horse's mouth. If the horse does not slow down in response to the squeezing of your hand muscles, add weight to its mouth by pulling back slightly, until the animal does react. Once the horse acknowledges your hand aid and begins to slow down, relax the hand muscles and allow your arms to follow the motion of its head and neck, so that the animal is rewarded through lighter contact.

You should think of punishment as the active use of your aids, not as an angry or overly severe response to a horse's bad behavior. A good example of incorrect punishment is seen when a horse stops in front of a jump and is beaten severely on the head or neck. Its rider will usually try to justify his behavior by referring to it as "punishment" for the horse's disobedience. This, however, is not punishment, but abuse, since the angry rider is trying to inflict pain, rather than correct an error with the appropriate application of his aids.

If your aids are applied too severely, the horse will become frightened and try to run, escaping in any direction available. Once a horse has decided to bolt, it is difficult to regain control and get it to concentrate on work, for it becomes solely concerned with avoiding further pain.

Timing is another factor in punishment. By promptly addressing a problem, you will let the horse know that you are alert and that you intend to be in control. If you miss the opportunity to punish for a small error, then it will gradually increase in severity and related problems will spring up. At that point, you will have to be much more forceful than if you had applied your aids sooner, when the error was small and isolated.

Punishment must therefore be: (1) applied at the proper time; (2) applied to the proper place; and (3) applied with the proper force. Reward has the same criteria, for it is just as bad to miss the timing, location, and degree of reward as of punishment. Reward, being the relaxation of your aids, is the only indication a horse has as to whether it is performing correctly or incorrectly. Humans often forget that animals do not understand most of what is said — that if an instructor tells a rider what to do, the horse has no idea what is about to be asked of it.

Imagine yourself as a deaf person in a room full of people receiving detailed instructions about an obstacle course. You cannot interpret anything being said. Everyone nods that they understand the instructions, then they leave the room to carry them out. You, however, are following the group with no idea of what is up ahead. In this situation, you are like the horse. How comforting it would be if someone took you by the hand and guided you through the obstacle course, just as a good rider gives his horse guidance with his aids; and how frightening it would be if no one helped you and, when you made mistakes, you were soundly beaten. This is the case with many horses that receive such poor guidance from their riders that they are never quite sure what they are supposed to be doing. You can imagine how frustrated and angry the horse becomes.

Riding is a partnership between man and horse. The basis of this partnership is reward and punishment, for it is man's means of communicating with his horse and the horse's means of registering whether it is performing correctly or not. The animal will learn to do exactly what you want it to do only when the incentives and restrictions of training are logical, consistent, and justly applied.

2

Flat Exercises For Hunters
and Equitation Horses

Categorizing Your Horse

Horses, like people, change from day to day. For example, yesterday your horse might have been a placid animal when the weather was warm, but today it might be wild when a brisk breeze is blowing. For this reason, you must categorize your horse every time you ride.

Each horse will fall into one of the following three basic categories: dull, normal, or quick. You can begin studying your horse's type long before you work in the ring. For example, if a horse hangs its head low in a corner of the stall and props one hind foot up, then it would appear to be a dull horse; but if it walks around and around the stall, sticking its head out the door and whinnying every once in a while, then it would appear to be a quick horse.

Similarly, if the horse stands completely still when being mounted and is reluctant to move forward from a firm squeeze of your legs, then it would seem to be a dull horse. But if it dances around while you are trying to mount and rushes off as you swing your leg over the saddle, then it would appear to be a quick horse.

Finally, as you are walking the horse to the ring, if it plods along with its neck stretched down and out and requires a great deal of encouragement from your legs, then it would appear to be a dull horse. But if the horse carries its head high and looks quickly from one object to another, or jogs rather than walks, then it would seem to be a quick horse.

Although you have not begun to work in the arena, you already have a good idea of what to expect and, using this knowledge, can avoid certain pitfalls. For example, when anticipating a dull horse, mentally prepare yourself to be assertive, so that you will be able to enliven the plodder on the flat and not wait until you are facing a course of jumps before you deal with its slowness.

If you have mounted what seems to be a quick horse, you can anticipate that it will want to rush when working at all the gaits and will overreact to your aids. By remaining calm and applying your aids softly and slowly, you can encourage the horse to relax; but if the animal does not respond to your tactfully applied aids by settling down within a reasonable period of time, you can longe it to release its excess energy.

Longeing

Longeing is exercising the horse in a circle on a long ("longe") line held by a person on the ground. When a horse is very quick or spooky on the way to the arena, most riders will try riding it rather than longeing it first, simply because it is annoying to have to go back to the barn, dismount, search for equipment, attach it to the horse, and trudge back to the arena on foot. In my experience, however, a horse that is very tense going to the ring rarely calms down within a reasonable time.

I much prefer longeing to struggling while mounted in order to control a nervous horse. When a horse pulls while longeing, it will meet with the restriction of *side reins*, which are composed of leather and elastic connected between the horse's bit and girth. The elastic provides a little give when the horse pulls, but there is only so far that the animal can stretch its neck before it meets the fixed restriction of the leather part of the reins. In contrast, when a horse fights your hands while you are riding, it is difficult to offer as much flexibility, for most riders feel threatened by an increase in pace when they ease off the reins on a quick horse. Only a very talented and experienced rider can provide both the flexibility and restriction necessary when a horse wants to charge forward.

Longeing also offers the psychological advantage of focusing the horse's attention on the equipment as the source of its restriction; whereas, if you have been pulling on the horse's mouth for an hour on the flat, the animal associates discomfort directly with you. The situation also holds true in reverse. If your horse has been pulling against you for a long time, your arms will begin to hurt, and, if you are like most people, you will become angry with the animal in direct proportion to your degree of pain. But if you longe the horse before you try to work it, you will have a more pleasant ride afterwards and not develop such ill will toward it. Even a very good rider benefits from first longeing a tense horse, for it spares him from expending unnecessary energy on horseback.

Side reins not only simulate good hands by offering some flexibility while keeping the horse in a frame, but will also help prevent the excited horse from drifting sideways and stepping on itself. They should be equal in length on both sides, since lengthening the outside rein does not create proper bending, as some people believe, but rather allows the horse to drift to the outside of the circle. If the

2-1. The side reins are correctly adjusted, allowing the head to be slightly in front of the vertical. On a young horse such as this, it is particularly important not to make the side reins too tight, since they can cause the animal to panic.

horse is correctly fitted in side reins, the elastic in the outside rein will both accommodate the horse's bend and offer enough support to prevent the animal from becoming overly bent.

Side reins should be adjusted so that the horse can keep its head slightly in front of the vertical (fig. 2-1). Never tighten them to the point that they force the horse to bring its head behind the vertical, for this overflexed position makes it difficult for the horse to see where it is going and pulls apart the vertebrae just behind the horse's ears, inflicting pain at that point (fig. 2-2).

Boots are another important consideration when longeing. Galloping boots and ankle boots will protect the horse's legs if the animal *interferes*, striking one leg with the foot on the opposite side; and bell boots will protect the horse's heels in case the animal *overreaches*, striking the heel of a forefoot with the toe of a hind foot (fig. 2-3). (If an excited horse is allowed to run on the longe line, it will tend to

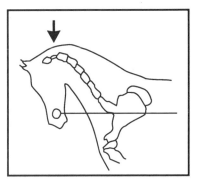

2-2. The side reins are adjusted too short, causing the horse to be overflexed at the poll. Notice the internal effect of overflexion indicated in the diagram. The arrow shows an uncomfortable stress point in the link joining the first and second cervical vertebrae, which are pulled apart as a result of overflexion.

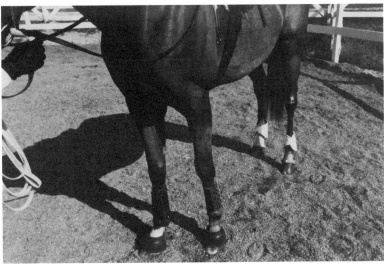

2-3. The horse is properly equipped with galloping boots (protecting the bones and soft tissue in the forelegs), bell boots (protecting the coronet band in each foreleg), and ankle boots (protecting the fetlocks in the hind legs).

bow out on the circle and interfere or overreach. For this reason, it is very important to keep the horse at a pace suitable for the size of the circle.)

I prefer a 30-foot longe line to the shorter ones. It gives the horse enough room to canter comfortably and allows you to have at least one extra loop left in your hand at all times, so that if the horse bolts, you will not be instantly pulled to the ground and dragged. Although some people slide the small loop at the end of the longe line over their hand and let it rest on their wrist, I prefer to hold the end of the line in my hand, so that I can quickly let go of it if necessary. I decided to do this after witnessing a young girl getting snared in her longe line and dragged facedown for about 150 feet through the mud before her horse stopped. It was fortunate she was longeing inside an arena. If the horse had not been corralled by the railing, there is no telling how far it would have run before stopping.

Try to hold on to the horse if it starts to bolt, for in most cases you will be able to get it under control. But if the extra loop you have hanging from your hand is sliding rapidly through your fingers and you can see that the horse has no intention of stopping, then at the instant the line runs out, open your hand and drop the end of the line.

The longe line should be held at the level of the horse's mouth, with a steady feel all the time, just as on a normal rein. The longe line, then, represents communication with your primary restricting aid — your hands. When the horse is traveling counterclockwise, the line is held in your left hand; and when the horse is traveling clockwise, the line is held in your right hand.

A longe whip measuring 11 feet or more, including both stock and thong, should also be used. Pointed at the horse's hocks and trailing them as the animal moves around the circle, the whip is used to drive the horse forward. The whip, then, represents your primary driving aid — your legs (fig. 2-4). Hold the longe whip in the opposite hand from the one holding the longe line.

To begin longeing, choose a place that does not have slippery or deep footing, since slickness often leads to interference between the limbs, and deep footing can injure soft tissue in the legs. The longe line should be wrapped into loops, each measuring about four feet in circumference, with the first loop being the one on the bottom. This allows you to drop one loop at a time from the top, preventing the line from getting tangled (fig. 2-5).

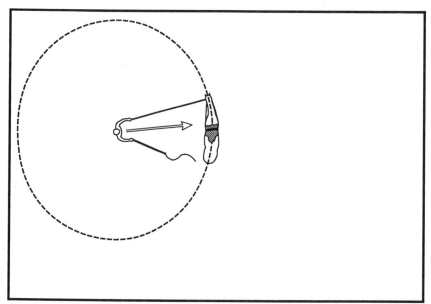

2-4. This top view of longeing shows the proper relationship of the trainer and equipment to the horse. In his left hand, the trainer holds the longe line and in his right hand he holds the whip, as the horse works counterclockwise on the circle. The trainer's chest correctly faces the horse's shoulder.

Thread the snap of the line through one ring of the bit and over the horse's head, attaching it to the top of the bit ring on the other side (see figs. 2-1, 2-2). This enables your hand to act on both sides of the horse's mouth. While you are attaching the longe line, hold the stock of the whip under your armpit, on the side away from the horse. This is the method used to carry the whip whenever you are working with a standing horse or are walking from one site to another. The thong should be wrapped around the stock and tied, so that the horse cannot get its feet caught in it (fig. 2-6).

Once the longe line has been threaded through the bit and attached on the opposite side, untie the thong of the whip and twist the stock until the thong is completely unwound. Then, drop a couple of loops of the longe line and quietly back away from the horse, moving toward its haunches, with the whip held perpendicular to the longe line. This makes the horse aware of the whip without having it in such close proximity that the animal dashes off (fig. 2-7).

2-5. The longe line is wrapped properly in preparation for work, with the handle on the bottom loop and the snap on the top.

2-6. The trainer holds the whip under her armpit, on the side away from the horse, to prevent frightening the animal as she checks the equipment. The thong is wrapped around the whip and tied with a half knot prior to work so that the horse will not get its feet tangled in it while walking to the arena. Notice in the boxed diagram how the stirrup leather is looped back and forth through the iron to secure the stirrup for longeing.

2-7. The trainer begins by letting two loops of the longe line slide through her hand and drop, while holding the whip perpendicular to the horse to prevent spooking it in the initial stage of work.

2-8. The trainer has moved from his original position, indicated by the gray shading, to a position in line with the horse's haunches in order to drive the horse forward with the whip and provide an "open door" to the left through which the horse can travel.

The horse will usually begin to move forward when its sees the whip, at which point you let a few more loops drop by allowing them to slide through your hand. If the horse has not begun to move, slowly bring the whip toward its hocks until it responds by walking forward. Allow the horse to travel on a large circle, with about 18 feet of line at the walk and up to 26 feet of line at the trot and canter.

When starting the horse on the circle, move the whip toward the hocks as soon as possible without spooking the animal. The whip should form one leg of a triangular shape made up of the horse's body, the longe line, and the longe whip. If the horse runs wildly from the whip, drop it on the ground until the animal has worked off some of its energy. Then, pick it up again.

On the other hand, if the horse ignores the whip and plods forward, move to a position in line with its rear end and motivate the animal by flicking the whip toward its hocks. By moving toward the rear of the horse, you give the animal an open door through which its forehand can travel (fig. 2-8).

If it ignores your movement toward its haunches and the motions of the whip, tighten the circle by slowly taking up a loop or two, until the horse is close enough to the thong to respect it. Once the

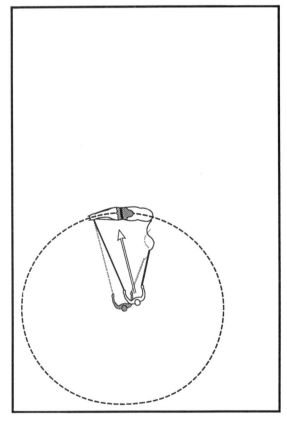

animal is working in a good rhythm, drop the loop or loops slowly to allow it to move back onto a wider, more comfortable circle. If it begins to ignore the whip again, bring it back onto a smaller circle. You can hit the horse lightly on the hocks with the whip to encourage it forward, but be prepared to get out of the way when you do, since a horse will sometimes kick out at the whip. Be persistent in your encouragement with the whip if necessary, but make sure the animal realizes when you are moving toward its hocks. (Remember that a horse's natural reaction is to kick anything that surprises it from behind.) By watching the horse's expression, you can tell if the animal is aware of your movements or is ignoring you.

Correct longeing requires your complete concentration. You must watch the horse's expression and monitor its rhythm incessantly, so that you will know what adjustments are necessary at each moment. For example, if the horse slides its haunches to the outside of the circle in an attempt to stop and face you, it is important to move to its rear end quickly. If you haven't been paying attention, you won't notice the problem developing and will not be able to react in time to keep the horse moving around the circle. You will then have to take up all of the loops in the line and start again.

Although you monitor the rhythm of the horse's haunches when longeing, your body should not be turned toward the haunches, but toward the horse's shoulder. This position enables your leg toward the rear of the horse to step around your other leg as you turn. For example, when longeing the horse counterclockwise, your right leg steps around your pivotal left leg (fig. 2-9). When longeing a well-trained horse, your pivotal foot will step in approximately the same place each time, for the horse will respond properly to the longe line and whip; but when longeing a horse that is inexperienced, you usually will not be able to remain in the center of the circle at all times. Instead you must move toward the haunches when necessary to motivate the horse, then move toward the shoulder when the horse is going forward properly. (Theoretically, by moving in front of the shoulder, you should be able to slow your horse. But in practice, if you place yourself too far to the front of the horse, it will stop, then turn and move in the other direction, getting the line wrapped around its head.)

The direction of longeing should be changed

2-9. When longeing, the trainer's foot toward the direction in which the horse is moving is the pivotal foot, and the opposite foot steps around it. In this case, the trainer's left foot is the pivotal foot and her right foot steps around it as the horse moves counterclockwise. This helps the trainer keep her balance, which is especially important if the horse bolts.

about every five minutes, so that the animal will not have stress on its body in one direction for too long. To change direction, place the whip under your arm or drop it on the ground, so that it won't spook the horse as you rewind the loops. Then, say "whoa" until the animal stops and rewind the line, placing each loop over the preceding one. Once you have gathered the loops all the way to the horse, unhook the line from the far side of its head, making sure you keep a hand on the reins once the longe line has been removed. Thread the line again, starting from the far side. After hooking the snap onto the bit ring, pick up the whip and begin to longe the horse in the new direction.

Longeing is not a cure-all, but it can be helpful in releasing some of the excess energy of a tense horse. However, the original use for longeing was not as a means of tiring the animal, but of training it. Traditionally, longeing has been used to accustom young horses to working under tack and to improve the balance and rhythm of horses of all ages. If the longe line is gradually shortened so that the horse is brought onto a smaller circle, the exercise will teach the horse to collect itself. The smaller circle is more stressful on the horse's body, however, and should only be maintained for one or two revolutions before the animal can return to the original track.

When the horse's equipment is adjusted properly and the person longeing the animal keeps it going forward in a steady rhythm at each gait, longeing correctly develops the horse's haunches and top-line. Four five-minute sessions, with a change of direction between each, is plenty of work on the longe line for normal training. With a tense horse, it may take another ten minutes, but if you longe longer than this you are risking lameness. Longeing is confining, and the same physical stress that quiets the tense horse can break it down if used to excess.

When you have finished longeing, take up the line by wrapping it in loops, with each new loop being placed on top of the preceding one. Tie off the line by wrapping the end of the last loop around the other loops, then sliding the snap hook through the small hole left at the top. You can then store the longe line by hanging it from the snap hook (fig. 2-10 A, B, C, D, E, F, G, H).

A

B

2-10 A, B, C, D, E, F, G, H. By holding the loop at the end of the line, rather than slipping it over your wrist, you will be less likely to become snared if the horse bolts (A). From this position, to begin wrapping the line, drop the whip in your opposite hand, then use that hand to wrap the loops as you slow the horse and bring it into the center of the circle. When you have finished wrapping the loops, the line should have the handle on the bottom and the snap on the top (B). Lift the snap and a few inches of line (C) and wrap them around the remainder of the line (D, E, F). When no more line is left, slide the snap through the small hole at the top (G). When the line is wrapped properly, you can hang it by the snap until its next use (H).

Unsnap both side reins from the bit, then take them off the girth. To prevent the horse from spooking from the dangling side reins, cross the ends with the snaps over the horse's withers until you are able to remove the other ends from the girth (fig. 2-11). Make all adjustments to side reins outside the barn, both when connecting the reins before work and when taking them off afterwards. A horse fidgeting in side reins may rear and fall backwards, which is particularly dangerous in a busy, paved barn aisle.

Wind the thong around the stock of the whip and tie half a knot to hold it in place (fig. 2-12). The whip can be hung on a wall or stored in a corner of your tackroom.

2-11. To prevent the side reins from dangling against the horse's legs and spooking it while you are removing the equipment, unsnap each rein from the bit and cross it over the withers before you remove the other end from the girth. The photograph shows the trainer removing a side rein from the girth, after the snap ends have been crossed over the withers.

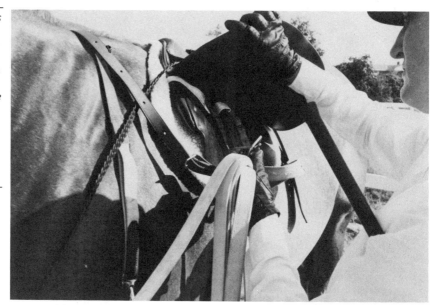

2-12. A half knot holds the thong around the stock of the longe whip. This makes the whip neat for storage.

Devising A Work Plan

A good rider evaluates the animal's strengths and weaknesses in the first few minutes of work, then spends the rest of the session practicing specific exercises to improve the trouble spots. This is the only way you can get the most out of your riding time, for each day you should seek to improve the horse at least slightly in one of its weak areas. If all goes well, the flat session lasts about 20 to 30 minutes, including several two-minute breaks which should be interspersed evenly throughout the session. If you are having difficulty, you can continue working the horse for up to another half hour, again including several breaks. Working longer than this becomes less and less productive. A horse that will not respond positively within an hour is either being ridden very poorly or is so excited and distracted that you should have taken the edge off of it by longeing beforehand.

Although you may have a specific exercise or two that you would like to practice that day, your general work plan should be formulated according to your horse's response in the first few minutes of work. For example, if the horse is a little dull that day, choose lively exercises, such as lengthening at the gaits, or practice upward transitions to promote obedience to your legs. The basic problem of lack of pace needs to be solved before you attempt any lateral exercises, since lateral movements tend to slow the horse down.

When you finally achieve the forward momentum you want, it might be so late in the training session that the horse is very tired. In this case, it would be better to end on a good note, having been successful in increasing the horse's sensitivity to the leg, than to attempt a more difficult movement on a tired horse.

Occasionally, the reverse situation occurs, in which your horse starts out working much better than expected and you find you can introduce a more difficult movement earlier than you had planned. The work plan, then, should be devised each day as you ride, for if you have a preconceived plan and are inflexible, you will not get the best results from your horse.

The Walk

Establishing Pace

When you enter an arena, allow the animal to stretch and relax at the walk on loose reins for a couple of minutes before you begin work. This gives the horse a good feeling about the ring, rather than making the animal think of it only as a workplace.

Then, take up the slack in the reins until you have a soft, but steady, contact on the horse's mouth, with the animal traveling in a long frame at the walk. Think of the ideal tempo for your particular horse and, through the use of your aids, ask the animal to stick to it. (If the tempo you are dictating turns out to be slightly slow or fast when the horse reaches it, you can make the necessary adjustments.) On a dull horse, dictate a marching rhythm that makes the horse's hind end work, but not a tempo so fast that the animal is encouraged to break into a trot. On a quick horse, dictate a steady rhythm that is slower than that at which the horse wants to travel, so that it encourages it to calm down and stretch for longer, more relaxed steps.

Mark the rhythm of the walk by silently counting 1,2; 1,2; 1,2; etc., as you mentally track the footfalls of the hind feet each time they strike underneath your seat. Although the walk is a four-beat gait, the feet fall too quickly to reasonably count them in fours, so only concern yourself with the footfalls of the hind two feet. (The front feet can only go where the hind feet push them, so if you control the hind feet, you control the horse.)

Motivating the Dull Horse

If the dull horse will not keep the proper tempo without being nagged by your legs, then supplement your leg aid with spurs or a stick. The horse should think: "If I do not move forward from leg pressure, then the rider will spur me; and if I do not move forward from the spur, then he will punish me with the stick." Finally, the horse concludes that it would be better to respond to the leg and avoid the spur and stick altogether.

I often see riders jabbing their horses every step with the spur. In this case, the rider is not using his reinforcements properly. If the horse doesn't respond to the spur, then punish the animal with the stick. If the stick seems to fall on lifeless flesh, then punish the horse more forcefully. You know you've accurately gauged the strength of the stick when the horse reacts with respect for it. If the horse ignores it, you have not hit the animal hard enough; and if it reacts to the stick with fear, then your punishment has been too harsh. Apply the stick with just enough force to get the performance you desire, for excess use of force creates new problems, such as anxiety and too much pace.

Controlling the Quick Horse

Quickness of movement is not only a by-product of nervousness, but also a perpetuator of it. If you can persuade the horse to physically slow down, the animal will usually become more mentally relaxed. This takes your complete concentration, for you must dictate every step on a quick horse, or else the animal will immediately resume a fast walk.

As discussed earlier, half-halts can be used to establish and maintain the proper rhythm at the walk, or they can be used during a downward transition to slow the horse gradually until it halts. Half-halts reprimand the quick horse, but halting is even more effective because it requires the horse not only to slow down, but to obey to the point of immobility. Therefore, when you ask the horse to halt, you further promote obedience to your aids.

In changing from a walk to a halt on a long frame, emphasis is on the horse's willingness to respond to your restrictive aids and stand still at the halt. Although engagement of the hocks is not an issue when the horse is asked to halt while in a long frame, the horse should nevertheless stand squarely and not stop with its hocks trailing behind.

Walking and halting several times teaches the horse to wait for you to dictate the rhythm. At the

halt, require the horse to stand immobile for four to six seconds, the same period of time used in competition. When schooling, if the horse is jittery and wants to move, you can say "whoa" in a low, calm voice, or reach down with one hand and pat the animal near its withers. This action does not solve the horse's nervous problem, but it does reassure the animal—particularly a young horse—and can calm it down a little.

If the horse wants to lurch forward into the walk again, or if it has pulled during the downward transition, the halt can be followed by backing. To back, apply leg pressure, but completely restrict any forward movement with your hands, so that the horse moves into the bit and, finding no forward escape, moves backward. At that instant, ease the pressure of your legs to allow the horse to step backward. On a very sensitive horse, you may not need to use your legs to motivate the animal, but may get the proper response from adding pressure in your hands alone. In this case, your legs simply maintain straightness of the hindquarters.

Backing requires the quick horse to submit completely, not only by prohibiting it from rushing forward, but also by making it concentrate on moving in the opposite direction from the one in which it would rather go. It works well in correcting horses that pull because it makes them activate their haunches in upward and backward steps, rather than allowing them to use their haunches in low, forward, bracing steps to exert more pressure on the bit.

On jittery horses that do not want to stand, backing may elicit the frightening response of rearing. A horse that is nervously dancing around, champing at the bit, or looking anxiously from one object to another should be longed to release some of its energy before it is restricted with halting or backing, both of which make it too easy for the animal to channel all of its energy upward.

The Importance of the Walk

The walk comes into your work plan time and

again when, for example, you practice a lateral movement at the walk before attempting it at the upper gaits; when you give your horse a break on a free rein; or when you collect the reins after a break and walk for a short while before picking up another gait. You do not have to walk the horse for long periods of time, but do practice the walk a little each day, so that your horse considers it to be a working gait and does not anticipate the trot by jogging whenever you pick up the reins.

Intersperse free walks into your work frequently, so that the horse can stretch and relax. If you do not do this about every five minutes, then its muscles will become so cramped that it will begin to fight you.

rather than bobbing upward as the horse takes the first step of the trot. Smoothness results when you use only the amount of leg pressure needed to reach the trot and when you maintain a light feel of the reins, rather than abruptly releasing all of the pressure on them during the upward transition.

The trot is the most useful gait in flatwork for a number of reasons. First, many exercises can be performed at this gait. Second, it is faster than the walk, so it is not as boring; and it is slower than the canter, so it is not as intimidating to the rider. Third, it enables you to prepare the horse for the canter and jumping. Finally, it can be used for longer periods of time than the canter without exhausting the horse.

The Trot

The Upward Transition to the Trot

Once you have established the proper pace at the walk, pick up the trot by squeezing with your legs and slightly easing off the pressure on the reins, so that as you ask the horse to go forward, you give it a comfortable place to go. The transition should be smooth, with the horse's head remaining steady,

Establishing Pace

Begin your work at the trot by dictating a rhythm with your legs. If the horse does not move at the proper pace, but is quick or dull, correct it the same way as you did at the walk: half-halting the quick horse until it responds to your restrictive aids and slows down; or pressing the dull horse forward with your legs (accompanied by spurs or stick, if necessary) until it reaches the proper pace (fig. 2-13).

2-13. When applying the stick at the posting trot, strike the horse during the sitting phase. This enables your weight to work with your leg, spurs, and crop as a driving aid and is less awkward than applying it while rising. Although the rider is applying the crop on the inside in order to demonstrate its application for the camera, it is best to carry the stick to the outside if you must use it on the flat in competition, since its application will be more discreet.

At the posting trot, coordinate the squeezing of your calves against the horse's sides with the sitting phase of each step, so that your two legs and seat act together as driving aids. Once the horse is moving in a nice rhythm at the trot for a few minutes in a long frame, collect it into a medium frame through the use of half-halts.

As the horse's body becomes shorter, it will be necessary to shorten your reins. If you do not, you will find your hands coming back toward your stomach to take up the slack, resulting in their being in an ineffective position (fig. 2-14 A & B).

Adding Bending and Transitions

Now you must choose between working on bending or transitions. If the horse is a normal type and willingly moves forward at a suitable pace for the trot when collected into a medium frame, you should choose bending as the next exercise, to test the horse's lateral suppleness. If the horse is a dull type and must be driven forward in order to maintain the correct pace in a medium frame at the trot, you should also choose bending movements as the next exercise, but only large, sweeping figures that

2-14 A & B. The rider's hands are correctly positioned just over and slightly in front of the withers, in a direct line between the rider's elbow and the horse's mouth. The hands should be two to three inches apart, with the thumbs tilted just inside the vertical (A). When the reins are too long, the hands become ineffective. It takes longer for the rider to add pressure to the mouth, since slack must be taken up first. The rider cannot use upper-body weight to reinforce the hands because there is no longer a direct line between the horse's mouth and the portion of the rider's back that is used as a brace during half-halts (B).

2-15 A & B. With her upper body on the same axis as that of the horse, the rider is aligned with the animal's center of gravity. (Notice that the buttons on her jacket are lined up with the center of the horse.) She is in balance with the horse as it travels around the curve (A). When the rider tilts the axis of her upper body inward, the horse's axis follows, so that the animal travels around the curve with its shoulder leaning in (B).

encourage the horse to maintain impulsion. On a normal or dull horse, then, the routine up to this point is the establishment of the proper pace at a walk and trot on a long frame; the collection of the horse into a medium frame at the trot while maintaining a suitable pace; then the incorporation of bending movements into the horse's work to test its lateral suppleness.

Care must be taken to make all bending movements large enough for the horse to maintain its balance on the curves. A small curving figure will usually cause the horse to lessen its pace, lean to the inside of the figure, and shorten its steps as it tries to catch its balance.

You should also be aware of the influence of your upper-body weight as the horse moves around a curving figure. You will find it particularly difficult to bend your horse if you lean toward the inside of the curve, for even though your inside leg may be firmly pushing the horse away, its effect will be canceled by your weight, as it forces the horse to lean to the inside of the figure in order to catch its balance (fig. 2-15 A & B).

Some horses will lean to the inside of a curve without any encouragement from the rider's upper body. For example, a typical "school horse" will often be in the habit of cutting corners. To counteract a horse's tendency to lean inward, shift the weight of your outside hip and upper body toward the outside of the curve, so that your weight acts as an aid and gives your inside leg added strength (fig. 2-16).

Finally, add transitions to your work to test the normal or dull horse's willingness to obey your driving and restricting aids. If you are on a quick horse, you will usually benefit more from proceeding directly to transitions after establishing the pace at the trot, since transitions are generally a stronger deterrent to excess speed than bending exercises.

Although your initial concentration is on downward transitions on the quick horse, you can soon combine bending exercises with transitions, such as performing a downward transition each time you cross the centerline during a serpentine. The combination of bending movements and frequent transitions is particularly effective in controlling a quick horse because: (1) a horse naturally slows down a little on a turn in order to keep its balance; (2) the horse's inside hind leg moves slightly to the side —farther underneath the horse—on a turn, causing the horse to take a split-second longer to place its foot than when it is traveling on a straightaway; (3) the slight lateral displacement of the horse's inside hind leg prevents the animal from using its haunches to brace against your hands; and (4) the transitions not only require the horse to submit to your aids by slowing down in reaction to the half-halts, but also to submit to the point that it changes to a lower gait.

2-16. The rider is correcting a horse that is trying to cut the corner by applying her inside leg at the girth, shifting both hands slightly toward the outside of the turn, putting more weight in her outside hip, and subtly tilting the axis of her upper body toward the outside of the curve. These aids bring the axis of the horse closer to the vertical, prohibiting the animal from leaning inward and cutting the corner.

2-17 A & B. During the leg-yield, the horse travels on a diagonal line that is at a 45-degree angle from the railing. The animal's head and neck should be slightly bent away from the direction of travel, while its body from withers to tail remains almost parallel to the rail. (The forehand should slightly precede the haunches.) The horse maintains the two-beat sequence of the trot, with the left foreleg and right hind leg striking together (A), followed by the right foreleg and left hind leg (B).

Lateral Exercises at the Walk and Trot

Leg-yield

To increase the suppleness of the horse, you can add other lateral exercises to your work program. The leg-yield is an elementary lateral exercise, which can be performed at either the walk or sitting trot along the long side of the arena or across the diagonal of the ring, with the horse positioned at no more than a 45-degree angle from the direction in which it is moving.

If the horse begins by traveling counterclockwise, then performs a leg-yield across the diagonal of the arena, your aids would be as follows (fig. 2-17 A & B):

- right indirect rein
- right leg behind the girth
- left leg at the girth

The horse's body remains straight during this movement, except for a slight bend at the poll away from the direction of travel. Your right hand bends the horse only to where the bulge of its right eye can be seen, while your left hand restricts the animal from rushing. Both hands are shifted slightly to the left to reinforce the right leg as it drives the horse toward the proper direction of travel.

To keep the animal's body from becoming bent from withers to tail, your right leg must be positioned behind the girth. Pressure exerted by the right leg creates the lateral movement in the haunches, while the at-the-girth position of the left leg prevents the horse from bowing its barrel toward the direction of travel and helps to maintain impulsion. As in all lateral movements, pressure from each of your legs changes as necessary to maintain the proper position and impulsion.

If the horse begins by traveling counterclockwise, then performs a leg-yield along the railing on the long side of the arena, your aids are as follows:

- left indirect rein
- left leg behind the girth
- right leg at the girth

To initiate the movement, bring the horse's forehand off the track by moving both hands slightly toward the inside of the ring, while slipping your left leg back into a behind-the-girth position and applying enough pressure to make the horse take the first step sideways. The animal should continue traveling down the long side of the arena with its body at a 45-degree angle from the railing and its left legs crossing in front of its right legs.

The function of the hands is critical at the start of the movement. In the span of a few seconds; they must: (1) half-halt the horse to balance it in preparation for the movement; (2) create a slight left bend at the horse's poll through a left indirect rein; (3) bring the horse's forehand off the track by moving together to the left; then (4) change the direction of travel by shifting to the right, creating lateral motion in conjunction with the left leg aid. Thus, there is a shift of the hands to the left, immediately followed by a shift to the right. This must be done subtly, or the horse's impulsion will be interrupted by the roughness of your hands.

If the horse tries to leave the track, your outside hand can be used as both a restricting aid and an opening rein for a moment or two, correcting the error by prohibiting forward movement while guiding the horse toward the proper direction. Your hands, then, change both their strength and position to make the adjustments necessary to maintain the leg-yield (fig. 2-18).

You may find it easier to perform this movement

2-18. The horse has become overly bent to the left in its head and neck while performing the leg-yield on a line running parallel to the railing. To correct this, the rider moves her right hand into a leading rein position, guiding the young horse in the proper direction. (Horses are often more willing to perform the leg-yield down the long side of the arena when they are positioned a few feet away from the railing, as shown, than when their tails are next to it.)

across the diagonal, as in fig. 2-17, since your legs remain in the same position as when you were traveling around the preceding corner of the ring; whereas if you choose to perform the leg-yield on the rail, you must change the position of both of your legs to initiate the movement.

Shoulder-in

The *shoulder-in* promotes control of the horse's inside hind leg, which is critical to the correct execution of a number of upper-level movements. I often refer to the shoulder-in as "more than a bend," since the horse stretches its inside hind leg a little farther sideways than the normal bend requires in order to sustain the correct position during each step of the shoulder-in. This causes it to lower its inside hip in collection, which can be very useful on a strong, stiff horse because it prevents the animal from bracing with this foot, using it as a base from which to pull against the reins.

The shoulder-in is executed at the walk or sitting trot on the long side of the arena. In a left shoulder-in position, the horse is moving on three tracks, with its left fore on one track, its left hind and right fore on a second track, and its right hind on a third track. You should concentrate on the centerline, formed by the left hind and right fore, and drive the horse's feet forward along that line to maintain the correct position. You can best do this by looking down the line and feeling the horse's left hind leg reach under your seat with each step (fig. 2-19).

To perform the left shoulder-in when moving counterclockwise, first balance the horse with half-halts, then bring both of your hands slightly to the left, moving the horse's forehand in that direction until the animal is at a 30-degree angle from the rail. The moment you displace the shoulders, press with your left leg in an at-the-girth position to begin lateral movement. (The at-the-girth position of your inside leg, coordinated with an inside indirect rein, causes the horse to be bent uniformly from head to tail. Note the difference between this and the behind-the-girth position of the inside leg during the leg-yield, which causes the horse to remain straight from withers to tail.)

2-19. In the left shoulder-in, the horse's left foreleg travels on one track, its right foreleg and left hind leg follow the second track, and its right hind leg is on the third track. The horse is bent to the left from head to tail, but looks a little stiff in its barrel, rather than having displaced its rib cage properly a little farther to the outside. The rider's collapsed left side also suggests that the horse is stiff against her left leg.

Throughout the movement, the driving aid is predominantly your left leg, although the right leg helps in maintaining impulsion. Your left leg and hand sustain a slight bend to the left throughout the movement; your right hand controls the pace and prevents the horse from "popping its shoulder" to the right; and your right leg prevents the haunches from swinging toward the rail, an error which would result in the horse's body becoming too straight from withers to tail so that the animal's feet would be tracking a leg-yield pattern.

For the left shoulder-in, then, move the forehand away from the track by bringing both hands slightly to the left, then sustain the movement with the following aids:

- left indirect rein
- left leg at the girth
- right leg behind the girth

Since all lateral movements tend to slow down a horse, you should follow them with straightforward work that encourages long steps and an energetic tempo.

Turn on the Forehand (Basic and Advanced)

The usefulness of the *turn on the forehand* is controversial. It was deleted from the Dressage Division rules in the 1990-91 *AHSA Rulebook* because many riders feel that it encourages the horse to lean on its forehand and lose impulsion in its haunches and therefore is a deterrent to collection. This opinion is not shared by all, however. Those who disagree feel that the turn on the forehand encourages the horse to remain active in its haunches, even when the animal's forward movement is very restricted, and thus promotes collection.

Although the turn on the forehand has been deleted in the Dressage Division rules, it has not been deleted from the AHSA Equitation Tests 1-19. Therefore, you will find specific information about both the basic and advanced executions of this movement in AHSA Test 11, p. 89.

The basic turn on the forehand, shoulder-in, and leg-yield are relatively simple to perform and are beneficial in the training of all hunters, equitation horses, and jumpers. Although more difficult movements such as the advanced turn on the forehand, travers, renvers, turn on the haunches, half-pass, and modified pirouette might be useful for training a hunter, they are usually reserved for horses that will also be performing tests of greater precision in equitation competition, or for jumpers whose courses demand concentrated power in the haunches.

2-20. The horse is bent around the rider's inside leg and travels on four separate tracks when performing the travers along the railing. Notice the straightness of the horse's head and of the rider's upper body in this correctly performed movement.

Travers (Haunches-in)

When the *travers (haunches-in)* is performed at the walk or trot along the railing of the arena, the horse's haunches are pressed toward the inside of the ring by your outside leg (fig. 2-20). When traveling counterclockwise, the aids for the travers are:

- left indirect rein
- left leg at the girth
- right leg behind the girth

To move into a left haunches-in from a straightaway, your right leg slides back into position

---

2-21. The renvers is the inverse position of the travers. The horse moves along the railing in four separate tracks, bent around the rider's outside leg.

and presses the horse's haunches off the track, while your hands move into a left indirect rein position, bending the horse toward the direction in which it is traveling. (If the horse resists the left indirect rein by stiffening its shoulders, use an outside opening rein to guide the shoulders toward the right, into the correct position.) Your left leg complements the left rein in sustaining a uniform bend throughout the animal's body and drives the horse forward in the movement. Your right leg holds the haunches off the track, while your right hand prevents the horse from rushing and works with the left hand to control the degree of bending.

In the haunches-in, the horse's body is approximately at a 30-degree angle from the wall, but the haunches are bent slightly more around the rider's leg than when performing the shoulder-in, so that the animal's feet travel on four tracks, instead of three. (Originally, the haunches-in was a three-track movement, but because of the difficulty of judging the less obvious degree of bending, the movement was changed to four tracks for dressage competition.)

To straighten the horse after the left haunches-in, bring its shoulder in line with its haunches by moving both of your hands to the left and resuming a direct rein; then press the horse sideways, back to the railing, with a leg-yield.

Renvers (Haunches-out)

The *renvers (haunches-out)* is the inverse position of the haunches-in, with the horse's tail turned toward the wall, instead of toward the inside of the arena (fig. 2-21). When this movement is performed along the rail, the horse's shoulders must be brought off the track as the movement begins, so that the haunches will not bump into the railing.

To perform the haunches-out at the walk or trot while moving counterclockwise on the long side of the arena, bring the horse's shoulders off the track into a left shoulder-in position. Then create a right bend with a right indirect rein while simultaneously sliding your left leg back to keep the haunches on the track. Sustain the bend and impulsion by firmly pressing with your right leg at an at-the-girth position, for it is difficult to bend the horse outward when it has just been bent inward on the preceding corner of the arena.

The aids, then, for the haunches-out while moving counterclockwise around the ring are:

- right indirect rein
- left leg behind the girth
- right leg at the girth

The travers and renvers are particularly beneficial for schooling a tense horse. Animals that have a keen temperament are often distracted by the smallest movement in or around the arena. The upper-level lateral movements, which encourage the horse's concentration, can work wonders in making a high-strung animal pay attention to its work. They also are physically demanding and rid the horse of excess energy sooner than less difficult movements.

Turn on the Haunches

Specific information about the *turn on the haunches* can be found in AHSA Test 17, p.100.

Half-pass (Two-track)

Another useful upper-level movement is the *half-pass*. The half-pass receives its name from being a half-forward and half-sideways movement—that is, the horse travels on a diagonal line that is at a 45-degree angle from the long side of the arena. The combination of the forward track and sideways track is the reason this movement is also commonly referred to as the "two track."

The half-pass can be performed at the walk, trot, or canter, although it would be unusual to incorporate it at the canter into the schooling routine of an equitation horse or jumper. When moving counterclockwise, in order to perform the half-pass across the diagonal, your aids are as follows:

- left indirect rein
- left leg at the girth
- right leg behind the girth

The left indirect rein creates a slight bend in the horse's neck. The left leg at the girth drives the horse forward during the half-pass; and the right leg in a behind-the-girth position initiates and sustains the lateral motion. To begin the half-pass, move both hands to the left to bring the horse's inside shoulder slightly off the track, just as in the shoulder-in. Then, when you immediately apply your right leg to begin the lateral movement, the horse's shoulders will be correctly preceding the haunches. The animal's body should be almost parallel to the long sides of the arena during the movement, with the forehand preceding the rest of the body only slightly.

The horse's right foreleg crosses in front of its left foreleg, and its right hind leg crosses in front of its left hind leg (fig. 2-22 A & B). Since it is difficult for most riders to position the horse properly and initiate the crossing of the legs when they first try this movement, it is best to begin at the walk, rather than at a faster gait, so that you have time to think about what you are doing and correct your errors.

Once you can perform the movement at the walk, try it at the sitting trot, encouraging your horse not only to cross the outside legs over the inside ones, but also to have a swinging, athletic motion during the crosses. By concentrating on an imaginary line from your left seat bone to a point at the end of the diagonal line on the other side of the arena, you will naturally shift your aids to move the horse laterally. You may, however, have trouble maintaining the slight bend in the neck and keeping the horse's shoulders in front of its haunches, since these are typical problems during the half-pass. If the horse starts to invert its bend or catch up to its shoulders with its haunches, use a left opening rein to correct these errors. As always, if impulsion drops radically during the movement, straighten the animal and drive it forward until the desired impulsion is regained, then attempt the movement again.

Although the half-pass can be beneficial in training a horse, it is a difficult movement that is performed badly by many riders and, for this reason, may hinder more than help a horse.

Teaching the movement to an equitation rider is more for the sake of rounding out his education than necessary for improving his horse, since there are other, easier movements that can teach the horse the basic concept of moving toward the bend, such as the advanced turn on the forehand, turn on the haunches, or travers.

If you believe the difficulty of the half-pass outweighs its benefits, do not hesitate to discard it from your schooling routine, since it is not included in any equitation tests and therefore is not mandatory for a hunter seat equitation rider to perform. However, if you find it useful in training your equitation horse or jumper, then incorporate the movement into your work.

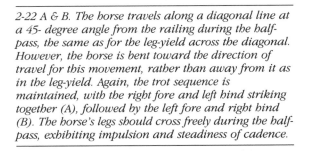

2-22 A & B. The horse travels along a diagonal line at a 45- degree angle from the railing during the half-pass, the same as for the leg-yield across the diagonal. However, the horse is bent toward the direction of travel for this movement, rather than away from it as in the leg-yield. Again, the trot sequence is maintained, with the right fore and left hind striking together (A), followed by the left fore and right hind (B). The horse's legs should cross freely during the half-pass, exhibiting impulsion and steadiness of cadence.

Choosing Lateral Exercises

When working a horse, it is not necessary to practice all of the lateral movements in each flatwork session. Instead, you should choose the ones which seem to address the horse's particular problems. For example, if an animal does not want to move away from the leg, practice the leg-yield or turn on the forehand. If the horse is quick or a little stiff to the inside, the shoulder-in will be helpful. To develop strength and suppleness in the haunches and increase your control over them, practice the turn on the haunches, travers, or renvers; or to test the horse's obedience and balance, perform the half-pass (fig. 2-23 A, B, C, D, E, F).

2-23. For the sake of comparison, the rider's aids and horse's position for the lateral movements discussed so far are depicted from a top view.

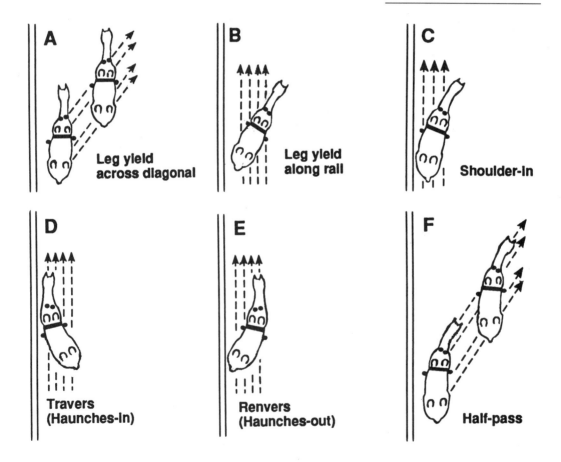

A — **Leg yield across diagonal**

B — **Leg yield along rail**

C — **Shoulder-in**

D — **Travers (Haunches-in)**

E — **Renvers (Haunches-out)**

F — **Half-pass**

The Canter

The Canter Depart

Following the use of lateral exercises and transitions between the lower gaits, your horse's resistances should have been resolved to the point that you can try a *canter depart*, which is an upward transition into the canter from the walk or trot. A basic way to make a horse take the correct lead is to turn its head toward the outside of the arena, then apply pressure with your outside leg in a behind-the-girth position. This causes the horse to strike with its inside foreleg in order to catch its balance. The easiest aids, then, for the canter depart when traveling counterclockwise are:

- right indirect rein
- left leg at the girth
- right leg behind the girth

These aids are effective for getting the left lead, but they lack the subtlety that is desired for show riding. A horse that has its head turned toward the outside of the arena during the canter depart usually looks as though it is falling onto the lead. To avoid this unbalanced appearance, use the following, more sophisticated aids for the left lead:

- left indirect rein
- left leg at the girth
- right leg behind the girth

Using this second set of aids, when you apply your right leg for the canter depart, the horse will not drift toward the inside of the arena, since the left indirect rein holds its shoulders toward the rail. When using either set of aids listed above, be careful not to let the horse gain speed and "run into the canter" from the trot. If it speeds up and becomes strung out, steady it to a slow, even trot, then ask for the canter.

A young horse or inexperienced rider will find it easier to pick up the canter from a slow sitting trot than from the walk. Once you have become proficient at the canter depart from the trot, attempt it directly from the walk, using the same aids as the second set listed above. The indirect rein should be applied only slightly, so that it does not noticeably turn the horse's head toward the inside of the arena, but simply prevents the inside shoulder from bulging inward. The application of your outside leg should also be subtle, providing enough pressure to create the canter sequence, but not so much that the horse moves through the canter depart with its haunches thrust toward the inside of the ring.

To prepare for the canter from the walk, collect your horse slightly. Collection accomplishes three things: (1) it increases the horse's vertical thrust; (2) it shifts the horse's center of gravity backward, lightening the forehand; and (3) it causes the horse's feet to strike closer together. Just as it is easier for a human to lift a heavy object when he is holding it close to his body than when he has to reach outward and lift it, it is easier for the horse to lift three legs during the canter depart when they are positioned close to the lifting hind leg than when they are far from it.

When you apply your aids for the canter—an inside indirect rein followed by an outside leg behind the girth—the horse may react to the pressure from your leg by throwing its head upward, rather than staying in a frame. To counteract its tendency to escape upward during the transition, I have found it beneficial to place the horse's nose lower than normal just prior to the canter depart, so that if the head rises a little too much, it will still be within an acceptable range. To position the nose lower, collect the horse and, two or three steps before the canter depart, squeeze a little harder with both legs and close your fingers, so that the horse puts more weight on the bit and tries to put its head down a little. When you feel that it is steadily on the bit with its head in a fairly low position, ask for the canter depart. As the horse lifts into the canter sequence, it will move its head upward into a normal head carriage, or, at worst, only slightly higher than desired.

Pace is an important consideration during and immediately following the transition into the canter. If you let your horse become too quick during the depart, either by running into the canter from the trot or by lunging into it from the walk, it will be much more difficult to prevent the animal from gaining speed at the canter than if you had controlled the pace more effectively during the upward transition. By imagining in advance the tempo you desire and concentrating on gradually building through the upward transition to that tempo, you can control the initial steps of the canter. If a horse disregards your effort to control the pace and runs into the canter, practice a series of closely scheduled downward and upward transitions, so that by isolating the problem, you can train your horse to perform the upward transition properly.

On a horse that has a serious problem with lurching into the canter, allow it to travel only six or eight cantering steps before asking it to perform a down-

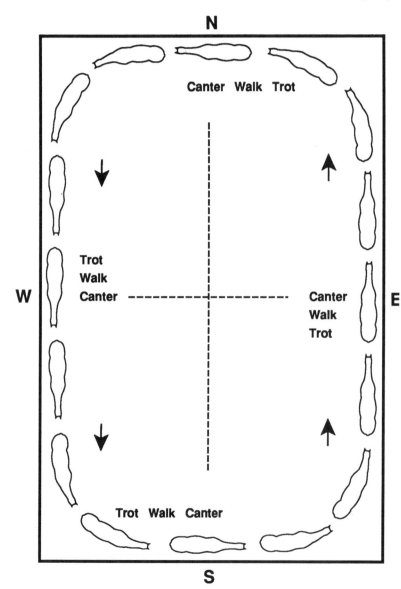

N

Canter Walk Trot

Trot
Walk
W   Canter

Canter
Walk
E   Trot

Trot Walk Canter

S

2-24. To practice upward and downward transitions, you can divide the ring into fourths and perform the transitions at each quarter mark. For example, when traveling counterclockwise, begin by picking up the left lead at the south end of the arena, then continue cantering until just before you reach the easterly quarter mark. Perform the downward transition through the trot, leaving enough room for all of the trotting and walking steps before you reach the middle of the long side of the arena. At the easterly quarter mark, pick up the canter again. You should go directly into the canter from the walk on an experienced horse, but can use a few preliminary trotting steps during the upward transition on an inexperienced animal. Perform the same sequence at each quarter mark for an entire circuit of the ring, then reverse direction and practice the exercise traveling clockwise.

ward transition to the walk. Maintain the walk until the horse is calm and moving in a steady tempo, then attempt the transition into the canter again. On a horse that is a little quick or slightly heavy on the forehand during the upward transition, but does not have a major problem, allow more room between one transition and the other (fig. 2-24).

At a prolonged canter, you must rely on half-halts to deal with an excitable or heavy horse. If you have done your homework well, no matter how tense your horse gets, it will not ignore the half-halts completely. Force of habit works for you. When a horse has practiced downward transitions at every quarter of the ring, it is accustomed to collecting itself frequently during the canter. The horse may be stronger on the bit than you would like, but it is a rare occasion when the well-schooled horse suddenly turns into a runaway.

The exercise requiring four downward and upward transitions for every revolution of the ring is as useful for training dull horses as quick ones. While the goal on the quick horse is to teach submission during the downward transitions and a relaxed, steady pace during the upward transitions, the goal on the dull horse is to make the upward and downward transitions prompt. You begin by collecting your horse, then asking for the upward transition with your outside leg. If the horse does not willingly respond, punish it with the spur or stick on the same side as your initial leg aid, using only the degree of punishment necessary to make the horse canter promptly.

Just before you reach the end of the first quarter of the ring, use half-halts to perform a downward transition, supporting the sides of the horse with your legs to keep the hocks engaged, rather than letting the animal brake sharply in front and drop its hocks out behind. Establish a marching rhythm at the walk for a few steps, then collect your horse in preparation for the upcoming gait and ask again for a canter depart. Each time you ask for the upward transition, encourage the dull horse to be prompt by immediately using a spur or stick if it lags; but be careful not to apply the aids with more force than necessary, or the horse will soon develop the oppo-

site problem of rushing through the canter depart.

Designating certain points in the arena for the performance of specific movements allows you to test the effectiveness of your aids and teaches the horse obedience. If you never make restrictions for yourself during schooling, you may be very surprised and embarrassed to find out in the show ring that your flatwork is not accurate. It is better to address a given problem at home, where you have the time to solve it.

Schooling Exercises Performed at the Canter

Flying Change of Lead

The *flying change of lead*, in which the horse changes from one lead to another while maintaining the canter, is difficult for many riders because it requires excellent coordination of aids, a good feel for the horse's balance and sequence of footfalls, and sensitivity to the animal's emotional state. A good flying change that is smooth and accomplishes a total change of the sequence of footfalls, known as a "complete switch," will occur only when the horse remains balanced approaching and during the change, when you apply your aids at the proper instant, and when the horse reacts willingly.

The flying change should not be introduced until the horse can perform the following exercises well: upward and downward transitions between the walk and the canter, the shoulder-in at the trot, and the turn on the haunches. Downward transitions prepare the horse to collect itself leading into the flying change; upward transitions prepare the horse to remain steady in its frame and tempo during and following the change of leads; the shoulder-in encourages collection of the haunches and lateral suppleness, which is especially important when the flying change of lead is performed between a bend in one direction and then another, as in the figure eight; and the turn on the haunches promotes control of the horse's rear end, which is essential to the successful change of lead in the horse's hind feet, as well as its front feet.

During the flying change, the horse switches the sequence of its footfalls in a moment of suspension following the placement of the leading leg. For example, if the horse changes from the right lead to the left lead, the moment of suspension follows the placement of the horse's right forefoot. For a split second, all of the horse's feet are off the ground, at which time you apply your aids, causing the horse to adjust the sequence of its footfalls so that its right hind leg begins the new sequence, rather than its left hind leg. Approaching the point at which the change occurs, the sequence of the horse's feet is left hind, right hind and left fore together, then right fore. Leaving the point at which the change occurs, the sequence of the footfalls is right hind, left hind and right fore together, then left fore (fig. 2-25 A, B, C).

It is easiest to teach the flying change on a half-turn. Canter the horse down the long side of the arena on the inside lead, perform a half circle to the middle of the arena, then follow a diagonal line back to the rail, asking for the flying change just as the horse returns to the track. The oblique angle on the approach to the rail will help you, since it encourages the horse to collect itself slightly and to change leads in order to keep its balance. This does not mean that the horse will automatically change, for many animals are content to remain on the former lead (counter canter) or alter the sequence of feet in front, but not behind (cross canter). (Following an attempt to change from the left lead to the right lead, the cross canter sequence of the horse's footfalls would be: right hind, left hind and left fore together, then right fore.)

2-25 A, B, C. *The photographic sequence shows the horse performing a flying change from the counter (outside) lead to the inside lead. A split second before the flying change, the horse's weight is carried solely by the right foreleg, which is the "leading leg" for the counter canter (A). Next, the horse changes the sequence of its feet so that its right hind leg, rather than its left hind leg, starts the new canter sequence (B). The final picture shows the horse in its first complete stride on the inside lead (C).*

You must apply your aids firmly, but not harshly, in order to make both an accurate and smooth flying change of lead. When changing from the left to the right lead, approach the change with your hands in a direct rein position, your left leg at the girth, and your right leg behind the girth. Both hands should be shifted slightly to the left so that the right rein acts as a neck rein, working in conjunction with the right leg to hold the horse on the left lead until the exact moment for the switch. Your right leg in a behind-the-girth position monitors the horse's right hind leg, guaranteeing the maintenance of the correct sequence of footfalls. It is particularly important for you to keep the behind-the-girth position as you near the end of the half-turn. If you move your right leg forward too early, the horse may anticipate the upcoming lead and lean to the right, becoming unbalanced and jeopardizing its chance for a complete switch.

During the moment of suspension preceding the stride in which the horse returns to the track, move your left leg to a behind-the-girth position and squeeze firmly, asking the horse to place its left hind foot down next, rather than continue the former sequence by putting its right hind down. Simultaneously, move your right leg forward to an at-the-girth position and relax the pressure of your right hand, so that it will follow the rolling motion of the forehand as the animal changes to the right lead. Then, place your hands in a right indirect rein position to create the proper bend for the small curve around which the horse will travel as it meets the rail (fig. 2-26).

2-26. *The horse begins the half-turn traveling on the inside (left) lead. In order to maintain this lead until the switch, the rider shifts both hands slightly to the left and keeps steady pressure against the horse's right side with his right leg in a behind-the-girth position. As the horse completes the last three-beat sequence before returning to the rail, the rider moves his right leg forward to an at-the-girth position and his left leg back to a behind-the-girth position, immediately giving the signal to change leads with his left leg aid. He eases the tension on the right rein as he applies his left leg, so that he will not bump the horse in the mouth as it switches to the new lead.*

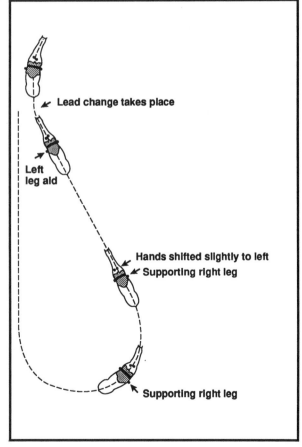

Lead change takes place

Left leg aid

Hands shifted slightly to left
Supporting right leg

Supporting right leg

The flying change requires adjustment of your aids at a specific instant, which makes it one of the more difficult movements on the flat. However, I think the main reason riders have trouble with it is that they try to teach it to the horse in the context of jumping a course of fences. Especially with a young horse filled with uncertainty about jumping, the introduction of a flying change at the end of a line of fences is more than the animal can handle, both emotionally and physically. A rider who attempts to perform flying changes on course with a horse that is not well-schooled on the flat is like a driver who fills his tank with gas (upward transitions) and heads toward the freeway (the course of jumps) without testing the brakes (downward transitions) or steering (bending).

Although some horses can be "thrown" onto the opposite lead by a rider shifting his upper-body weight that direction, most horses respond by changing the sequence of their front feet only. Even those that do change all four feet look unattractive, for they lean sharply to the inside of the turn as they try to catch their balance. It is worth it, then, to properly teach the horse to perform flying changes to both the left and right before it must do them on a course. This not only means applying the aids at the proper place and time, but also making sure the animal is traveling in a balanced frame as it approaches the place at which the change should occur. A horse that is too heavy on its forehand, lacking support from its hocks, will not have enough elevation during the moment of suspension to allow all of the feet to change sequence.

The flying change of lead is discussed several times in this book. In Chapter 3, information is provided about the flying change during the figure eight on the flat (Test 12), during a test of lead changes on a line (Test 14), and as part of jumping obstacles on a figure-eight course (Test 7). Suggestions for teaching a difficult horse to perform flying changes at the end of a line of fences are offered in Chapter 6 under the topic *Horse Problems*.

Counter Canter

The counter canter is required of all competitors being considered for an award in the USET Junior/Young Rider Medal Class and may be used to test riders in other upper-level equitation classes. Specific information about the execution of this movement is in AHSA Test 16, p. 95.

Modified Pirouette

The *pirouette* is a turn on the haunches at the canter. When it is performed in dressage competitions, the horse's pivotal foot should fall in exactly the same spot each time, or ever so slightly in front of that spot. This movement is unneccesarily restrictive for training equitation horses and jumpers and for this reason is modified so that the turning radius of the pivotal foot can be as much as fifteen feet. Technically, this is no longer a pirouette, but should be called a *modified pirouette*

As in the turn on the haunches to the left, the aids for the modified pirouette to the left are:

- left indirect rein
- left leg at the girth
- right leg behind the girth

The modified pirouette is preceded by a series of half-halts to shorten the stride of the horse and shift its center of gravity backward. As you begin the turn, look toward the direction in which you are turning and keep your shoulders back and hands up. You want as much lightness in the horse's front end as possible, for the lighter the forehand, the more precise the turn will be (fig. 2-27 A, B, C, D).

If you can perform the turn on the haunches well at the walk, then the modified pirouette at the canter will not be very difficult for you to learn. This movement is extremely beneficial for jumpers, providing excellent preparation for classes with tight turns. Although the modified pirouette is useful in training an equitation horse, I am reluctant to suggest that a rider use it when warming up before

A

B

C

D

2-27 A, B, C, D. The rider half-halts the horse to slow and balance it in the stride preceding the modified pirouette. Her eyes indicate the anticipated direction of travel for the turn (A). The rider's aids are applied to initiate the turn, and the horse responds properly with a light forehand and a slight shift of its axis toward the inside of the turn (B & C). The horse continues around the turn with a light forehand and steady cadence (D). (Notice how difficult it is for the rider to balance and turn her horse when her reins are so long. This is particularly evident in the second photo, in which the hands appear to be trapped against her stomach. A shorter rein would allow her to be more subtle, as well as effective, with her aids.)

most equitation classes, since a horse's temperament usually gets keener and its stride shorter when it is required to perform abrupt turns. However, if I feel that a turn required in an equitation class is so tight that the horse might overshoot it without special preparation just prior to going into the ring, then I would use the modified pirouette in warm-up. Basically, you should try to prepare the horse with the more strenuous exercises at home, so that you can ease off a little at the show and have the ideal combination of accuracy and relaxation in the horse's performance.

General Suggestions

The Horse's Good and Bad Sides

Just as humans are right-handed or left-handed, horses are usually better coordinated and more supple on one side than the other. Use a horse's good side to help its bad side improve. For example, if a horse's bad side is the left and the horse is very stiff moving around the corners of the ring when traveling counterclockwise, first work on a supling movement such as a left shoulder-in to address this stiffness, then change direction and perform the same movement on the horse's good side. The animal may not be very responsive to the aids when applied to the left side, but will respond better when asked to do the same movement the other direction. Using the good side has two functions: (1) it helps you to teach the horse the proper execution of the movement; and (2) it enables you to reward your horse by using your aids more softly than when you were correcting stiffness on its bad side.

Drilling the horse only on its bad side is a mistake. Since the animal's lack of coordination makes it difficult to perform the movement, you may find yourself in the position of applying all punishment and no reward. In this case, the horse will become more anxious and perform the movement worse, instead of better.

Let The Slower Gaits Help You

When you are having difficulty controlling your horse, drop to a slower gait and work there for awhile. For instance, if your horse is tense when you are working on flying changes, do not repeatedly force the animal to attempt the change of lead, for it will only become more upset. Go back to the trot or walk and work on some supling exercises at these slower gaits. Then, when the horse is more relaxed and obedient, try the difficult movement again.

Variety Prevents Boredom

A variety of exercises keeps the horse from getting bored, so be creative when you work on the flat, blending one movement into the other rather than going around the arena several times between one exercise and the next. Change direction frequently to check the horse's lateral resistances on each side, and perform many downward and upward transitions to test your horse's obedience and teach the basic idea of collection (fig. 2-28 A & B).

Forming a Well-rounded Schooling Program

Although I suggest specific exercises for both quick and dull horses, they are intended only as a general guide. For example, downward transitions are extremely helpful in regulating the pace of a quick horse, but this does not mean that you must never practice lengthening the horse's stride. The preponderance of your work should address the horse's particular problems, but you do not want your horse to go into competition without a well-rounded education on the flat. By practicing movements that expose the horse's weaknesses, you obtain a clearer picture of the animal's development, which will help you determine how far you are off the mark in your competitive aspirations.

Altering Your Plan

Never hesitate to go back to easier movements when you find the tougher ones are beyond the present capabilities of your horse. By going back to something the horse knows well, you reassure the animal. An easier movement can regain confidence and relieve tension in both you and your horse. To press ahead at all costs is never the answer. This is particularly true if you or the animal are very tired.

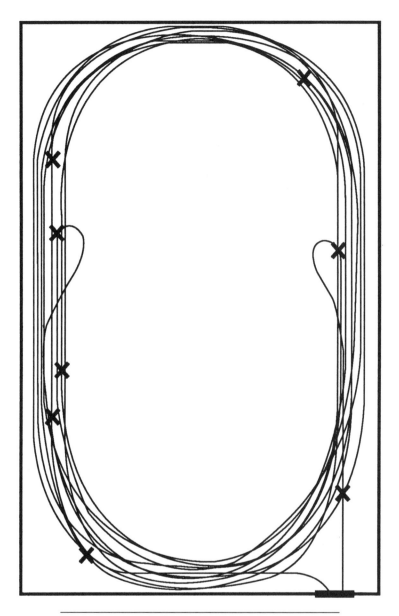

2-28 A. A top view of a bad work pattern shows the rider going around and around the arena performing few transitions (indicated by the symbol X) and rarely changing the direction of travel.

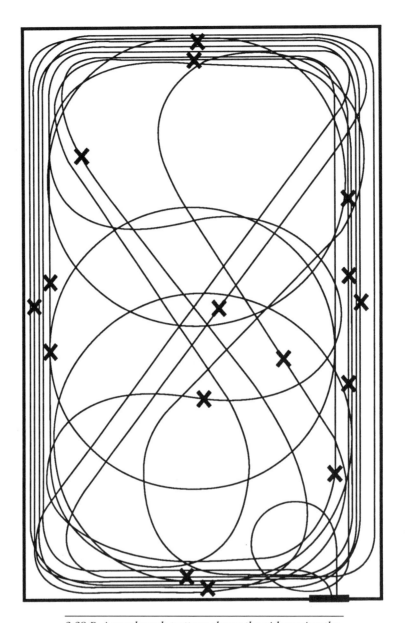

2-28 B. A good work pattern shows the rider using the inside of the arena as well as the track. Changes of direction are numerous and are accomplished through patterns such as the half-turn in reverse, the change across the diagonal, and the serpentine, as well as the typical half-turn. Transitions are also frequently practiced.

3

AHSA Tests 1-19: Tips for Training and Showing

TEST 1. *Halt (4 to 6 seconds) and/or back.*

During the test of the halt, the judge is as concerned with the downward transition as with the halt itself. When a horse correctly performs this test, its hocks stay engaged throughout the downward transition, until the halt is completed with the horse standing squarely on all four legs. In order to keep the hocks engaged, you must maintain pressure with your calves against the horse's sides and may even have to increase that pressure if the horse begins to pull on the reins and drop its haunches out behind. The combination of a supporting leg and multiple half-halts encourages the horse to stay in the proper frame and not elongate its body.

When the downward transition is correctly performed, you feel the horse's hind feet dance beneath your seat. This lilting feeling is caused by the hocks' circular movement as they remain engaged. If you do not experience this, but instead feel that the horse's back is flat and its hind feet are striking behind your seat, then you know the horse has lost the engagement of its hocks. This incorrect position of the animal's hind legs compromises your ability to perform specific movements accurately, since your control over the horse decreases as the hocks lose their engagement.

The degree of collection necessary at the halt depends upon the difficulty of the segment of the test immediately following the halt. For example, if the end of a test calls for the rider to halt and then exit the arena at a sitting trot, the horse could successfully perform the final segment while collected into a medium frame. However, if a test asks the rider to halt and then pick up the counter canter, a short frame would be necessary at the halt, in preparation for the difficult movement that follows.

The main points judged during the test of the halt are: (1) smoothness and straightness during the downward transition; (2) accuracy of the halt—that is, halting at a designated place; (3) a square stance; and (4) immobility for 4 to 6 seconds. Owing to its usefulness as a test of obedience, the halt is frequently asked for by judges in gauging all levels of riders.

The second portion of Test 1 is backing. Horses have a natural distaste for moving backward because they don't like to step into an area they cannot see. You may notice this if, when dismounted, you try to make a horse step backward. The animal's initial reaction will often be to raise its head and plant its hind feet firmly in objection (fig. 3-1).

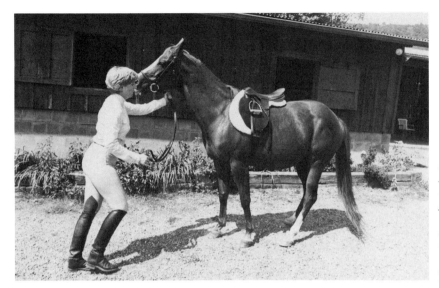

3-1. When asked to back up, this horse stubbornly resists by planting its hind feet and raising its head. Many horses have a natural dislike of backing, probably because they are reluctant to step into an area they cannot see.

3-2. The horse is backing properly by moving its feet in diagonal pairs, staying straight throughout its body and steadily remaining in a frame.

When mounted, if you simply pull on the reins to make your horse back up, you probably will get the same reaction of head raised and feet stuck. To overcome this problem, you must think of backing as another aspect of the impulsion you have been creating in all of your forward work. The only difference is that the impulsion is now being channeled in the opposite direction.

To prepare to back, take a steady hold on a short rein. Then, applying leg pressure to press the horse into the bit, keep a firm feel on the reins so that the horse cannot take even a single step forward. Motivated by your leg, but unable to escape forward, the horse will attempt the backward route, at which moment you should ease the pressure of your legs (and hands, if possible) to reward the horse. From that point on, use only enough leg and hand pressure to continue the backward movement for the required number of steps in a steady tempo.

In response to the aids, the horse's steps should be deliberate, with the feet moving backward in diagonal pairs. The hooves should not drag, nor hurry backward; rather each step should be in a definite rhythm that demonstrates your complete control of the horse (fig. 3-2).

When backing is not followed by another test, you must count the number of steps the horse takes going backward and be sure it walks forward the same number of steps to resume its starting position. When backing is used within a series of tests —for example, "Jump fences 1, 2, and 3, halt, back four steps, trot fence 4, and exit the arena at a sitting trot"—the horse is not required to take the same number of forward as backward steps, but instead assumes the next gait immediately after the backward steps.

In this typical multiple test, if your horse becomes anxious at the halt preceding backing, try not to become panicked yourself. A tense horse requires a very calm rider, one whose apparent lack of anxiety assures the animal that there is no reason to worry. Never rush from one movement to the next. Instead, take time to calm the horse and prepare for the next part of the test.

If your horse is so excited at the halt that there is no way you can stop its squirming for a full four seconds, at least make sure the animal goes in the right direction for the next movement—backward, not forward or sideways. This way, you will only be faulted for a brief halt, rather than for incorrect steps during the backing test, which is a greater error.

Most horses naturally slow down as they back, due to their concern about moving into a space they can't see. This gives you the opportunity to settle into a slower tempo if you are on a quick horse. Following the backing steps, try to maintain this relaxed tempo when forward motion is resumed. By establishing a slower tempo and dictating it with your aids—that is, through half-halts and applying your aids softly and slowly—you can consciously restrict the speed of each step.

It is important to realize that the speed at which your aids are applied is as important to the horse's reaction as the force of the aids. Especially on a tense horse, if your aids are applied too quickly, the animal will overreact and instantly go above a suitable rhythm. You will get the best results only when you feel confident enough to use time liberally, in both training and showing.

Nervousness often causes riders to react too quickly or too forcefully with their aids, resulting in rough or imprecise performances. Backing is a very precise movement, usually requiring the horse to take a specific number of steps designated by the judge. The rider who uses his time wisely to think through and monitor this process will surpass the anxious competitor who is too hurried to think clearly or apply his aids tactfully.

TEST 2. *Hand gallop.*

The *hand gallop* is a three-beat gait which is faster than the canter. The horse should move with bold, flowing strides during the hand gallop, but the pace should not be so fast as to appear unsafe for the size of the arena. As the horse changes from the canter to the hand gallop, you should rise into two-point position to free its back at the increased speed.

At the hand gallop, just as at the canter, the horse's body is straight on the straight sides of the ring and bent on the corners. When traveling on straightaways, you can extend your horse's stride at the hand gallop to between 12 and 13 feet; but on the corners of the ring, you should collect the horse to a slightly shorter stride to help it maintain its balance.

Shorten your horse's stride by opening your hip angle slightly as you approach a corner, so that the weight of your upper body helps your hands and arms restrict the horse's horizontal motion. As the horse's hocks become more engaged and the forehand rises slightly in response to the your restricting hand, arm, and upper-body weight, the distance between the footfalls of the horse's hind and front feet will be shortened, enabling the horse to be balanced on the corner while maintaining the same tempo (fig. 3-3). As the horse starts to move out of the corner toward the long side of the arena, relax the pressure on its mouth by moving your hands slightly forward, easing the restriction of the forehand and allowing the animal to strike farther forward with its front feet. As the horse's frame lengthens, close your hip angle forward to follow the more horizontal motion (fig. 3-4). The collecting and lengthening of the horse's frame should not be obvious, but only used as subtle, balancing techniques.

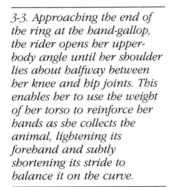

3-3. Approaching the end of the ring at the hand-gallop, the rider opens her upper-body angle until her shoulder lies about halfway between her knee and hip joints. This enables her to use the weight of her torso to reinforce her hands as she collects the animal, lightening its forehand and subtly shortening its stride to balance it on the curve.

3-4. As the horse departs the end of the ring and hand-gallops down the long side of the arena, the rider closes her hip angle forward to match her center of gravity as closely as possible to that of her horse. Her shoulder is correctly aligned directly over her knee and toe.

The main problem riders have during the hand gallop is the horse getting too "strong" by pulling and going faster. If you feel this problem coming on, open your hip angle slightly when going down the long side of the arena, so that you can subtly use your upper-body weight to brace against the strong horse. Performing a series of half-halts on the approach to the corner will help you bring the horse back to the proper pace. This is particularly effective if the arena is rectangular rather than oval. If worse comes to worst, you can circle the animal to slow it down, but this is usually obvious to the judge.

If your horse tends to get excited around other galloping animals, don't start out at peak pace. As you pass in front of the judge on a straightaway, increase your horse's pace, then settle back to a speed that is below normal as you move into the corner. Better to be slow and controlled than to start at the normal pace for the hand gallop and increase to a speed out of control.

Again, the use of downward transitions as a training technique at home is invaluable. If your horse has been taught daily to collect itself in reaction to your half-halts, it is much less likely to ignore your aids and run off in the show ring.

Test 3. *Figure eight at trot, demonstrating change of diagonals. At left diagonal, rider should be sitting the saddle when left front leg is on the ground; at right diagonal, rider should be sitting the saddle when right front leg is on the ground; when circling clockwise at a trot, rider should be on left diagonal; when circling counterclockwise, rider should be on the right diagonal.*

The figure eight is made up of two circles of equal size, joined by a short, straight juncture. The middle of this juncture is known as the *center point* of the figure. You should initially establish the center point by approaching it at the sitting trot, then posting as your shoulder crosses it.

The most important aspect of performing the figure eight is having a plan. An unthinking rider will start toward the figure with no idea where he is going, other than that he will first turn in one direction, then another. In contrast, a smart rider figures out exactly where he will go beforehand. He selects markers throughout the ring, such as a patch of dirt or the wing of a fence, to help him remember where his center point will be and where each quarter of each circle is. When it is his turn to perform the test, he simply rides according to his plan and does not have to worry that his pattern might be inaccurate.

When planning a figure eight, you must consider where you would like to go and what obstacles might be in the way of achieving two identical circles, each approximately 50 to 60 feet in diameter. A judge has already figured this out when he calls for the test, for he would not ask for the figure eight unless the competitors had enough room and a reasonable path on which to perform it. Although a judge will usually say at which end of the ring he would like the test performed, he will not provide detailed instructions about the pattern.

However, a judge may specify that the figure eight be performed with the rider facing him. In this case, the center point of the figure should be in line with the judge as he stands in the ring or sits in the judge's box, so that he can see you head-on when you change the horse's bend and switch diagonals.

Start collecting and straightening your horse during the last quarter of the circle before the center point. Once you hit the center point, at which time your horse should be straight from head to tail, start bending and gradually lengthening your horse's stride until you reach the end of the first quarter of the new circle. At this point, you should be on the proper length of stride and in the correct bend for the remainder of the circle.

Your eyes are extremely important in Test 3, for if you aren't looking ahead, your won't be able to sight your predetermined markers. Look to the center point when you are halfway around each circle, keeping your eyes rivetted there so that you can make the necessary adjustments each step to put

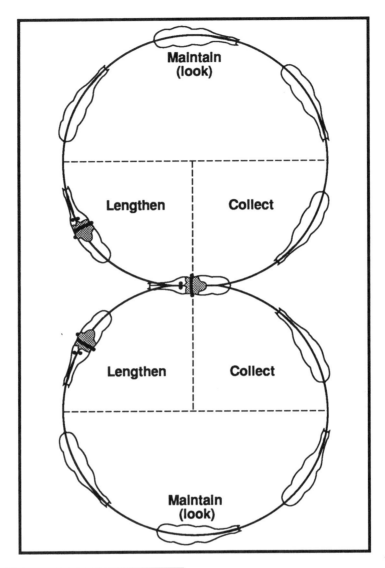

3-5. From a top view, you can see the proper placement of the rider's aids for the figure eight. In each direction, use an inside indirect rein and an inside leg at the girth to bend the horse, while keeping the outside leg in a behind-the-girth position to prevent the animal from shifting its haunches to the outside of the figure. The horse's body should be bent to match the curve of each circle, except when the horse crosses the centerline of the figure, at which point the horse should be held straight with a direct rein and both legs positioned at the girth. (If you change to your new leg position a moment before you change your hand position as you leave the center point, you will prevent your horse from anticipating the upcoming direction of travel and falling toward the inside of the circle.) It is important to collect the horse in the quadrant preceding the center point, to balance it for the change of bend. Once the animal has changed its bend, press it forward to resume the original length of stride. The horse should be traveling with the correct length of stride by the time it completes the first quadrant and should maintain this length of stride for the following half of the circle. Be sure to look toward the center point when you are half of the circle away from it, so that you will have plenty of time to make the necessary adjustments to be precise and balanced as you meet the centerline.

your horse on target. Although you are looking directly at the center point, you will be able to spot your marker for the beginning of the fourth quadrant by using your peripheral vision. Being deadly accurate to the center point is particularly important if the judge is right on the centerline (fig. 3-5).

Of course, getting the correct diagonal is very important. You should change from one diagonal to the other as your shoulders cross the center point at the end of the first circle. If you sit for one extra step at the center point instead of rising in the usual rhythm, you will automatically be on the proper diagonal. Although you should be able to check your diagonal in each direction through feeling it, it is acceptable to check it with a glance while keeping your head up. It is incorrect to drop your head or lean over the horse's shoulder to look.

TEST 4. *Figure eight at canter on correct lead, demonstrating simple change of lead. This is a change whereby the horse is brought back into a walk or trot and restarted into a canter on the opposite lead. Figures to be commenced in center of two circles so that one change of lead is shown.*

To establish the center point of the figure eight when it is to be performed at the canter, approach the figure at the sitting trot, then pick up the canter as your shoulder crosses the center point. The change of lead following the first circle should occur as your shoulder crosses the center point again. This means that all walking or trotting steps must take place before that point. From practicing downward transitions, you know approximately how many feet it takes your horse to move downward from one gait to another. From practicing upward transitions, you know how many feet it takes to get the horse into the canter after the aids are applied. Add these two pieces of information together to determine how long it will take you to prepare your horse for the new lead at the center point.

If the judge has not designated in which direction to begin the figure eight, you have the advantage of choosing the lead change according to how well your horse takes a particular lead. For instance, a horse might readily pick up its right lead, but might not be as reliable in taking the left. In this case, you should start the figure eight with a circle to the left, since you would have a long initial approach to the center point in which to prepare the horse for the more difficult canter lead. Then, when the horse comes around the circle and has only a few steps in which to change leads, you will be more confident about picking up the easier lead.

Your eyes are very important during this test, even more so than in Test 3, because everything happens much quicker at the canter than at the trot. You may glance to check your lead, but is is preferable to know the leads through feel, so that your eyes are free to sight each predetermined marker without interruption.

The size of each circle in the figure eight at the canter should be about 50 to 60 feet. If the judge calls for a figure eight at the trot to be followed by a figure eight at the canter, the path of travel should be identical for both tests.

TEST 5. *Work collectively at a walk, trot, or canter.*

Test 5 reveals the quality of your position, use of aids, and knowledge of the principles of flatwork at the three basic gaits. The most important feature of the rider's position is his leg, since this is the foundation upon which all else depends. The ball of the foot should be placed on the stirrup iron and the heel pressed down and in, just behind the girth. (I rest my foot against the side of the stirrup nearest the horse. I have also seen placement in the middle of the stirrup or against the outer edge. Any of these should be acceptable, as long as the stirrup does not turn during work and the leg is not contorted due to the foot position.)

The stirrup leather falls vertically and the stirrup iron rests perpendicular to the girth when the leg is positioned properly. When viewed from the side, there is a direct line from the rider's knee to the toe of the boot. The toe is turned out slightly in keeping with the rider's conformation, but it should not be turned so far that it causes the back of the calf to come into contact with the horse.

Contact is distributed evenly between the inside of the rider's calf, the inner knee bone, and the inside of the thigh. The calf rests against the flesh of the horse, just behind the back edge of the girth. The rider's base of support, the thighs and seat, should be securely forked just behind the pommel.

The torso is carried erect with the shoulders dropped and the collarbone raised. The rider's eyes look on a line parallel to the ground and are focused in the upcoming direction of travel. The hands and arms follow the motion of the animal's head and neck, giving a flexible, elastic appearance. There should be a direct line from the rider's elbow to the horse's mouth.

The judging standards for Test 5 depend upon the sophistication of the riders on hand. For example, emphasis for young or inexperienced riders is on basic position and use of the aids to accomplish

---

3-6 A. Collection can be used to advantage in a crowded arena. Rider X foresees a collision between himself and riders W and Y as they all try to pass through the narrow gap between two fences. To avoid the problem, rider X collects his horse, allows rider W to pass him, then turns to the left of the fence on the diagonal line and works his way to an open spot behind horse V.

3-6 B. Lengthening the stride is another technique that is useful in a crowded arena. Rider X realizes that if he does not make a move he will be crowded out of the judge's line of sight by rider W. To prevent this, rider X lengthens his horse's stride and passes rider W, arriving at a clear spot behind rider V in time to be seen by the judge.

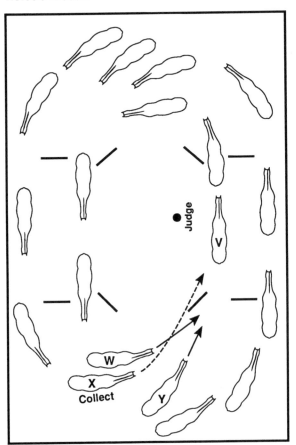

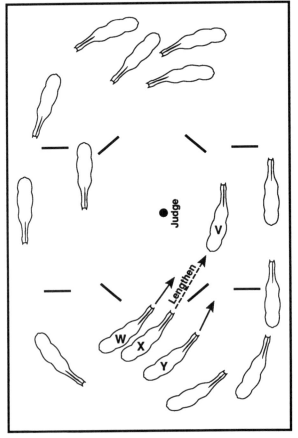

an even rhythm in the gaits, smooth transitions, bending, and most importantly, sufficient control of the horse. For more advanced riders, the elements of impulsion, collection, and precision also come into play.

We have already dealt with these principles of

3-7 A. *Rider X circles his uncooperative horse to avoid passing in front of the judge until he can correct the problem. Rider Z has hidden his misbehaving horse behind rider Y's animal, so that the judge cannot see his horse or his number.*

3-7 B. *When your horse is performing well, make sure the judge can see you. Riders Z, W, and X are in good positions to be seen by the judge. It is often difficult for a judge to see the horse, rider, or number from a judge's box outside the ring when the competitor is directly against the rail, as in the case of rider Y; and it is impossible to see a competitor when he is blocked by another, as in the case of rider V.*

flatwork, so let's turn to the element of showmanship. At the walk, many riders allow their horses to drag along in a dull rhythm, as though the horse were taking a break. The rider who maintains impulsion will not only stand out in this crowd of sleepers, but will also have an edge on his competitors because his horse will be prepared for anything the judge might suddenly request.

You should make good passes in front of the judge at all of the gaits, for no matter how well you ride, if the judge doesn't see you, you will not get a ribbon. Plan your passes ahead of time so that you do not find yourself blocked from the judge's view by other competitors. In fact, in top competition, when the flat classes are crowded, one competitor will often try to block another during a pass, so that someone who might have had a chance at a ribbon will go unseen. It is not necessary to take on an

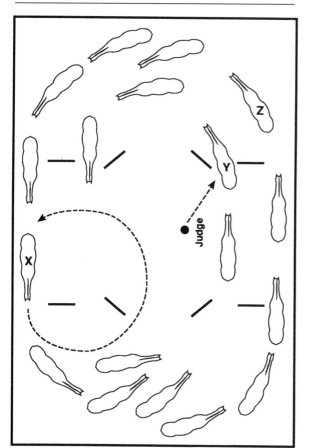

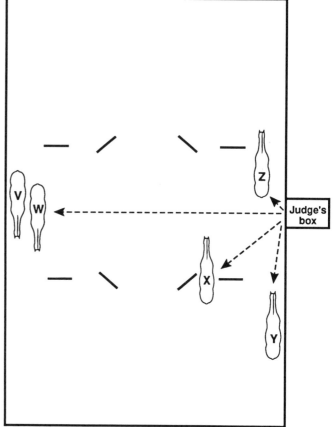

overly assertive attitude by trying to block out other competitors, but neither should you be so naive as to end up being the one who gets blocked.

If you are smart, you will collect or lengthen your horse's strides when necessary to put yourself into

3-8. To avoid the misbehaving horse symbolized by X, the rider on horse W can either circle behind it as he bears it approaching or can take a different path, allowing the horse to pass at a distance.

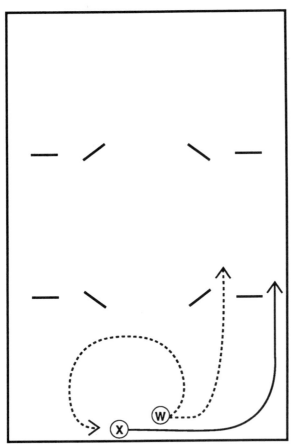

a clear spot (fig. 3-6 A & B). If your horse begins to act badly, you can circle to avoid passing the judge, or can duck behind another competitor to hide your problem, as well as your number, until the horse settles down (fig. 3-7 A & B).

Be aware of what is going on with other competitors in the ring—for example, a horse that is pinning its ears back as though it wants to kick, or one that seems about to run off with its rider. By choosing a different path, such as circling, or taking the path on the inside, instead of the outside of a jump, you can move away from problems that are coming up fast on your horse's tail (fig. 3-8).

Test 6. *Pull up and halt (4 to 6 seconds).*

I find this test odd. The rider must pull up in order to halt, so I can't see the difference between this and Test 1. Usually Test 6 is used in conjunction with Test 9 as part of a work-off. Therefore, I will discuss them together later.

Test 7. *Jump obstacles on figure eight course.*

A figure-eight course requires a horse to change leads either on the ground or in the air, according to how the fences are set (fig. 3-9 A & B). When the horse must switch leads on the ground with a flying change at the center of the figure eight, prepare through collection. Use half-halts to lighten the forehand and shorten the horse's stride, balancing the animal for the switch. If you hold your outside leg back and both your hands away from the direction of the upcoming lead on the approach to the center point, you will discourage your horse from changing too early or switching in front but not behind (fig. 3-10).

If the horse does cross canter, immediately half-halt and apply your outside leg aid again, giving the animal a second chance to switch behind. This, however, interrupts the stride once more, making it increasingly difficult for the animal to meet a suitable take-off spot to the upcoming fence. It will also be harder for you to see a good distance to the fence if you are preoccupied with correcting the awkward-feeling cross canter. It is much better to get the job done the first time and allow plenty of time to calculate the approach to the upcoming obstacle.

To make the horse land on a specific lead, use an outside leg aid, the same as for the canter depart.

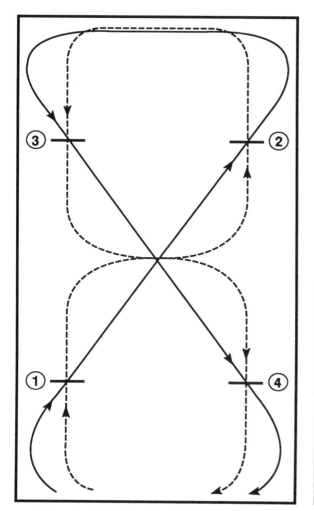

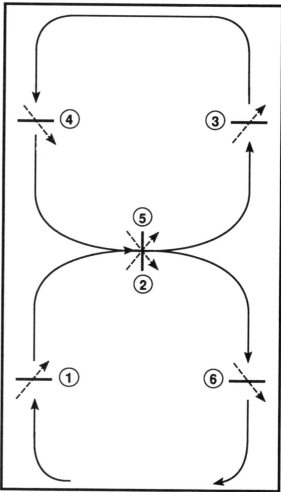

3-9 A. *The arrangement of the fences requires the horse to either perform a flying change of lead in the middle of the ring (dotted line) or jump the fences at an angle and travel across the diagonal lines on whatever lead the horse lands on following the first fence on each line (solid line). Both are difficult tests of precision, but jumping fences at an angle is generally considered the more difficult of the two. In order to take the difficult option, you must make sure the fences are far enough off the rail to allow you to travel on a direct line both approaching and following each fence.*

3-9 B. *This arrangement of fences requires the horse to either change leads in the air over the middle fence (with the path indicated by the solid lines) or to jump the fences at an angle across the two diagonal lines (as indicated by the dotted lines). Again, in order to successfully ride the diagonal path across the arena, you must be sure that the fences are set far enough from the railing to allow a straight approach to and from each fence. There must be enough space between the fences and the railing to assure the horse that it will not bump into the long side of the arena.*

3-10. The rider has shifted her hands away from the upcoming right lead and is keeping her right leg in a behind-the-girth position to hold the horse onto the left lead until the exact moment for the flying change. Notice that her weight is shifted to the left to reinforce her other aids.

3-11. The top view shows the rider's aids used in midair to make the horse land on the right lead. The predominant aid is the rider's left leg, which signals the horse for the right lead, the same as during the canter depart. The hands reinforce the left leg by shifting slightly to the right, so that the left hand acts as a bearing rein, while the right hand functions as an opening rein. The bearing action of the left rein against the horse's neck tips the axis of the horse slightly to the right, making it nearly impossible for the horse to land on the left lead.

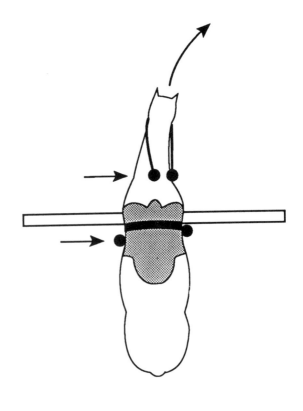

Pressure from your left leg causes the horse to land on the right lead, and vice versa. By shifting both hands in the air slightly toward the direction of the upcoming turn, you can increase the intensity of the signal to land on the desired lead. Outside rein pressure acts as a neck rein, while the inside rein's movement toward the turn acts as an opening rein (fig. 3-11).

Look for the upcoming turn while you are in the air, over the fence. If you have an exceptionally good eye, you can look in the direction of the upcoming turn before you jump the obstacle. Although this will give you extra time to concentrate on the turn to the next fence, it does involve some risk. Horses usually go where the rider is looking, since most people subconsciously shift their bodies toward their focal point. If a horse is very sensitive, it will pick up on your early preoccupation with the upcoming turn and drift in that direction, possibly running out at the fence. If you realize the potential for this, you can make sure you control how much weight you cast toward the direction of the turn and receive the benefit of looking as early as possible, without encouraging a runout.

TEST 8. *Ride without stirrups, or drop and pick up stirrups.*

Riding without stirrups requires a sound position and physical fitness. To be secure enough on your horse to perform this test well, you must practice regularly without stirrups at the posting trot and sitting trot (see pp. 165-9).

When performing this test, keep your lower legs positioned as though your feet were in the stirrups. The only allowable modification is that when posting or jumping a course of fences, you can hold your knees slightly higher than usual to give your torso the extra support your stirrups would normally provide. This change in the knee position should be slight, so your legs do not appear to be cramped.

On the flat, your upper-body position is the same as for the walk, trot, and canter with stirrups; but on course, the upper-body angulation is a little different. Instead of approaching the fences in two-point position, with no contact between your seat and the horse, use a *modified three-point position*, in which your crotch touches the saddle to give added support in compensation for the absence of stirrups. In modified three-point position, your upper body angulation should be about 10 degrees in front of the vertical, just enough to take some of your weight off the horse's back.

The rougher the horse's gaits on the flat or the greater the horse's thrust over fences, the more difficult Test 8 will be. It takes strength, balance, coordination, and concentration to ride well over fences without stirrup support. Although jumping without stirrups will familiarize you with this test and give you self-confidence, the most beneficial preparation comes from daily work on the flat without stirrups.

As for dropping and picking up the stirrups, this used to be a common test. I don't see it used anymore, but I've noticed that many riders have no idea how to retrieve a stirrup when they lose it on course. This tells me that the lack of use of this test has resulted in riders not considering this an important skill. However, the AHSA Rulebook clearly states in the Equitation section, "The following constitute major faults and can be cause for elimination: (a) a refusal; (b) loss of stirrup; (c) trotting while on course when not part of a test; and (d) loss of reins." Three of these faults are considered serious errors by even the most inexperienced competitor. Yet the importance of the fourth, the loss of a stirrup, gets overlooked by many riders until they sadly realize that it cost them a class. If for no other reason than to be able to regain your stirrup quickly before the judge notices you've lost it, you ought to have this skill.

The following procedure will help you locate a stirrup. First, feel where the iron is by lightly tapping the inside of your foot against it. Once you have determined the height of it through this method, you can raise your foot up and slip your toe into the stirrup without having to look or reach down. When a test calls for you to drop and pick up your stirrups, tap the irons simultaneously, then slip your toes into both at the same time.

TEST 9. *Jump low obstacles at a walk and trot as well as at a canter. The maximum height for a walk obstacle is 3'. The maximum height and spread for a trotting obstacle is 3'.*

Test 9 and Test 6 ("Pull up and halt [4 to 6 seconds]") are frequently seen together in work-offs over fences. The instructions are often something like, "Without stirrups, jump fences 1, 2, 3, and 4. Halt. Back four steps, then trot fence 5." (You can see that there is no need to add "pull up" to the command to halt, so judges usually don't.)

When called upon to halt between fences, you must consider several things while formulating your overall plan. First, determine whether the preceding fences require you to maintain a strong pace to the fence that will be jumped just before the halt (fig. 3-12). Normally, you will be able to collect your horse and drop the pace slightly on the approach to the fence preceding the halt, so that the downward transition will be easier to accomplish (fig. 3-13).

By shortening the animal's stride through collection, you make it possible for the horse to look

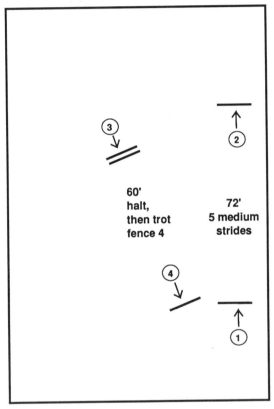

3-12. The long distance between fences 3A and 3B requires a great deal of impulsion on the approach to the in-and-out. This will make it difficult to perform the halt between fences 3B and 4.

3-13. When the element preceding the halt does not require a tremendous amount of impulsion, the halt becomes much easier. To ride this test well, you would collect your horse between fences 2 and 3. Then you would look for a slightly deep spot to fence 3, so that your landing would be "soft," without too much momentum leading into the halt.

good jumping from a slightly deeper take-off spot. In other words, a shorter stride, with its increased vertical motion, matches a shorter take-off and more vertical thrust at the obstacle. Also, when the horse is traveling on a shorter stride, you will tend to see deeper spots. This phenomenon is known as "shortening your eye." (The opposite is also true. By lengthening the horse's stride, you will "lengthen your eye" and find longer take-off spots to obstacles. Of course, this comes in handy when you're having a bad day, tending to see all of your spots either too short or too long. By changing the horse's degree of collection, you can suddenly bring your eye back to normal. If your spots are tending to be too deep, lengthen your horse's stride on course; if your spots are too long, collect your animal a little.)

With the horse more collected and leaving from a deeper spot, you can expect to land closer to the fence preceding the halt. This soft landing, with less forward thrust, is helpful in bringing the horse to a halt. It is smart to plan to halt a little earlier than necessary so that you will have extra room if you need it. If your horse ignores your restricting aids, you will have an additional stride or two to deal with the problem. On the other hand, if your horse reacts promptly, you can add a little leg during the downward transition and ease forward to the halt. Remember that providing space in which to correct potential errors is a major key to successful precision work.

Following the backing portion of the test, the next consideration is how to maintain the trot all the way to the obstacle. Too little leg can result in "chipping in," whereby the horse adds an unnecessary step at the base of the fence. The passive leg can even result in the competitive disaster of stopping in front of the fence. On the other hand, if you are too assertive with your legs, you can cause the horse to break into the canter and even leave out a stride, which may result in your "getting left," with your upper body being so far behind the horse's motion at take-off that you hit the animal in the mouth and/or back in midair.

To avoid problems at a trot fence, leave plenty of room on the approach so that you will have time to get the horse into a steady tempo. Ideally, you'd like to leave 20 feet or more between the point of the halt and the upcoming jump. One aid that will make this possible on a strong horse is a pulley rein (fig. 3-14). Although a horse should be obedient enough to stop in response to a direct rein aid, when the closeness of the fences (three or four strides) demands an immediate halt, you may have to use a pulley rein to ensure that your horse will stop. It is better to be a little rough and get the job done than to let the horse pull you too close to the upcoming trot fence. The pulley rein should be applied firmly and close to the horse's neck. Though severe, this rein aid is preferable to the high, sawing hands that you often see during work-offs (fig. 3-15).

Count slowly to five at the halt, then calmly signal the horse to resume the trot. A nervous, hurried rider doesn't give himself time to think, so he often makes a stupid mistake that could easily have been avoided if he'd only taken a little more time. A hurried rider also creates anxiety in his horse. Overly quick aids prevent the horse from concentrating on the fence and often cause the animal to commit an error. You should approach precision work methodically and give your horse calm, firm, second-to-second communication.

Once you have eased your horse into the trot from the halt, try to maintain a distinct rhythm all the way to the fence. I've found that posting is preferable to sitting to a fence for two reasons. First, posting helps you dictate a clear rhythm to the horse. Second, and most importantly, the horse associates the up and down motion of posting only with the trot, so the gait you desire is quite clear. The sitting trot is easily confused with the preparation for a canter depart. A horse may break into the canter, not because it is trying to rush the fence, but because it actually believes you want it to canter. By posting, you make your intention much clearer.

Some riders claim that sitting to the fence helps them feel when the horse is leaving the ground and, thus, prevents them from getting left. I find it easier, however, to follow the motion of the horse when posting approximately 20 degrees in front of the

3-14. The pulley rein can be used to stop a horse quickly; but too often the animal gapes its mouth, advertising the severity of the rider's hands. For this reason, you should only use a pulley rein if you cannot stop the horse on time with a direct rein.

3-15. The pulley rein is a preferable alternative to this picture of the rough, sawing hands of a desperate rider who has lost control of the horse.

vertical than when sitting just a couple of degrees in front of the vertical. If a horse begins to jump earlier than expected, you can simply keep your seat out of the saddle, rather than sitting that step. Both sitting and posting are acceptable in the show ring. It's a matter of personal preference.

As for controlling the last steps before take-off, it is important to make the horse trot all the way to the fence. The animal can canter the very last step and not be too heavily faulted; but there is a serious penalty if any of the preceding steps are cantered.

The reason for this is that a horse may canter the very last step because it is adjusting its feet for take-off in the pattern it is accustomed to using at the canter, an error which is considered to be a horse's bad habit, rather than a major riding mistake. (If your horse consistently canters the last stride to a trot fence, you may be able to remedy this problem by working through cavalletti and an X fence, which encourage the horse to maintain the trot sequence until take-off. See pp. 104-10). If the horse canters the last two or three steps, however, it shows that the rider is not in control. As always, lack of control is heavily penalized.

Test 9 can also be performed at the walk, with the horse marching up to the fence and hopping over it. If the tempo of the horse is slow at the walk, the animal will usually stop at the obstacle, not realizing it is supposed to jump it. The horse must be guided absolutely straight to the fence in a brisk, but steady-cadenced walk, so that it will walk every step to the fence and not break into a trot before jumping.

You can encourage the horse at take-off with a "cluck," which is a clicking sound made with your mouth. The cluck, if applied each time you use your stick in schooling, will become linked with the stick in the horse's mind, so that when you need an additional aid in competition, but don't want to use the overt action of your crop, you can cluck to your horse and initiate a forward response from the association of the two aids.

On landing after the walk or trot fence, the horse should be cantering. If you've ever seen a horse land trotting after a fence, you'll know why this is not correct. It looks very disjointed and, lacking the rolling motion that serves as a shock absorber, is extremely uncomfortable for the rider.

TEST 10. *Dismount and mount individually.*

Test 10 is fairly simple for riders who regularly mount from the ground. It may prove to be an embarrassment, however, for those who think that a leg-up from a groom is the only way to get on a horse.

To dismount, put both reins in your left hand and get down in either of two ways: drop your right stirrup and swing your right leg over the horse's croup to the near side, then drop the left stirrup and slide down; or drop both feet out of your stirrups and vault to the ground on the near side. Either way is acceptable, but sliding down is preferable on a young or spooky horse.

To mount, turn to face the horse's rear end, holding the reins in your left hand. Grab some mane in your left hand, also, to avoid pulling on the horse's mouth when mounting. Grasp the back of the stirrup iron with your right hand and turn it toward yourself, inserting your left foot in the iron and turning the toe of your boot into the girth, so that your toe won't poke the horse's flesh as you mount (fig. 3-16). Then grasp the cantle of the saddle with

3-16. To mount correctly, place the toe of the boot into the girth to prevent poking the horse in the flesh.

3-17. The rider supports her weight on her knees for a moment or two before gently settling onto the horse's back. Her right hand rests on the front of the saddle flap to help her keep her balance while supported in two-point position by only one stirrup.

your right hand and, aided by one or two bounces on your right foot, pull yourself up above the saddle and swing your right leg over the horse. Do not land heavily on the horse's back, but gradually sink into the saddle; then separate your reins into their proper position for riding. Find the other stirrup iron by feel, rather than looking for it or reaching down to position it on the foot. As mentioned earlier, you can locate your stirrup by lightly tapping the inside of your foot against the iron. This will let you know how high you must raise your foot to reach the iron.

Horses that are not usually mounted from the ground may not want to stand still during this test. Even if your horse is mounted from the ground regularly, it may try to move around, particularly if you habitually mount incorrectly, poking the

horse's flesh with your toe. In either case, you must keep a short rein while mounting so that the horse will have contact against its mouth and not be free to roam forward.

You must also consider your horse's back when mounting. A horse with a sensitive back may try to move forward as you mount, or may sink down several inches to avoid your weight. To minimize these reactions, whenever you mount you should keep your weight on your knees for a second or two before settling into the saddle. This way, the horse won't associate mounting with pain (fig. 3-17).

It is important to mount properly, not only for competition purposes, but also to avoid an accident at home. If your horse is anxious about being mounted from the ground, use a mounting block

3-18. *The rider is jeopardizing her safety by facing the horse's head, maintaining overly long reins, having no grip on the mane, and poking the horse with her toe as she mounts.*

until the animal becomes more relaxed. For safety reasons, this is preferable to having someone hold the horse while you are trying to mount it from the ground, since a nervous animal is likely to panic if firmly restrained.

When the horse is more relaxed, try mounting it from the ground. If you are short and find it difficult to scale your horse, let your stirrup leather down several holes to make the iron easier to reach with your foot. (Lengthening the leather is not standard procedure for mounting in competition, but it is preferable to the rider remaining on the ground, unable to mount when asked to do so by the judge.) Under no circumstances should you face the front of the horse when mounting. This position is dangerous because it makes it impossible for you to catch up to your horse if the animal moves forward. As a result, you could easily be dragged (fig. 3-18).

TEST 11. *Turn on the forehand.*

The turn on the forehand is a lateral exercise in which the horse's hindquarters circle around the forehand in a steady cadence through 90, 180, or 360 degrees. Initiated from the halt, the turn on the forehand can be performed in either of two ways: the horse moving away from the direction it is bent (basic) or the horse moving into the direction it is bent (advanced). A competitor is correct whether he bends his horse outward or inward; but whichever way he chooses, he must stick to that method throughout the turn and not let the horse slip from being bent in one direction to the other.

Whether performing the basic or the advanced method, if the railing were on the horse's right side, the animal would move its haunches to the left to complete a 180-degree half-turn on the forehand.

The horse's neck in the basic turn is bent slightly toward the rail with a right indirect rein (fig. 3-19). Your right leg should be drawn back about four inches behind the normal left leg position in order to activate the haunches into sideways movement.

The aids for the basic turn on the forehand to the left are as follows:

- right indirect rein
- right leg behind the girth
- left leg at the girth

If you maintain a behind-the-girth position with your right leg throughout the movement, your horse's body will remain basically straight from withers to tail during the turn, rather than being bent around your right leg. However, the bending in the horse's neck and the motion of the animal's legs during the turn will make the horse appear slightly bent from head to tail.

While your right hand maintains the bend in the neck and your right leg pushes the haunches to the left, your left hand and leg restrict the horse from stepping forward or backward, respectively, or from moving hurriedly to the left. The horse's steps should be in a steady rhythm, with the right foreleg turning and stepping in place (not stuck to the ground and twisting), the left foreleg stepping around the right foreleg, and the right hind leg crossing the left hind throughout the turn. It usually takes about four steps to make a half-turn on the forehand on a willing horse, but the number will vary somewhat with each animal. Therefore, don't be concerned with the specific number of steps as much as with the maintenance of a steady tempo throughout the test and the successful completion of the turn.

For the advanced turn on the forehand, the horse's neck is slightly bent to the left as the animal stands with the railing on its right side (fig. 3-20).

Basic Turn On The Forehand

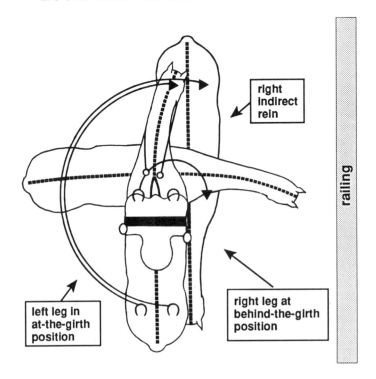

3-19. The aids for the basic turn on the forehand are described in the boxes. The movements of the horse's feet are indicated by the solid lines connected to the hoofprints. The neck remains bent throughout the movement, until the animal is straightened as it meets the rail.

right indirect rein

railing

left leg in at-the-girth position

right leg at behind-the-girth position

Use a left indirect rein, which is the opposite direction from the previous rein aid, but position your legs the same as before.

The aids for the advanced turn on the forehand to the left, then, are as follows:

- left indirect rein
- right leg behind the girth
- left leg at the girth

When you press with your right leg, the horse's body will bend slightly around your left leg as the animal moves to the left, into the bend. The horse's feet step in the same pattern as described above. This method of turning on the forehand is more difficult than the first because it requires the horse to move into, instead of away from, the direction in which it is bent.

Although the horse should not walk forward as an evasion of your aids during the basic or advanced turn on the forehand, the pivotal forefoot may move slightly to the side during the turn so that the horse is tracking a small half-circle with the pivotal foot, rather than stepping in place. There is no rule as to the size of this half-circle, but, generally speaking, a turn in which the pivotal foot remains within a 9-inch radius is acceptable.

Throughout the turn, the horse's neck should remain in a steady, slightly *flexed* position — that is, the neck should be slightly arched as a result of the head being positioned just in front of the vertical, with the poll being the highest point on the curve of the neck. If you keep constant pressure with your calves throughout the turn, you will be able to maintain the horse's proper head carriage; but if your leg pressure is intermittent, the horse will stop moving fluidly through the turn and will usually begin to raise its head obstinately. A constant rhythm is your best friend through any lateral movement. It prevents many problems and minimizes the ones that do arise.

Advanced Turn On The Forehand

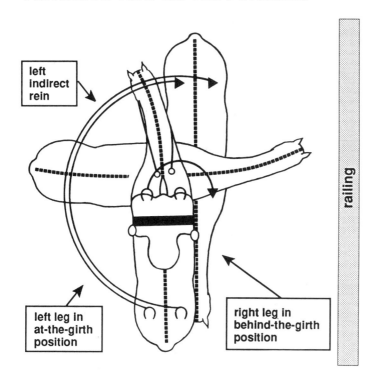

left indirect rein

railing

left leg in at-the-girth position

right leg in behind-the-girth position

3-20. During the advanced turn on the forehand, the rider's legs remain in the same position as for the basic turn; but the direction of the indirect rein is changed, so that the horse's neck becomes bent toward the direction of travel. The animal's feet track the same pattern as during the basic turn.

TEST 12. *Figure eight at canter on correct lead demonstrating flying change of leads.*

When changing from the left to the right lead with a flying change at the center point of a figure eight, you should begin with a left indirect rein, left leg at the girth, and right leg behind the girth as you approach the center point. Just before you reach the center of the figure, straighten the horse by adding pressure on the right side of the horse's neck with a neck rein, while easing the tension of the left rein. When the neck rein on the horse's right side is used in conjunction with your right leg at a behind-the-girth position, the pressure of the aids will keep the animal from anticipating the lead change and falling prematurely into the new lead or into a cross canter. At the instant the horse has completed the third beat of the canter sequence with its leading leg and is in a moment of suspension, position your aids as you would for an upward transition into the right lead, moving your hands into a right indirect rein position, moving your right leg forward to an at-the-girth position, and moving your left leg back to a behind-the-girth position. The left leg is the active aid, giving the animal the signal to switch leads the moment that it reaches the behind-the-girth position.

If your horse does not change leads properly the first time, try the exercise again, making sure you are pressing firmly with your left leg. The emphasis should be on your outside leg, not your hands, during the flying change. The hands help collect and balance the horse, but it is the leg that motivates the animal to switch leads.

The timing of your outside leg is very important. Remember, it must press against the horse the split second the animal completes the three-beat sequence of its feet, which is the exact instant when the horse's four feet are suspended above the ground. This is the only moment in which the horse can change to the new lead.

It helps if you silently count the footfalls a few strides before the change: "one, two, three...one, two, three...one, two, three...." This will make you acutely aware of the sequence and help you apply the outside leg aid at the proper moment. Your timing will be correct if you leave the leg that will be giving the signal in an at-the-girth position as you think "one, two, three" several times, then move this leg to a behind-the-girth position between the count of "three" and "one." If you are either too late or too early, the horse will stay on the first lead.

If you think you are using your legs strongly enough and at the proper time, but are still not getting the change of leads, check to see if you are riding the proper figure-eight pattern of two circles joined by a straight section at their juncture. If you are riding across the center of the figure obliquely, the lack of an acute turn will make it easy for the horse to stay on the wrong lead (fig. 3-21 A & B).

As discussed in Test 7, it is essential that you not let the horse anticipate the upcoming turn that follows the change of leads and thrust its weight toward the new lead. When the horse shifts its weight inward just prior to or during the switch, it often ends up in a cross canter. A second more of straightness and balance will allow the horse to switch the sequence of all four feet.

The flying change is difficult for both horse and rider. To perform it correctly, the horse must be well-coordinated, balanced, and obedient. To achieve the change of lead in all four of the horse's feet, the rider must have good timing, a sensitive feel for his horse, and an educated approach to the application of his aids. For this reason, the easier test of the simple change (Test 4) is used by judges much more often than the flying change (Test 12), which is generally reserved for testing top-level riders.

TEST 13. *Execute serpentine at a trot and/or canter on correct lead demonstrating simple or flying changes of lead.*

The serpentine is not used as a test as often as the figure eight, since it requires more space and can be hard to perform in a show ring filled with jumps. However, it is an excellent movement to incorpo-

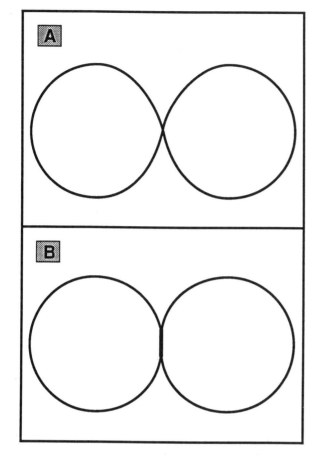

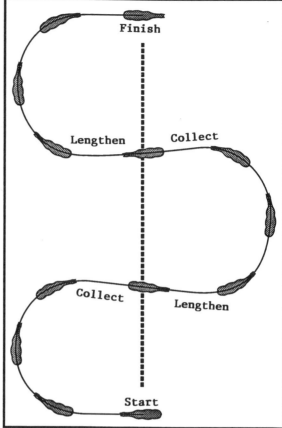

3-21 A & B. When you cross the center point on an oblique line, it is easy for the horse to avoid the flying change and begin the second circle on the counter lead (A). By traveling straight down the centerline a step or two before the center point, you create a more acute curve at the beginning of the second circle and encourage the horse to change leads (B).

3-22. Collect the horse slightly as you approach the centerline to balance it for the upcoming change of bend; then press it forward as you depart the centerline, to regain the initial length of step. These alterations must be very subtle, with the tempo remaining the same as the length of stride changes. Otherwise, the pace will appear erratic.

rate into daily work because, like the figure eight, it alternately supples each side of the horse. Also, when performed with an even number of loops, it provides an interesting way of changing direction.

As in planning any figure, mentally divide the ring so that each section of the figure will be equal. A serpentine usually consists of three or four loops. The figure begins and ends as the rider's shoulder crosses the centerline, and any change of diagonals or leads should occur on the centerline. As with the figure eight, all transitional steps preceding a new lead during a simple change occur before the centerline, so that the new lead is taken as the rider's shoulder crosses it.

To keep the horse balanced through each change in the direction of bending, collect it by half-halting the last few steps before the centerline. As you move away from the centerline, press the horse forward with your legs to regain the original length of step (fig. 3-22).

TEST 14. *Change leads on a line demonstrating a simple or flying change of lead.*

Changing leads on a straight line is difficult because the horse must respond solely to your aids, without any indication of direction that would cause it to take a particular lead. You will see simple changes performed through both the walk and trot at horse shows, but the classically correct simple change is only through the walk. The trot is reserved for inexperienced horses and riders.

Usually two changes of lead are required, which means the animal actually canters on three leads. If the test is to be performed down the centerline and you are allowed to choose the beginning lead, plan for the first change of lead be the easiest. For example, if your horse switches more easily from the left to the right lead than vice versa, then start on the left lead. The reason is that a horse is more likely to be lacking in impulsion and a little sleepy in its responses during the first switch than during the second. However, if the test is to be performed next to the railing on the long side of the arena, start off on the inside lead as usual.

If the test is to do flying changes, use the "one, two, three" silent counting sequence discussed under Test 12 to help find the proper moment for the switch. I also find that slightly raising the hand on the side of the upcoming lead, just as the horse is switching, helps to keep the animal straight down the line, counteracting its tendency to fall toward the new lead.

All precision work demands that your eyes be active. You must find a focal point and ride straight to it, not letting anything distract you from that line. By fixing your eyes steadily on the focal point, you will immediately notice if your horse is drifting in one direction or the other. If you look somewhere else, you won't notice how far you have gone off the line until it's too late to make the necessary corrections.

When planning simple or flying changes on a line, divide the ring into sections, starting with the place at which you will pick up the canter and ending at about 20 feet before the last possible place you can

3-23. Two changes of lead on a line are indicated by the symbol X. When beginning on the left lead at "start," the horse canters directly to the first X and performs a flying change at that point. If simple changes are required, all steps at the walk or trot should occur before X, as indicated by the dotted lines. At the completion of the test, the horse should halt squarely on the line and stand immobile for 4 to 6 seconds. As in all precision work, collection will not only provide greater control of the horse, but also offer more time to make corrections during the test. The horse's steps are shortened through collection, giving the competitor on a horse in a short frame more steps to work with than one on a horse in a medium or long frame.

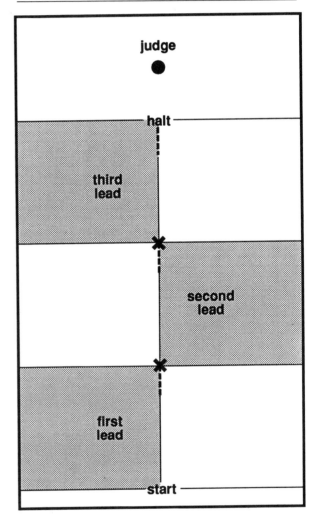

halt. Divide the line equally and make mental notes of objects in or around the arena that will let you know exactly where the changes should occur. As in all figure work, the steps performed at the lower gait during a simple change should precede the points you have designated in dividing the arena — that is, the horse should begin a new lead at each designated point (fig. 3-23).

The extra 20 feet at the end of the ring allows you a margin for error. If your horse is slow in taking the leads and overshoots the designated points, or if it is strong and pulls you past the markers, you will still have enough room to fit in all of the lead changes, provided the horse's dullness or pulling are not so severe as to negate a 20-foot margin.

On the other hand, if your horse performs well and you are able to do the upward transitions at exactly the designated points, then halt at the place you had planned. Leaving an extra 20 feet will be viewed by the judge as a sign of the horse's obedience, since it is always more impressive to see an animal halt in the open than stop simply because it has run up against the railing. If the judge happens to be standing at the end of the line during your test, it would be wise to allow a little more than 20 feet between yourself and him. The worst scenario would be trampling the judge with your disobedient horse.

Test 15. *Change horses. (Note: this test is the equivalent of two tests).*

Test 15 is considered to be the most difficult of Tests 1-18. For this reason, when it is used in classes which require "two or more tests of the top four competitors," such as the AHSA Hunter Seat Medal Class and AHSA Adult Equitation Class, it is counted as two tests.

When performing Test 15, ignore your instincts to correct the horse and instead concentrate on getting along with it. If the strange horse is not well trained, try to get the most out of it that you can without irritating the animal. Sometimes the results of this strategy are very good; but other times they are not good at all, since chance plays such a large

part in this test.

Many riders feel disoriented by a strange horse's gaits, size, responses to the aids, or, in the case of a class involving fences, the jumping style of the animal. The more experience you have on a variety of horses, the less intimidated you will be by these differences. In time, you will learn to put horses into categories — such as a puller, a quick horse, a short-strided horse, and so forth — and will be able to ride the unfamiliar animal based on your general knowledge of its type.

If the judge will allow it, use your own saddle on the new horse, so that you'll be comfortable and correctly fitted. Don't let the owner of the strange horse adjust any of the animal's equipment for you. Although my competitive experiences in the Equitation Division were generally good, I nevertheless found that people were sometimes not honest when handing an unfamiliar horse to me.

Be wary of competitors who try to tell you about their horses. Let it go in one ear and out the other. All that matters is your ability to get along with the new horse for a limited amount of time. Common sense and concentration will be your best guides.

Test 16. *Canter on counter lead. (Note: no more than twelve horses may counter canter at one time).*

At the counter canter, instead of traveling around the arena on the inside lead as usual, the horse will travel on the outside (counter) lead. The movement is difficult, not only because it demands good balance and coordination in the horse, but also because it is opposed to what the horse has previously been trained to do. Force of habit, as well as uncertainty about its balance, makes the horse want to switch back to the inside lead, particularly on the corners of the ring.

The horse starts the counter canter sequence by pushing off with the hind leg toward the inside of the ring. When traveling counterclockwise, the horse starts with its left hind leg, followed by the right hind and left fore striking together, then the right fore (the leading leg) striking alone. The horse

3-24 A & B. The horse is correctly bent to the outside at the counter canter. It is collected into a short frame that enables it to remain balanced on curves during this difficult movement (A). When performing the counter canter amongst a group of competitors, it is wise to shift the horse's haunches far enough to the outside of the arena that the horse will not be able to place the hind leg that is nearest the rail underneath its body and switch leads (B).

is bent slightly from head to tail toward the leading leg (fig. 3-24 A & B).

The aids for the counter canter when traveling counterclockwise are as follows:

- right indirect rein
- right leg at the girth
- left leg behind the girth

Your hands, in a right indirect rein position, bend the horse slightly to the right; your right leg at the girth aids your hands in maintaining the bend to-

ward the rail; and your left leg, in a behind-the-girth position, starts and maintains the sequence of footfalls. The left leg presses the horse's haunches toward the railing at the start of each stride, so that the horse will not be able to move its right hind leg underneath itself far enough to change the sequence of its feet to the opposite lead. If you move both your hands slightly toward the rail as you approach the ends of the arena, the left rein will act as a neck rein to reinforce the pressure of your left leg and hold the horse on the counter lead.

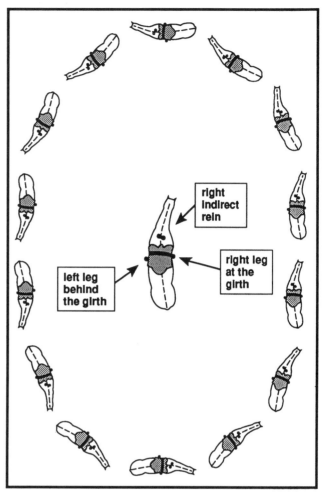

right
indirect
rein

left leg
behind
the girth

right leg
at the
girth

*3-25. The diagram shows a
top view of the horse's
position and rider's aids
during the counter canter in
a counterclockwise direction.*

You should feel the horse's left hind foot beneath your seat each time it strikes the ground. By monitoring this foot, you can control the sequence of the footfalls, both on the straight sides of the arena and the corners, so that the horse remains on the counter canter in a clear, three-beat sequence. When traveling counterclockwise, the animal should be slightly bent toward the right on the straight sides of the arena and wrapped around your right leg a little tighter on the turns to prevent switching leads (fig. 3-25).

Collection is necessary to sustain the counter canter, since a horse in a long frame will lose its balance and switch leads on the corners. However, take care not to let the horse's shoulders, neck, and head become too light through collection, since lightness in the forehand makes it easy for the horse to switch from one lead to another. If you sense that the animal is preparing to change leads, press it forward and toward the rail with your leg that is toward the inside of the arena. As the horse responds by stretching its head and neck out and down, follow this movement with your hands. Allow the horse to shift its center of gravity forward enough to add a little weight to the forehand, making it less tempting to switch leads. However, do not allow the horse to add so much weight to its forehand that it loses its balance and is forced to switch.

When first training a horse to perform the counter canter, begin on the inside lead, then make a half-turn back to the track and continue cantering in the new direction on what has become the counter lead (fig. 3-26 A, B, C, D). Pull the horse up before the corner and reward it for remaining on the counter lead with a one-minute break. Next, begin the same way, but ask the horse to perform the counter canter around the first corner you meet, making sure that you do not ride so deeply into the corner that the horse is inclined to switch leads. From this you can progress to riding the horse around both corners of the short side of the arena. Finally, teach your horse to pick up the counter canter to begin with and continue cantering around the entire arena on the counter lead.

There are performance techniques that will help you attain and maintain the counter lead in competition. If you find yourself on the short side of the arena when the judge calls for this test, turn your

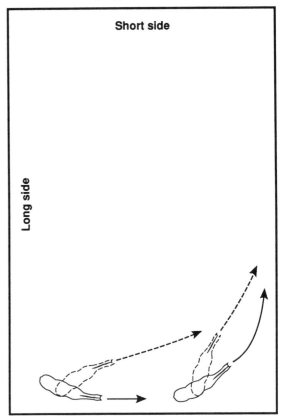

3-26 A, B, C, D. The counter canter should be introduced in stages. First, canter down the long side of the arena on the inside lead, then perform a half-turn and counter canter back down the long side (A). Next, perform the half turn, then counter canter around one corner (B). Finally, perform the half-turn, then counter canter around the two corners of the short side of the arena (C). Once you are able to counter canter around an entire short side, you will be prepared to go around the whole arena (D).

3-27. If you are on the short side of the arena when the judge calls for the counter canter, make it easier for the horse to pick up the lead by angling it toward the long side. Your angle will not have to be as acute when you are traveling on the last half of the short side (the horse to the right) as when you are on the first half (the horse to the left).

horse toward the upcoming long side as subtly as possible before you ask it to canter (fig. 3-27). The reason you should do this is that it can be mentally confusing and physically difficult for the horse to pick up the outside lead when the track around the short side of the arena so clearly dictates the need for the inside lead. By steering your horse onto a straighter path, you will not only make it easier for the animal to initially pick up the counter lead, but also to maintain it through the remainder of the short side.

It is very important to know exactly what is going on around you during the counter canter. If someone is having trouble with a horse ahead, note this and immediately try to steer clear of the problem. For example, a bad-tempered rider in front of you may abruptly jerk his horse to a halt if the animal switches off of the counter lead. If you are oblivious to this situation, you may end up cantering into the rump of the competitor's horse.

It is also important to sense trouble approaching your horse's tail and get out of the way as it comes by. This is not as easy at the counter canter as when your horse is on the regular lead, since it is next to impossible to circle back and allow the other competitor to pass without your horse switching to the inside lead. However, you can carefully steer your horse away from the approaching problem, so that the competitor with the misbehaving horse will have a wider path in which to pass.

Ride around a rectangular arena as though it were an oval, so that the horse can ease along the soft turns of the egg-shaped pattern, rather than be encouraged to switch on the acute corners of the rectangular ring (fig. 3-28 A & B). It also helps to start the counter canter away from other horses and to try to maintain as great a distance as possible between your horse and others throughout the test, so that your animal won't be distracted and switch leads.

Since a horse's main defense is its ability to kick with its hind feet, it will often move its rump slightly toward another horse that is coming up from behind, about to pass. If you are on the rail on the counter lead and your horse moves inward toward a passing horse, your animal may switch leads in order to catch its balance. To counteract this tendency, keep firm pressure against the horse with your leg that is toward the inside of the ring. By pushing the horse's haunches in the direction of the rail with each step and positioning both your hands slightly toward the rail so that they aid your leg in prohibiting a drift toward the inside of the ring, you can generally prevent the horse from switching.

The counter canter is a difficult test of obedience and should be ridden with great care, since a moment's slip in your concentration or in the horse's balance will result in a change of leads.

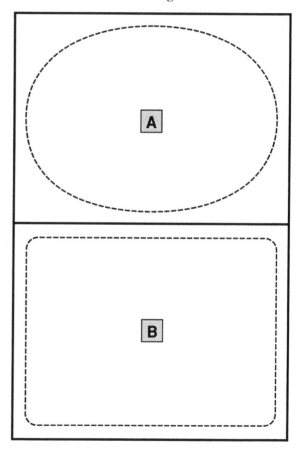

3-28 A & B. It is easier to maintain the counter canter when traveling on an oval path (A) than when going deeper into the corners on a rectangular pattern (B).

TEST 17. *Turn on the haunches from the walk.*

The turn on the haunches can be executed through 90, 180, or 360 degrees, but is usually tested as a 180-degree half-turn on the haunches (fig. 3-29). During this movement, the horse's forehand should move in a steady cadence around the horse's inner hind leg, which is the pivotal foot.

The aids for the turn on the haunches performed in a counterclockwise direction are as follows:

- left indirect rein
- left leg at the girth
- right leg behind the girth

The pivotal foot (left hind) is not required to step in the same spot each time it leaves the ground, but may move slightly forward, so that it forms a small half-circle having a radius of no more than 9 inches. The right hind foot steps around the pivotal left hind, while the right foreleg crosses over the left foreleg.

Both of your hands should be shifted slightly to the left, so that the left hand can act as a subtle opening rein, while the right hand works as a neck rein. The left hand aids the left leg in creating and maintaining a bend to the left. The left leg not only maintains the bend, but also prevents the horse from slowing down or stepping backwards during the movement. The right rein, acting as a neck rein, helps push the horse sideways toward the bend, as well as restricting the animal from stepping forward; and the right leg pushes the horse sideways

Turn On The Haunches

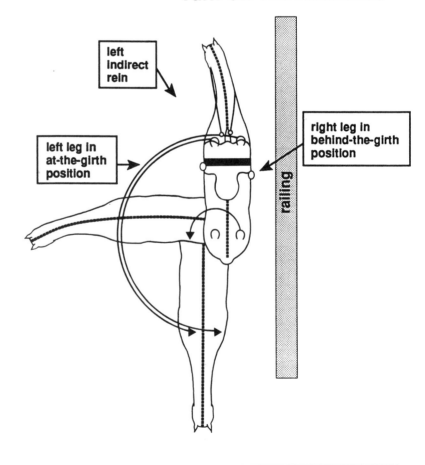

3-29. During a turn on the haunches, the horse moves toward the direction it is bent. The diagram shows the aids of the rider and the movement of the horse's legs during a turn on the haunches moving counterclockwise. When performing the turn in a clockwise direction, the rider's aids and horse's bend would be reversed.

and, along with the left leg, prevents the horse from stopping or stepping backwards.

Requiring the horse to move toward the direction it is bent, the turn on the haunches is an excellent preparatory exercise for horses that must perform tight turns on courses. The same aids as those used for the turn on the haunches are applied to equitation horses and jumpers when neat turns are required: the outside leg and hand prevent the horse from bulging around the turn, the inside leg and hand maintain the bend to the inside of the turn, and both hands work together to guide the horse around the turn. (The inside hand can also be used in a more overt leading-rein position if you need to execute a very tight turn in a jumper class.) The turn on the haunches is a preparatory movement for the modified pirouette, which more closely resembles a tight turn on course because it is performed at the canter.

The turn on the haunches is a good test of your coordination. If your inside leg becomes predominant, the horse will not move toward the bend; and if your outside leg completely overrides your inside aids, the horse will change its bend to the outside during the movement. If your hands do not restrict the forward movement and channel it sideways, the horse will simply walk forward; and if the hands are applied too harshly, the animal will stop or back up.

Since you are primarily being tested on your ability to smoothly change straightforward energy into sideways energy, the regularity of the horse's steps throughout the turn is more important than anything else. You should concentrate on maintaining an even rhythm throughout the turn. If you must choose between the two, it is better to let the horse swing wide on the turn to maintain a constant rhythm than to restrict the horse to a tight radius and lose the rhythm.

The horse's bend to the inside of the turn must be maintained throughout the entire exercise. It is a major fault for the animal to switch its bend from one direction to the other during the movement. If the horse tries to change, move your left hand farther to the left to lead the horse around the turn, preventing it from moving its head and neck to the

3-30. When teaching a horse to perform the turn on the haunches, an opening rein can be used to provide a clearer sense of direction through the turn. The rider is pictured using a left opening rein.

right and popping its shoulder to the left (fig. 3-30).

A teacher can help a rider learn the correct feeling of the outside aids by simulating their pressure and effect as follows:

> *Standing on the side of the horse that is away from the direction of the turn, the teacher places one hand on the rider's calf*

and the other on the horse's neck. Then, the teacher asks the rider to apply the aids for the turn on the haunches and pushes with both hands to increase the pressure of the rider's aids (fig. 3-31).

In response, the horse will move properly through the turn, and the rider can get the correct feel of the shoulders preceding the haunches in a steady tempo around the turn. This teaching tool demonstrates how much leg pressure is needed, for if the teacher must press hard against the rider's calf to push the horse through the movement, then it is apparent that the leg is not active enough.

TEST 18. *Demonstration ride of approximately one minute. Rider must advise judge beforehand what ride he plans to demonstrate.*

Prepare for this test by thinking up an innovative arrangement of movements that will blend together well and highlight your skills. You might do something like this:

Without stirrups, enter the ring at a posting trot. Halt halfway down the long side of the arena. Back four steps. Pick up the counter canter. On the far side of the ring, perform two simple changes of lead. Halt. Pick up the canter on the inside lead and perform a four-loop serpentine, with flying changes of lead. At the end of the serpentine, perform a downward transition to the working trot sitting. Lengthen the horse's stride at a posting trot down the long side of the arena. Perform a downward transition to the halt at the end of the long side, then exit the arena at a sitting trot.

This test could be made harder by adding flying changes on the line or simpler by using the inside lead instead of the counter canter around the corner. Of course, there are many other movements that could add interest to the test. The reason I find the demonstration ride appealing is that it allows you to use additional movements, such as a half-

pass, that you never see in the normal course of a show.

I think Test 18 would be an excellent choice as the last test in the Medal or Maclay Finals. It would allow top-level riders to demonstrate their particular strengths and would be more interesting to watch than normal tests, in which all of the riders are required to perform the same movements.

3-31. By pressing against the rider's outside leg and the horse's neck, a teacher can help a student learn the correct feeling of the turn on the haunches.

TEST 19. *Verbal Test—Question(s) regarding basic tack and equipment, stable management, or anatomy of the horse. The same questions(s) asked of each rider.*

A good source for this information is The United States Pony Clubs, Inc., 893 S. Matlack St., Suite 110, West Chester, PA, 19382-4913.

4

Basic Courses for Hunters and Equitation

A Systematic Approach to Jumping

A training program incorporating flatwork, cavalletti, gymnastic exercises, and practice over single lines, as well as entire courses, is the tried-and-true method that has produced many of the finest horses and horsemen in America. Although the initial element in your training program is flatwork, this does not mean that the horse must be performing upper-level movements before it is introduced to jumping. It is not even necessary to teach it flying changes before you start jumping gymnastics or single lines of fences, since the horse should always be halted on a straight line after these exercises to convey the principle of collecting at the end of a line. The horse should, however, be correctly performing basic exercises on the flat before it is asked to jump. It should be able to keep a steady pace at each gait, perform lower-level bending exercises, and perform upward and downward transitions properly.

Overly ambitious riders and trainers introduce jumping too early, before the horse is either mentally or physically prepared to carry the rider's weight over obstacles. This often results in the horse developing an unorthodox style of jumping that departs from the classical ideal of a rounded back, outstretched neck, and tightly folded legs with the forearms held parallel to the ground or higher (fig. 4-1).

4-1. This horse demonstrates good jumping form, with knees held high, hooves tucked, and the topline forming a convex arc as the neck stretches out and down to counterbalance the hindquarters. Photo: Pennington Galleries

The person who causes form faults by rushing the horse into jumping is usually the very one who tries to correct the problem with a quick fix, such as poling. This approach seldom works. Some horses may be momentarily tuned, so that they jump the first few fences in a class well, before reverting to their original style; but in many cases, poling does nothing to alter the horse's form in the show ring and only makes the animal excited or angry. In fact, some horses will become so opposed to being poled that they will not jump any fence if a person is standing near it. This is hardly the cooperative arrangement between horse and human that produces a winning performance.

Often, when people speak of a horse having "bad form" over fences, they are referring to the contortion of its body to clear the rails when it has been placed poorly for take-off. Even a very nice horse can be made to look bad if it is placed at a spot so far from or so close to the fence that it cannot clear the rails without diving or twisting in the air. Your skill in placing the horse at a suitable spot is the most critical factor affecting the horse's form in the air. Therefore, if you are not accurate in your placement of the horse, you should not blame the animal for poor form, but should work on improving your *timing*—that is, your ability to adjust the horse's stride to meet the proper take-off spot—so that you will give the horse a reasonable opportunity to jump well. (See "Developing a Better Eye," pp. 161-5, for a full discussion of learning to find a suitable spot.)

There are times, however, when a rider places his horse at a suitable point for take-off, but the animal still does not jump well. This would truly be considered "bad form," since the animal could not jump well from a reasonable spot. Although form faults are difficult to correct, this type of horse can usually benefit from being worked over gymnastic exercises, which are designed to teach the horse to use its body properly at take-off and in the air.

Some horses, like some people, are just not good athletes and will show little improvement when regularly schooled over gymnastics. But most horses respond positively to this training, not only because the series of fences improves the horse's form and fitness, but also because the cavalletti that precede them help to teach the horse evenness of pace.

If you start with flatwork, then progress to cavalletti, gymnastics, and lines, you will have prepared your horse well for the challenges of a full course. I am not saying that every horse will have a wonderful jumping style if it is brought along this way, but each horse will develop the best jumping style that it possibly can within its natural limitations.

Cavalletti

When starting an inexperienced horse over fences, let the animal become comfortable first with a single pole on the ground. There are four options for introducing the pole: (1) walk a large circle and cross the pole once each circuit; (2) walk a figure eight, using the pole as the center point of the figure; (3) cross the pole at a walk and quietly pull up on a line, then reverse with a small turn and cross the pole again; or (4) walk the pole and make a series of sweeping half-turns back to it, uninterrupted by the halt (fig. 4-2 A, B, C, D).

Walking over the pole on a continuous circle breaks up lateral resistance on the side of the horse toward the inside of the turn (fig. 4-2 A). The figure eight offers the additional benefit of resolving resistances on both sides of the horse (fig. 4-2 B). These exercises are useful for introducing nervous or strong horses to the pole.

Pulling up at the end of the line simulates collection following a line of fences and is also useful for settling a tense horse. The small turn that follows breaks up lateral resistance on the inside of the turn and further stresses collection (fig. 4-2 C).

Sweeping half-turns encourage the horse to go forward and maintain impulsion, while gently promoting lateral suppleness around the broad turns. This is a good exercise for a normal or dull horse (fig. 4-2 D).

At the walk, the horse should have a steady, marching rhythm. It is not necessary to rise into

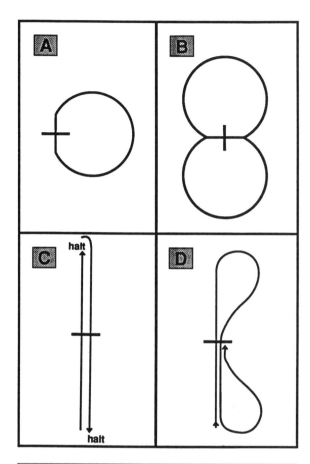

4-2 A, B, C, D. The diagram shows four options for introducing a ground pole to a horse: circle (A); figure eight (B); halting at the end of each line (C); and continuous half-turns (D).

4-3. As the horse crosses the pole at the walk, the rider maintains three-point position, but inclines her upper body forward to relieve some of her weight from the horse's back.

two-point position as your horse crosses the rail at a walk, but you should close your hip slightly forward two or three steps before the pole to lighten the weight of your seat on the horse's back as the animal approaches and crosses the rail (fig. 4-3). Follow the motion of the head and neck with your hands when the horse stretches down and out to observe and cross the rail, so that it learns to expect a sensitive, following hand, rather than a hard, restricting hand that interferes with its balance over a jump.

Once the horse is relaxed walking over the pole, pick up the trot and perform one or more of the same exercises. They may be performed at either the sitting or posting trot, although I prefer the posting trot for all pole exercises. On a horse that is inclined to be dull, the posting trot allows you to squeeze with your calves at the same moment your seat touches the saddle, so that your legs and weight work together as driving aids. Do not pump up and down, driving the horse predominantly with your seat, but rather apply your weight subtly as a secondary aid, coordinating it with the primary driving aid of the legs.

The posting trot is also beneficial on a tense horse. When you are in the rising phase, all of your weight will be removed from the nervous horse's stiff back; and, during the moments in which you sit, if you support your upper-body weight on your crotch and touch the saddle lightly, you can minimize your weight upon the horse's back.

Posting can also help you slow the pace of a quick horse. By posting slightly slower than the actual tempo, you will encourage the horse to lessen its pace to match the tempo you are dictating. You cannot completely fall behind the beat of the horse, or your weight will suddenly land hard on the animal's back, becoming a rough, driving aid. You can, however, post on the slow side of the tempo to regulate the pace subtly.

When the rail is approached at the trot, rise out of the saddle in two-point position two or three steps before the pole and maintain this position until all of the horse's feet have crossed the rail. This will prevent your seat from pounding on the horse's back when each of the feet lands with a small jolt after the rail (fig. 4-4).

Poles in a Series

Once the horse is relaxed crossing a single pole, place several rails at random sites in the arena and incorporate them into your flatwork to further accustom the animal to them. The next step is to place three poles close enough to one another for the horse to put one forefoot between each two poles. When the poles are set in a series, they are referred to as *cavalletti*. Measuring from the inside of one pole to the inside of the next, the distances will be approximately 4'6" to 4'9" for horses, 4'3" for large ponies, 3'9" for medium ponies, and 3'3" for small ponies.

Trot through the cavalletti poles, then adjust the distances if necessary to comfortably fit your animal's length of step, making sure that the measurements are the same for each space. For example, all of the spaces could be adjusted from a measurement of 4'6" to 4'8", but it is wrong to leave the first space measuring 4'6" and change the remaining spaces to 4'8". (If you have an inexperienced, tense, or bold horse, it is possible that the animal may try

4-4. The rider rises into two-point position several steps before the rail and holds this position until all four feet have crossed the rail at the trot.

to jump all three poles, rather than step between them. In this case, add two more poles to discourage the error.)

Keep adding poles the same distance apart until you are able to trot over six poles in succession, with the horse moving in comfortable steps in a steady rhythm. To begin with, you simply want the horse to place one front leg anywhere between each pair of poles. But as your horse begins to understand the exercise and gain confidence, ask for more precision, adjusting the animal's steps on the approach so that its feet will land exactly halfway between the first pair of rails and continue to land in this position throughout the remaining poles. This placement of the feet creates the ideal setup for the gymnastic exercises that will follow.

If the horse lengthens or shortens its steps within the cavalletti, it will inevitably bump into the rails or add an extra step between the poles, signaling you that it is out of rhythm. If the distances between the poles are set too short or too long, the horse will commit the same errors, in which case you must adjust the poles to your particular horse's needs.

One of the most important features of cavalletti is that they encourage the animal to "seek the ground" with its head and neck, for the horse becomes focused on the poles as it tries to place its feet between them. This aspect of cavalletti training promotes the development of the proper *bascule*, which is the horse's use of its outstretched head and neck to counterbalance its hindquarters in the air (fig. 4-5).

Cavalletti are additionally effective in developing the horse's athletic ability because the increased action, as the horse raises its feet over the poles, develops strength in the muscles, flexibility in the joints, and elasticity in the horse's back, all of which are essential to an athletic jumping effort. The horse can be made to work harder if you use elevated cavalletti that measure six to eight inches from the top of each pole to the ground. Most people, however, lay jump poles on the ground, since this requires no special construction. When using jump poles, be sure to check their alignment before the horse approaches them each time, making sure that one or more has not been kicked away from its original position.

4-5. The horse stretches its neck downward to focus on the cavalletti poles. This promotes the proper bascule, in which the horse counterbalances its hindquarters by stretching its neck out and down while in the air over a fence.

Adding Crossed Rails

Once a horse is working well through the series of six poles, set a pair of standards at each side of the final pole. Then, using the final and next-to-last pole, make an obstacle between the standards by crossing the poles. This construction is commonly referred to as *crossed rails* or an *X* (fig. 4-6). For horses, the space between the last (fourth) pole in the series and the obstacle should be double the distance between any two cavalletti poles. This does not hold true for pony distances, however. (See fig. 4-6 for pony measurements.)

Initially, set the X at 1' height in the middle for inexperienced horses and 6" for inexperienced ponies to invite them to jump. The X can be raised incrementally as the animal gains confidence. The maximum height of the center of the X for the following exercises should be 1' for small ponies, 1'3" for medium ponies, 1'6" for large ponies, and 2' for horses.

After moving several times across the poles and over the X fence, the animal will be accustomed to trotting the cavalletti and immediately setting itself up to jump. Following each time it crosses the last pole, sit lightly in the saddle, with your upper body inclined forward so that you can stay with the motion as the horse leaves the ground. If you close your upper body too far forward, ahead of the motion at take-off, you will burden the forehand with your weight and make it much more difficult for the animal to jump (fig. 4-7 A, B, C, D, E, F). On landing, your hips should stay with the motion, rather than the hip angle opening up and your seat dropping

4-6. The diagram shows how six cavalletti poles (indicated by the numbered circles at the top) are rearranged to make four cavalletti poles and an X-fence. Measurements between the elements are given for both horses and ponies.

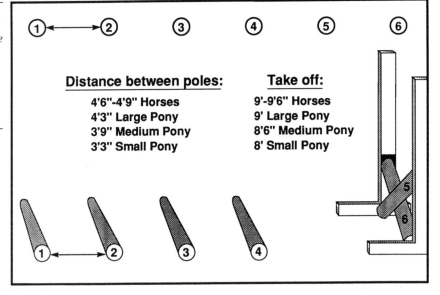

Distance between poles:

4'6"-4'9" Horses
4'3" Large Pony
3'9" Medium Pony
3'3" Small Pony

Take off:

9'-9'6" Horses
9' Large Pony
8'6" Medium Pony
8' Small Pony

4-7 A, B, C, D, E, F. The rider helps her horse maintain its balance by staying with its motion on the approach to the fence (A), at take-off (B), and in the air (C). In contrast, when the rider is ahead of the motion, she overloads the horse's forehand on the approach to the fence (D), at take-off (E), and in the air (F).

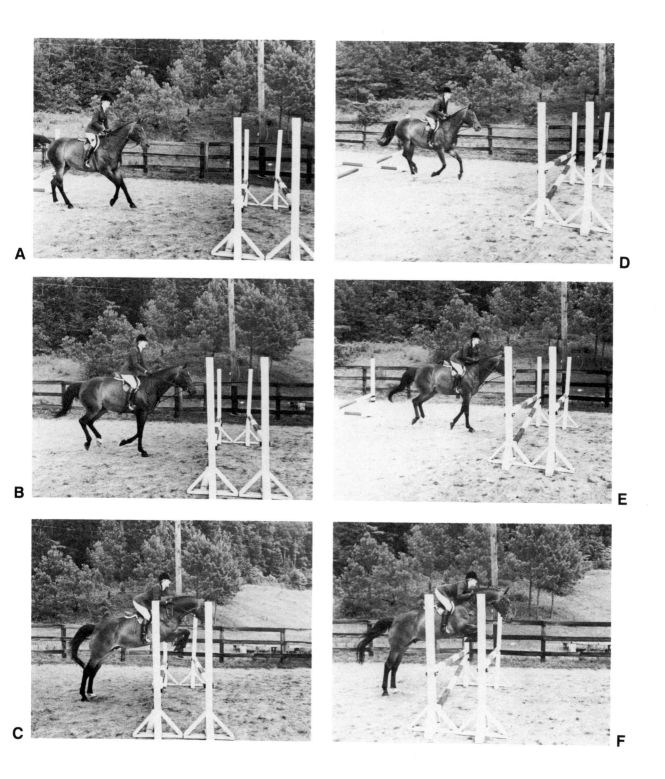

A

B

C

D

E

F

back into the saddle before the horse's feet have touched ground (fig. 4-7 G & H).

The X fence sets the animal up for gymnastic exercises. Its construction holds the horse to the middle, starting it on the proper line toward each successive obstacle. It also puts the horse into the canter sequence on landing, so that it can jump any upcoming, larger obstacles more easily.

The cavalletti poles and X fence are beneficial to the horse and rider in many ways. By creating a perfect take-off spot each time to the X, the cavalletti rails increase the horse's confidence and promote good jumping form. For the rider, cavalletti provide timing practice, requiring adjustment of the horse's trotting strides about 20 to 30 feet away from the initial rail in order to position the horse correctly for its first step over a pole. Since you must approach the poles at the proper speed in order to place the horse's feet correctly between them with each step, the spacing between the poles allows you to evaluate your sense of pace. If your horse is too slow or too fast on the approach, you can detect the mistake immediately after entering the cavalletti as the animal fumbles through the poles.

The cavalletti and X also enable you to practice the *mechanics* of riding over fences — that is, heels down and lower legs held snugly in place; knees aiding the lower leg in supporting the upper body weight; seat being held out of the saddle from take-off until landing; upper body staying with the motion of the horse; hands following the horse's neck as it stretches forward; and eyes maintaining a straightforward line. Through such a simple and controlled exercise, you can practice the style you will need to be successful over more difficult obstacles.

G

H

4-7 G & H. The rider's hips are with the motion on landing, so that her seat feels the saddle, but does not land heavily on the horse's back (G). The rider's hips have fallen behind the motion, an error known as "dropping back." Notice the horse's angry reaction to the seat banging against its back (H).

Gymnastics

Gymnastics are exercises performed over a series of fences for the purpose of increasing the strength and agility of the horse. In the following exercises, the gymnastic routine is preceded by cavalletti poles and approached from a trot. Gymnastic exercises can also be set up without the cavalletti and approached at a steady canter, with the distances between the elements lengthened at least a foot more than when they are approached from the trot. Gymnastics are not only useful for teaching the horse and rider the mechanics of jumping, but can also be helpful in proving to a rider that he needs to do very little to help the horse jump.

Horse Exercises

It is best to start with a simple one-stride distance from the X to a narrow ascending oxer. This gives the horse the least opportunity in which to develop balance problems, such as falling on the forehand, or rhythm problems such as rushing (fig. 4-8). Your initial objective is to make the horse as comfortable as possible through the exercise. The distances provided in fig. 4-8 are suitable for starting most horses and ponies in gymnastic training. However, since each animal has a slightly different length of stride, these distances must be adjusted to suit a particular animal's stride perfectly.

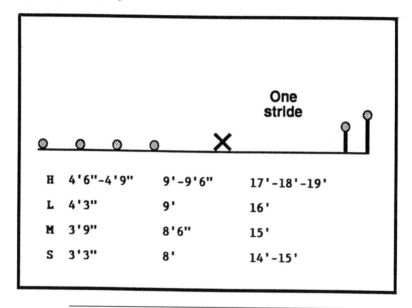

H	4'6"–4'9"	9'–9'6"	17'–18'–19'
L	4'3"	9'	16'
M	3'9"	8'6"	15'
S	3'3"	8'	14'–15'

4-8. *Four cavalletti poles and an X-fence set the horse up for the one-stride distance to an ascending oxer. Measurements between elements are provided for horses (H), large ponies (L), medium ponies (M), and small ponies (S). To the left are distances between the cavalletti poles; in the middle are distances for the take-off to the X; and to the right are measurements for the one-stride distance. (Note: When there is a range of measurement in the diagrams—as in the horse distances above—the measurements accommodate animals with a short, medium, or long natural stride.)*

Use only poles when setting gymnastic fences, rather than solid elements such as a brush box, coop, wall, or gate. Poles are not only easy to adjust, but also will readily fall to the ground if a horse crashes into them (fig. 4-9).

The starting height for the rear rail of the oxer depends upon the animal's size and level of experience. In general, if you begin six inches lower than the maximum height over which you school your hunter, you will have a safe starting point. In the beginning, keep the front rail of the oxer six inches lower than the rear. The slope of the rails will encourage the animal to come forward to the fence and clearly show it that the obstacle has width. The width of the oxer should be very narrow for an inexperienced rider or animal—about two feet wide for horses and one foot wide for ponies. This discourages the animal from diving between the rails.

So far, we have made the necessary preparations for gymnastic work: adjusting the cavalletti to the horse's natural length of step; setting an X as the regulating fence for the horse's initial take-off; and adjusting the distance between the X and oxer to comfortably fit the natural stride of the horse. Once the animal is moving confidently through the exercise, you can increase the difficulty by shortening the distance between the X and oxer in increments no greater than six inches at a time. Make sure that both the front and back rails of the oxer are moved closer to the X, so that only the distance between the X and the oxer has been changed, not the width of the oxer.

Shortening the distance between obstacles forces the horse to make a more powerful vertical thrust at take-off and/or shorten its stride between fences. You must be careful, however, not to close the distance so much that it becomes an impossible trap, causing the horse to crash or jump oddly to clear the rails. Although six-inch adjustments seem to be small, it usually takes only three or four of them

4-9. An oblique view shows four cavalletti poles leading to an X-fence, followed by a one-stride distance to an ascending oxer.

before the horse begins to have difficulty with the shorter distance. If the animal does get into trouble, adjust the distance back to the original, comfortable striding so that confidence can be regained (fig. 4-10 A, B, C).

Having jumped the narrow oxer several times as the distance between fences was gradually shortened, the animal should be comfortable jumping a fence with width. Now you can begin to widen and raise the oxer to influence the development of the horse's power and form. First, move the back rail away from the front rail. (This and all other adjustments in the following discussion, both horizontal and vertical, will involve three-inch adjustments for ponies and three- to six-inch adjustments for horses. Your choice between a three-inch or six-inch adjustment for a horse will depend upon the animal's athletic ability and level of confidence.) Pulling the back rail away from the front one forces the animal to use a greater horizontal thrust to clear the fence (fig. 4-10 D).

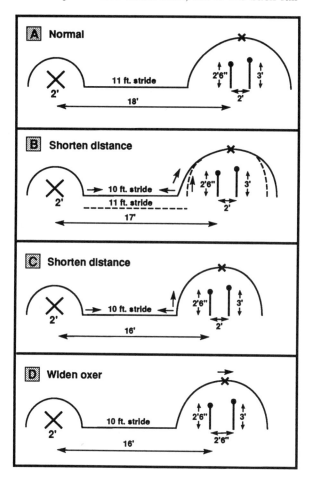

4-10 A, B, C, D. The diagrams in figure 4-10 A through H show how altering the distance between fences or changing the height or width of fences affects the horse's jumping style. The X-fence remains two feet high at its center and stationary throughout this exercise, while the oxer's dimensions and position are changed. The initial one-stride gymnastic is set to allow a horse with a medium-length stride to take one comfortable 11-foot stride between the X-fence and ascending oxer, when the gymnastic is approached at a trot. (A 12-foot stride would be normal if the exercise were approached at a canter.) The small symbol "X" above the oxer marks the peak of the horse's arc in the air (A). If the exercise is shortened to 17 feet, the horse must either take one 11-foot stride and take off closer to the oxer or shorten its stride to 10 feet to leave the ground the same distance from the oxer as before. The arrows show that when the stride is shortened to 10 feet, the horse's jumping effort is more horizontal than when the horse stays on an 11-foot stride and must use a vertical thrust to clear the front rail (B). If the exercise is shortened to 16 feet between the fences, the horse is forced to shorten its stride to 10 feet to be able to jump the oxer without knocking down the front rail. The shortened distance results in the horse having to both shorten its stride to 10 feet and thrust vertically off the ground (C). By moving the back rail six inches away from the front rail of the oxer, you can encourage the horse to stretch its body horizontally in the air, as indicated by the arrow above the fence. This promotes the proper bascule, as the horse stretches its neck down and out to counterbalance its hindquarters. You should always widen a gymnastic oxer while the fence is in ascending structure, so that the horse can clearly determine the new width on the initial approach (D).

Once the animal is jumping the wider oxer with confidence, raise the front rail of the obstacle step-by-step until it is level with the back rail, forming a square oxer. This will require either two three-inch adjustments, with the animal jumping over both heights, or one six-inch adjustment (fig. 4-10 E). If the horse or pony jumps the square oxer in good form and with complete confidence, the back rail can be raised. This will force the animal to have a stronger vertical thrust off the ground to surmount the greater height, but will also allow the motion to be directed somewhat horizontally—that is, the animal's motion will not have to be as vertical to clear the first rail as it would have to be if the oxer were square (fig. 4-10 F).

Once the animal has gone through the exercise with the back rail raised, you can pull the back rail away from the front rail again. Let's imagine that at this point you decide you do not want to raise the fence to a height any greater than that of the back rail. To adjust the fence to the maximum level of difficulty while maintaining this height, keep widening the obstacle step-by-step, until the fence is as wide as the back rail is high (fig. 4-10 G). Once the animal has jumped the fence at its maximum width, the front rail can be raised step-by-step until the oxer becomes square again, causing the animal to work harder to clear the first rail by demanding a stronger vertical thrust (fig. 4-10 H).

4-10 E, F, G, H. Once the new width has been established, you can raise the front rail of the oxer until it is even with the back rail, forming a square oxer. The arrow indicates the increased vertical thrust that is necessary to clear the front rail when the oxer is squared (E). The height of the rear rail can be raised, requiring more power from the horse, but allowing the animal to use an easier, more horizontal thrust than if the oxer were squared (F). The oxer can be widened to encourage the proper bascule over this larger fence (G). By raising the front rail, you will require the horse to demonstrate power in its vertical thrust at this fairly large obstacle. Notice that the horse's length of stride between the fences has shortened once more to enable the animal to leave the ground at a reasonable take-off spot in front of the oxer (H). Generally speaking, a horse must leave the ground at least as far from the obstacle as the height of the front rail in order to avoid knocking that rail down. A horse will rarely leave the ground closer than three feet from any fence, even a very small obstacle, such as the X-fence.

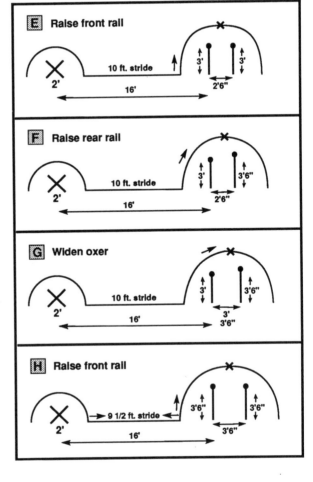

In short, the fence adjustments should be made by raising the rear rail, widening the obstacle, then raising the front rail, in that order, until you arrive at the desired height and width. By raising the rear rail first, you allow the horse to gauge the new height of the obstacle, while taking an easy path that is a blend of horizontal and vertical motion. In spreading the fence, as the second step, you use the far rail to define the width of the obstacle. Finally, by raising the front rail until it is even with the rear one, you test the horse's power and agility over the now familiar dimensions.

Generally speaking, both the height and width of an obstacle in a gymnastic setup should not exceed the measurement of the maximum height of the fences in the hunter division in which the animal shows:

Small Ponies   2'3"
Medium Ponies   2'6"
Large Ponies   3'
Children's Hunters   3'
Adult Amateur Hunters   3'
Junior Hunters   3'6"
First Year Green   3'6"
Second Year Green   3'9"

The exception applies to horses that are shown in classes with fences set higher than 4 feet. Although a Regular Working Hunter may be required to jump fences up to 4'6" in competition, the maximum height for a gymnastic exercise for a Regular Working Hunter should be 4 feet. (Gymnastic fences for jumpers should also be set no higher than 4 feet.) If you normally show your horse in equitation classes, but not in one of the hunter divisions, use the height limit in your most demanding equitation class as your maximum height and width for the gymnastics. The maximum dimensions stated above are only guidelines. If you have set a fence well under these, but your animal appears to have reached its athletic or emotional limits, do not raise or widen the fence any further.

The goal of the exercise described above is to teach the horse the proper mechanics of jumping.

The cavalletti encourage the horse to maintain a steady rhythm when approaching an obstacle and force the horse to adjust its center of gravity backward quickly at a fixed take-off point, which has been determined by the placement of the X fence. Through this restrictive approach, the horse learns to combine quick reflexes and power at take-off, as opposed to increasing its pace to a fence and using speed to hurl itself over the initial obstacle.

Numerous adjustments can be made to gymnastic exercises according to what you are trying to accomplish. For example, if the animal jumps poorly from a normal take-off spot and is only comfortable jumping from a long spot, your main concerns would be to teach the horse to engage its hocks and shift its center of gravity backward at take-off and to use its hocks powerfully to thrust its body upward. This would involve shortening the distance and raising the rails, to create a more vertical thrust.

If a horse does not follow through properly in its arc—that is, does not keep its knees high, legs tightly folded, back rounded, and head and neck stretched down and out—then widen the obstacle to encourage the horse to stretch in the air. If you reach the width limits listed above, but the horse is still not using itself, you can widen the fence a little more; but be careful not to make the fence too wide for its height, since this will encourage the horse to dive between the rails. As a rule of thumb, the width should not exceed the height by more than a foot for horses or more than six inches for large ponies. I would not suggest widening a fence beyond the height of the obstacle when working with a small or medium pony.

Lengthening exercises can also be used to encourage the horse to take longer strides rather than adding an extra stride at the base of an obstacle. To make the horse lengthen its stride, set the distance between the X and oxer so that the horse must extend its stride a little to reach the take-off spot, but not so long that the animal will find it easier to add a step. In this case, you must press the horse forward with your legs between fences to encourage it to lengthen to the proper spot, making it very difficult to shorten and add a stride.

After the horse is jumping well over a one-stride distance, introduce two strides between the X and oxer (fig. 4-11). From these early lessons with one-stride or two-stride distances, you can build a variety of combinations, using several oxers and even extending the distances to three strides or more (fig. 4-12). Notice in fig. 4-12 that for each successive position, you must add one foot in length. This

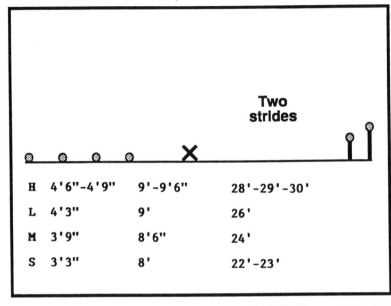

H   4'6"–4'9"   9'–9'6"   28'–29'–30'

L   4'3"   9'   26'

M   3'9"   8'6"   24'

S   3'3"   8'   22'–23'

4-11. The distances for a two-stride gymnastic are shown for horses (H) and large (L), medium (M), and small (S) ponies.

	1st distance	2nd distance	3rd distance
X	One Stride	One Stride	One Stride
H	17–18–19	18–19–20	19–20–21
L	16	17	18
M	15	16	17
S	14–15	15–16	16–17
X	Two Strides	Two Strides	Two Strides
H	28–29–30	29–30–31	30–31–32
L	26	27	28
M	24	25	26
S	22–23	23–24	24–25
X	Three Strides	Three Strides	Three Strides
H	41–42–43	42–43–44	43–44–45
L	38	39	40
M	35	36	37
S	32–33	33–34	34–35

4-12. The distances listed are a "mix and match" chart for any combination of one-stride, two-stride, and three-stride gymnastic distances between an X-fence and three oxers. For example, to set a one-stride, two-stride, one-stride combination for a large pony (L), use the one-stride measurement of 16 feet from the column marked "1st distance," the two-stride measurement of 27 feet from the column marked "2nd distance," and the one-stride measurement of 18 feet from the column marked "3rd distance." These distances are intended to be used as a starting point. Adjust them as necessary to suit your particular animal's stride or to influence it's jumping style.

accommodates a slight increase in impulsion that occurs throughout a gymnastic exercise, resulting in a natural lengthening of stride.

By setting short-to-long distances or long-to-short distances, you can teach the horse to make instantaneous stride adjustments. As a rule of thumb, your alterations from the normal gymnastic distances should not be greater than one foot per stride when either shortening or lengthening. However, you should not just subtract one foot per stride to make a short distance, then add one foot per stride to the following distance to make it long, since shortening or lengthening one distance will change the way the following distance rides, even if you don't change the footage in the following distance.

For example, suppose you initially set four cavalletti poles and an X followed by three oxers, with the distances between the jumps being 18 feet, 19 feet, and 20 feet to accommodate the horse's natural lengthening of stride (fig. 4-13 A). If you decided to change the last two distances to a short-to-long arrangement, then you would only have to change the measurement of the middle distance, since the final distance would ride longer than before as a result of the decreased momentum the horse would have from shortening its stride.

On the other hand, if you started with the same initial setup and wanted to change the last two distances to a long-to-short arrangement, once again you would only have to change the measurement of the middle distance, since the increased momentum needed to negotiate this longer distance would make the final distance ride shorter (fig. 4-13 B). (Although the measurement between the last two oxers would remain constant, the position of both fences would change, since if you only moved the second oxer, the distance between it and the third oxer would not remain the same as before.) You could change the distance between the last two oxers if you wanted to make the final distance ride a little longer or shorter; but it is wise not to adjust this distance until you see how difficult the change in the preceding distance has caused the final distance to ride when the final distance is set according to the normal measurement.

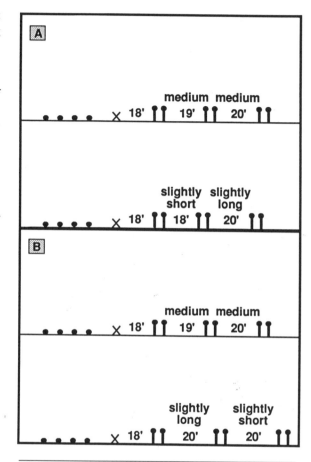

4-13 A & B. Whenever you change one distance within a combination, it will affect the way the other distance or distances ride. For example, if you began with the combination set at 18 feet, 19 feet, and 20 feet, then reduced the middle distance to 18 feet, you would not only cause that distance to ride shorter than before, but would also cause the following distance to ride longer, since the horse would be approaching it with less momentum (A). Conversely, if you lengthened the middle distance from 19 feet to 20 feet, you would not only cause it to ride longer, but would also cause the following distance to ride shorter, since the horse would be approaching it with more momentum than before (B).

The exercises that I use the most involve the cavalletti and X followed by three oxers. I always use a one-stride distance between the X and first oxer when other oxers are to follow because I think it offers the most stabilizing setup for gymnastic training. If the animal is fairly inexperienced or tends to have a dull pace, set one stride between the first and second oxer then two strides between the second and third oxer to encourage the horse to continue its forward movement through the exercise (fig. 4-14 A).

To test a horse's coordination and concentration and to encourage it to balance itself at the end of a line of obstacles, use a two-stride to one-stride distance between the first and third oxer. This creates the alternation of a one-stride distance following the X, then a two-stride distance, and back to a one-stride distance, requiring the horse to quickly perceive the shorter distance between the last two obstacles (fig. 4-14 B). It is important for a horse and rider to feel comfortable through combinations using one stride followed by two strides and vice versa, since these are commonly used in equitation and jumper courses.

To tighten a horse's form and sharpen its reflexes, use all one-stride distances. Be very careful not to set the fences too close or too high, for the horse will really be in trouble if it is overfaced within such a quick succession of fences (fig. 4-14 C).

Occasionally, you can use a three-stride distance following the initial one stride between the X and first oxer (fig. 4-14 D). This will gauge your horse's willingness to sustain a steady pace when it has more time to gain speed. This setup is particularly beneficial when working with quick horses, as a test following the preceeding exercises. It will show you whether or not your horse has learned that it can approach the fences in a steady tempo and clear them. If the horse tries to run, return to one of the earlier exercises in which it has less time to gain momentum.

A				
H	17-18-19	18-19-20	30-31-32	
L	16	17	28	
M	15	16	26	
S	14-15	15-16	24-25	

B				
H	17-18-19		29-30-31	19-20-21
L	16		27	18
M	15		25	17
S	14-15		23-24	16-17

C				
H	17-18-19	18-19-20	19-20-21	
L	16	17	18	
M	15	16	17	
S	14-15	15-16	16-17	

D			
H	17-18-19		42-43-44
L	16		39
M	15		36
S	14-15		33-34

4-14 A, B, C, D. The measurements are for the gymnastic exercises I find to be most useful: one-stride, one-stride, two-stride combination (A); one- stride, two-stride, one-stride combination (B); one-stride, one-stride, one-stride combination (C); and one-stride to three-stride combination (D).

Rider Exercises

Most "rushers" — that is, horses that run to fences — are topped by a nervous rider who panics when the horse grows tense and who increases the problem by reacting too quickly and strongly with the aids. The rider usually pulls hard on the mouth of the animal to restrain it, while leaning too far forward to the fences to make sure he will not get left behind on take-off. The unsympathetic hands cause sheer panic in the horse, while the inclined body encourages the horse to run. In fact, it is common to see a nervous rider drive his horse to a fence by pressing his upper body forward to the quick tempo of the horse's last steps before take-off. It's as though the rider is so nervous he can no longer concentrate on anything other than getting from one side of the fence to the other.

If this description fits you and your horse, try to find a placid animal on which you can practice low gymnastic exercises, set no higher than three feet. First, knot the end of the reins around a clump of mane, so that when you drop them as you cross the second pole, they will not sag so far downward that they get caught in the horse's feet as it jumps. When your reins are absent, you will probably fear that if you cannot pull on the horse's mouth, the animal will tear through the fences in a mad gallop, even though you know you are now riding a calm horse. To reassure yourself, remember that the reins are only a few inches away and can be easily retrieved if anything goes wrong during the exercise; but try not to use them at all if possible.

Unable to slow the horse with your hands, you will become acutely aware of the effect of your upper body on the horse's pace. You will notice as you approach the exercise that if you lean forward, the horse will become quicker. You will then react naturally by opening your hip angle, so that your upper body goes back to its correct, original position. In most cases, this will immediately result in the horse slowing its pace. Through repetition of this exercise, you can learn to resist inclining too far forward on the approach to fences, inadvertently using your upper body as a driving aid.

I have found it interesting that asking a rider to pull back on imaginary reins further slows the horse in the gymnastic exercise. As you draw your hands backward, you will naturally open your hip angle and shift your weight to the horse's rear, causing the animal to shift its weight that direction, too, and not run on its forehand (fig. 4-15 A, B, C, D).

Another gymnastic exercise that will teach you to use minimal movement with your upper body over fences is a series of *bounces*, which are fences with no strides between them. Bounces are best set as a series of small X fences, rather than oxers, since the shape of the X holds the horse straight down the line, enabling you to concentrate on matters other than steering. The bounces can be set alone or following cavalletti (fig. 4-16).

When approached from the trot, the distances between the X's should be approximately 9 to 10 feet for horses, 9 feet for large ponies, 8 feet for medium ponies, and 7 feet for small ponies. Set the center of each X a foot off the ground for a horse or large pony, nine inches for a medium pony, and six inches for a small pony. As the animal rocks back and forth during the multiple jumping effort, you must adjust your center of gravity to match your animal's. These adjustments occur quickly, but subtly; and if you are not syncronized properly, the exercise feels very awkward. Through practice, you will eventually learn to keep your balance in the air, much as a person on roller skates learns how to adjust his balance so that he won't fall down (fig. 4-17).

Bounces can be negotiated with the rider holding the reins or with the reins knotted around a clump of mane. When the reins are taken away, you can keep your hands in normal position, or you can practice jumping with your arms extended outward or with both hands on top of your hunt cap, to accentuate the feeling of seeking your center of gravity in the air (fig. 4-18 A & B).

4-15 A, B, C, D. The rider steers the horse into the gymnastic exercise by holding the reins in normal position (A). As the horse steps over the second pole, she drops the reins, the end of which are knotted around a clump of mane to prevent them from drooping toward the horse's front legs (B). Unable to use her reins during the last step before take-off, she instinctively opens the angle of her upper body, allowing the backward shifting of her weight to steady the horse (C). At take-off, her upper body is correctly with the motion of the horse, rather than ahead of it (D).

4-16. Distances for four cavalletti poles and a series of four bounces are listed for horses (H) and large (L), medium (M), and small (S) ponies.

H	4'6"-4'9"	9'-9'6"	9'-10'	9'-10'	9'-10'
L	4'3"	9'	9'	9'	9'
M	3'9"	8'6"	8'	8'	8'
S	3'3"	8'	7'	7'	7'

4-17. Striped poles will help guide the rider down the middle of the cavalletti and bounces. The center stripe should always be painted the lighter color to catch the rider's attention.

4-18 A & B. Practicing over bounces with your arms extended will help you discover the correct placement of your upper body above the horse at take-off, in the air, and on landing (A). Another method of finding your balance is to perform the exercise with your hands on your hunt cap (B). Both exercises encourage support of the upper body with a steady leg position. As in fig. 4-15 A & B, you should steer the horse to the cavalletti with your reins, then drop them as you cross the second rail.

Conclusion

Gymnastics can be fun if they are introduced properly. They offer a means of focusing on a particular fault, rather than having to deal with many problems at the same time. For example, if you have trouble keeping your heels down over fences, you can concentrate on doing only this within the gymnastic setup, since the fences are set in such a way that the horse's straightness, tempo, and take-off point are predetermined by the cavalletti and X, before you reach the first of the gymnastic fences.

Gymnastic exercises are also a nice change for the horse. They break up the monotony of galloping down lines with many strides between the fences and make the animal think harder about what it is doing. On a dull horse, this will result in quicker reflexes as it wakes up a bit to negotiate the closely set fences; while on a quick horse, the result is often a slower animal because it concentrates on the multiple fences, rather than just thinking of running.

There is the odd horse that is unnerved by gymnastics. Typically, this is the animal that has been overfaced in competition, particularly horses that have been shown in the jumper division without being properly prepared. In this case, progress may be slow, but gymnastic exercises are perfectly suited for rebuilding the confidence of a ruined animal.

A weekly routine for most horses includes a day of gymnastics, a day of schooling lines and/or courses, four days of flatwork (one of these days can be hacking in the woods), and one day of rest. Brief sessions of flatwork—about 10 minutes of work interspersed with 1 or 2 breaks lasting about a minute each—should always precede the jumping activities.

Striding Between Fences

In the early 1960's, hunter courses were frequently set in a field with the fences so far apart that the number of strides between them was of no concern. You simply maintained a steady hunting pace around the course, often built on uneven terrain, and tried to find a bold, but safe, take-off spot to each fence. The open field allowed a horse to reach a true hunting pace. Riders who rode too slowly were strongly penalized, based on the idea that an overly slow pace during a hunt would cause you to fall behind the field of horses and get lost in the countryside.

All of this began to change in the latter half of the decade. More and more hunter classes were held in arenas, which required less land, allowed the classes to run in a shorter time, provided level and more controllable footing, and gave the rider a greater advantage over his horse, since a railing aids steering and pace control. This containment, however, necessitated the measurement of strides between fences, for it soon became apparent that poorly set fences resulted in bad performances and accidents.

Today, the correct measurement and setting of courses is one of the most important and complicated elements in putting on a successful horse show. Any serious rider or coach should understand the basic principles of course designing, so that he can set good practice courses at home and correctly analyze courses at shows.

Course measurements for horses are based on a 12-foot stride as the standard. When jumping a line of two fences, a horse will generally land about 6 feet from the first obstacle, take 12-foot strides between the fences, then take off 6 feet before the second obstacle. Therefore, the combination of the landing and take-off distances gives you an extra 12 feet that must be added to the total footage of the strides. For example, if a horse takes four 12-foot strides between the fences and has a 6-foot landing and 6-foot take-off, the measurement for the line would be 48 feet plus 12 feet, or 60 feet in all for the 4-stride line.

From this standard measurement, the lines in hunter courses are lengthened 6 inches to a foot per stride when the height of the fences or the level of the horses' ability warrants it (fig. 4-19). For example, a children's hunter, which is restricted by the AHSA from jumping higher than 3 feet, would

Distances between fences for horses

Strides	3' Children's Hunter	3'6" Jr./Am. Hunter	4' Regular Working
1	25	26	27
2	36	37	38
3	48	49'6"	51
4	60	62	64
5	72	74'6"	77
6	84	87	90

4-19. The standard footage between fences is given for horses competing in the Children's, Junior, Amateur, and Regular Working Hunter divisions in a level ring with good footing. Adjustments to these distances should be made when the lay of the terrain, quality of footing, size of the arena, or other elements affect the horses' ability to perform in the standard striding.

not need as much momentum on course as a regular working hunter, which is required to jump at least 4' in A-rated sections. The children's hunter would comfortably move between the fences in the standard 12-foot striding; while the regular working hunter would naturally take longer strides between the fences—about 1 foot longer each stride—in keeping with the momentum necessary to jump the bigger fences. The junior working hunter would jump fences halfway between the heights of the children's and regular working hunters and would travel about 6 inches farther each stride than the children's hunter. A horse's take-off and landing spots will actually be slightly farther from the fence as the height of the obstacle is raised; however, when figuring distances for horses, you use a 6-foot landing and take-off and alter the length of the strides to accommodate the height of the fences.

The addition of 6 inches to a foot per stride is also appropriate for upper-level equitation riders. However, in equitation classes the courses are not set entirely with the longer distances as in the hunter classes, but rather alternate the long distances with some normal and some short ones to test the rider's ability to adjust the horse's length of stride promptly, yet smoothly.

Pony distances have been controversial for years. In the past, many horse shows have not altered the distances between the horse and pony classes, except for in-and-outs, which must be adjusted to meet AHSA requirements. This generally resulted in the large ponies having to gallop too fast to make the horse strides, the medium ponies being at about the right pace when adding one extra stride each line, and the small ponies having to race around the course even with the addition of an extra stride each line.

To deal with this problem, course designers sought a formula to use for calculating pony distances. Until recently, this formula was based on a 9-foot stride for small ponies, a 10-foot stride for medium ponies, and a 11 1/2-foot stride for large ponies. These calculations applied to the number of strides only, not to the take-off and landing, which were still calculated at 6 feet each. For example, when figuring four strides between fences for a medium pony, you calculated a 6-foot landing from the first fence, four strides at 10 feet each, and a take-off spot 6 feet from the second obstacle, totaling 52 feet (fig. 4-20 A).

In October, 1990, *Horse Show Magazine*, the official publication of the AHSA, published a list of suggested distances for ponies. These distances are based on a compilation of information provided by notable course designers for pony competitions. In some cases, the distances vary greatly from those that would be derived through the older method of calculation. Members of the AHSA Pony Committee are confident that the new distances will solve some of the pace problems that pony riders have had in previous years and will promote good riding and safety (fig. 4-20 B).

Distances between fences previously used for ponies

Strides	Small Ponies	Medium Ponies	Large Ponies
1	20	22	24
2	30	32	34
3	39	42	46'6"
4	48	52	58
5	57	62	69'6"
6	66	72	81

4-20 A. In the AHSA Rulebook, pony distances in one-stride and two- stride in-and-outs must be set according to the figures listed. Until recently, the distances for three or more strides for ponies were based on a 9-foot stride for small ponies, a 10-foot stride for medium ponies, and an 11-and-a-half-foot stride for large ponies, as shown in the diagram.

New distances between fences for ponies

Strides	Small Ponies	Medium Ponies	Large Ponies
1	20	22	24
2	30	32	34
3	41	43'6"	46
4	51	54	57
5	61	65	69
6	72	75'6"	80'6"
7	83	87	92

4-20 B. The new distances for ponies are based on averages of a compilation of several course designers' figures. You can see that in some cases the footage varies greatly from that used in previous years.

Analyzing Distances

When analyzing distances, there are many important considerations besides the measurements between the fences. They include the size of the arena, the quality of the footing, the lay of the land, the position of objects in and around the arena, and the types of fences used at each location.

A suitable size for an arena for hunters and equitation horses is at least 240-feet long and 120-feet wide. If the arena is smaller than this, it will be difficult for the horse to travel down the lines in the standard striding, since it would be hard to gain enough momentum out of the corners to the first fence in each line. If the competition area is much larger than these measurements, such as on an outside course, the standard striding will ride a little cramped.

Footing is always an important consideration, not only in determining how the lines will ride, but also in regard to your horse's soundness. Deep footing bogs a horse down and makes it difficult for the animal to travel between the fences in the standard striding. It can cause pulled muscles, tendons, and ligaments and be a threat to your horse's soundness not only at the show, but permanently, if the injury is serious enough. Course designers usually shorten the distances between fences when the footing becomes overly deep either from sand that has loosened under impact during the show or from deep mud caused by relentless rain.

Muddy footing not only presents the problem of pulling on the horse's legs, but also of being slick, which makes jumping fences and turning corners quite difficult. Slippery footing intimidates the animal, causing it to shorten its stride and tempting it to stop at the fences. If the horse tries to stop at the last moment, it can skid into the fence, cutting or puncturing itself or, in rare cases, damaging its bones.

Ice is another dangerous condition, combining slickness and hardness and causing accidents involving both soft tissue and concussion to bones in the foot and leg. In short, don't jump a horse on ice. Even if the temperature isn't as low as the freezing point, the horse's performance can be drastically affected by cold weather. A chilly breeze makes most horses "feel good" and sometimes elicits a buck and a squeal of delight as the animal releases some of its excess energy. In cold weather, it usually takes much longer to work a horse down to the quiet emotional level you would like, particularly if the weather has just turned cold. A horse will want to "gain down the lines," progressively lengthening its stride between the fences, rather than maintaining even strides between obstacles. The lines, then, will ride shorter than normal unless you open your body angle and steady the horse with your hands, restricting it from lengthening. Even then, the horse may get the best of you. In this case, longeing or a controlled hand gallop will be your quickest and most effective solution.

The slope of the terrain is another consideration. Traveling uphill drains impulsion, while traveling downhill makes it easy for the horse to lengthen its stride. The exception to this is very hard or slick footing on a downward sloping terrain. If the footing is so hard as to be uncomfortable (such as red clay in the summer) or slick (such as short, dry grass), the horse will protect itself from the concussion or slipperiness by taking shorter strides. In these cases, a line will ride longer than normal, even though it is being jumped downhill.

The position of other horses or of objects in or around the ring may also affect the way a line rides. Generally, a horse will want to take longer steps traveling toward other horses at the in-gate than when traveling away from them. A horse may also react to sounds or moving objects and change its length of stride. A few things that typically distract a horse are the movements of people near the ring, particularly noisy children; a loudspeaker set close to the arena; decorative flags used to mark off areas such as the concession stand and secretary's booth; or a judge's umbrella, particularly if a strong wind causes it to billow. A horse show photographer may even spook a horse and capture the animal's horrified expression for posterity! The horse's normal reaction is to shorten its stride as it ducks away from these distractions; but if the horse is terrified, it may lengthen its stride and try to run away.

The type of fence used at each location is a very important consideration when determining the difficulty of the lines. For example, a 48-foot distance between two vertical fences would ride as three medium strides on a horse with a 12-foot stride (fig. 4-21 A). If the last fence on the line were an oxer instead, the line would ride a little longer, since the center of the horse's arc would not be over the first rail of the oxer, but between the first and second rail (fig. 4-21 B). If both fences on the line were oxers, then the distance would ride even longer, with the horse's arc coming earlier on the first fence and later on the the last (Fig. 4-21 C).

In general, verticals encourage a horse to go forward and oxers slow a horse down. (Note: An exception is gymnastic work, in which the horse builds impulsion through the oxers as it naturally increases from the very restricted pace which led into the exercise.) On course, two oxers in a row will rob a horse of impulsion and make the line ride longer than if the horse's arc peaked at the same two places over verticals. Also, a square oxer will tend to slow a horse down more than an ascending oxer, particularly when the fences are big.

A triple bar, which is sometimes used in equitation classes as well as jumper classes, encourages

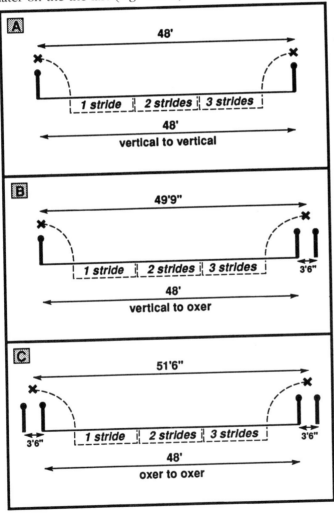

4-21 A, B, C. Although the fences in each of the diagrams have a distance of 48 feet between them when measured from the base on the landing side of the first fence to the base on the take-off side to the second fence, each of the lines rides differently because of the construction of the fences. In the first diagram, the peak of the horse's arc (indicated by the symbol "X") occurs directly over each vertical fence (A). When the second fence is changed to an oxer, the peak of the arc occurs between the two rails, making the 48-foot distance ride the same as a 49'9" distance between two vertical fences (B). If both fences were oxers, the 48-foot distance would ride the same as a 51'6" distance between two vertical fences (C).

the horse to lengthen its body in the air, so that the animal lands in a long frame, on a long stride. It is more difficult to collect the horse when moving from a triple bar to a vertical fence than when moving from an oxer or from a vertical to a vertical fence.

An oxer can be helpful when placed at the end of a normal or short line. The width of the fence slows the horse in the air, making it easier for you to collect in preparation for the upcoming corner. Also, the horse can be a little deep to an oxer and usually maintain the correct form. However, oxers can present a problem when they are placed at the end of a long line, for the horse may not be able to meet the take-off spot accurately and may dive through the rails from an overly long spot.

Vertical fences are easy to negotiate when the horse can leave from a normal or long spot; but many horses hang their forelegs, knock the top rail down, or even stop when placed too deep to a vertical fence. You can see, then, that you approach different fences in different ways. You would like to meet an oxer, either square or ascending, from a normal to slightly deep take-off spot; on the other hand, it is preferable to meet a vertical from a normal to slightly long spot. When approaching a triple bar, try to find a slightly deep spot, since this will discourage the horse from becoming too long and flat in the air.

Walking Courses

Before you ride over a course, walk the distances on the lines to determine how each line will ride. In order to do this correctly, you must be able to walk a 3-foot step and know by feel that it is accurate. Practice beforehand by stretching a measuring tape on a floor and walking beside it with your eyes focused straight ahead. Count your steps as you walk, then stop after several steps and see how many feet you have covered according to the tape measure. The footage on the tape should measure three times the number of steps you took. For example, 12 feet would equal 4 steps at 3 feet each.

To figure how a distance will ride, walk the distance from where the center of the horse's arc will occur on one fence to where the center of its arc will occur on the next. Over a vertical fence, the center of the horse's arc is directly above the fence; over an ascending oxer, in which the first rail is three- to six-inches lower than the second, it is about two-thirds the distance from the first rail to the second rail; over a square oxer, it is halfway between the two parts of the obstacle; and over a triple bar, in which three ascending rails form the fence, it is over the last rail (fig. 4-22 A, B, C, D).

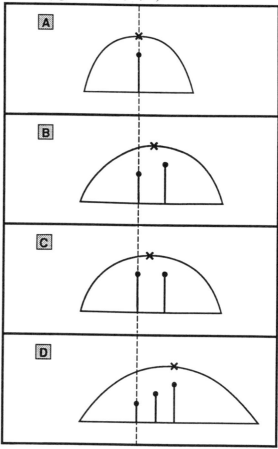

4-22 A, B, C, D. The peak of a horse's arc occurs directly above a vertical (A), approximately two-thirds the distance from the front to the back rail of an ascending oxer (B), halfway between both parts of a square oxer (C), above the last rail in a triple bar (D).

To walk distances to determine horse strides, begin by standing on the landing side of the first fence in the line. Note where the center of the horse's arc will be according to the type of fence, then walk two 3-foot steps to establish the approximate landing point. When calculating from a vertical fence or triple bar, you can back against the fence, then walk forward two steps to find the landing point. When an oxer is used, you must visually estimate a 6-foot distance from where the center of the horse's arc will be.

Mentally designate the landing spot by counting "one, two" for your initial 3-foot steps. Then begin counting the actual strides, thinking, "*one*...two, three, four" for the first 12-foot stride, "*two*...two, three, four" for the second 12-foot stride, "*three*...two, three, four" for the third 12-foot stride, and so on, until you are within take-off range for the upcoming fence. Finally, count the last steps to see if the take-off is set normally, which would be two steps (6 ft.) to the center of the horse's arc (fig. 4-23).

When analyzing distances of three strides or longer, if you are only able to take one 3-foot step before reaching the center of the second fence, then the line will "ride short" — that is, the horse will have to travel on strides shorter than 12 feet to end up at the correct take-off spot (fig. 4-24 A). If you count two steps and still have room for one more step before reaching the center of the horse's arc, the distance will "ride long," and you must lengthen each of your horse's strides beyond 12 feet to reach the proper take-off spot (fig. 4-24 B). If you have two extra steps left, then you must choose between riding a very long line or adding an extra stride and riding a very short line, with the decision depending upon the horse's length of stride and jumping ability (fig. 4-24 C). Finally, if you have three extra steps left, you must either ride a tremendously long line, or add a stride and ride a slightly short line. The latter is usually the better decision even when there are five or six strides on a line, since you don't want your horse to run to the fences (fig. 4-24 D).

4-23. To accurately walk distances between fences, you must know how a three-foot step feels. When walking from vertical to vertical, as in the diagram, you would begin by taking two three-foot steps from the first vertical fence to mark the landing point. (Each step is represented by gray half-circles.) Then, count the strides as follows: "One. . .two, three, four" to mark the first stride; "Two. . .two, three, four" to mark the second stride; "Three. . .two, three, four" to mark the third stride. At that point, when you walk the final two steps to the fence, you will realize that the take-off is exactly six feet, which means that the line is a normal three-stride distance for a horse.

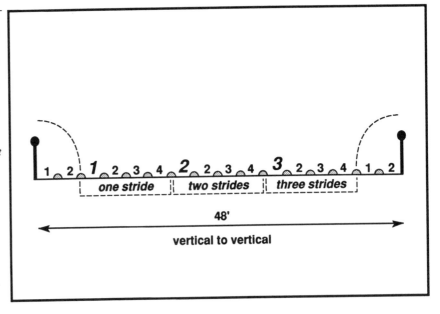

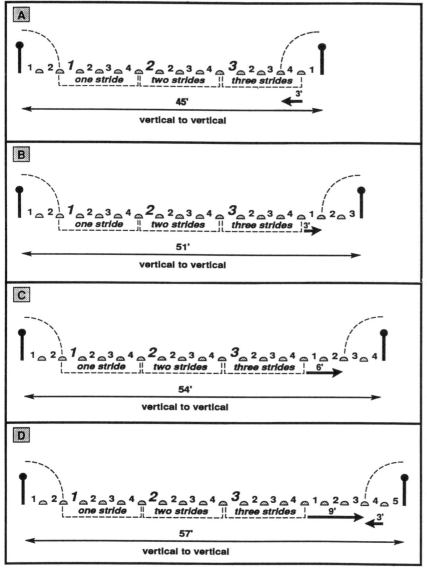

4-24 A, B, C, D. When walking a line, if you have only one step left for take-off instead of two, then you know the line will ride short. In this example of a three-stride distance, you would have to collect the horse to an 11-foot stride to ride the line properly. The horse would then be able to accommodate the three-foot less than normal footage by deducting one foot for each of the three strides (A). If you had an extra step left before take-off, then you would have to gallop the horse on a 13-foot stride down the line, covering the extra three feet by adding a foot per stride (B). If there were two extra steps left before take-off, you would have to increase the horse's stride to 14 feet to make the distance, with the extra six feet being covered by the horse extending two feet per stride (C). Finally, if there were three extra steps left before take-off, the horse would have to travel on 15-foot strides to make the distance, or add one stride and cover the distance in 11'3" strides. To make the 15-foot strides, most horses would have to run. The better option is to collect the horse 9 inches per stride and ride the distance in four moderately collected strides (D).

The degree to which the horse's strides must be adjusted depends on how many strides there are between the fences. For instance, if you have only three strides between fences, then shortening or lengthening the take-off spot by three feet will force the horse to collect or extend its stride one foot per stride; whereas if there are six strides between the fences, the horse would need to alter its steps only one-half foot per stride to reach the correct spot.

Once you have analyzed the course according to 12-foot increments, adapt your plan to the length of stride your horse actually takes. If the animal has a stride longer than 12 feet, long lines will ride normal, medium lines will ride a little short, and short lines will ride very short. Conversely, if your horse is short-strided, short lines will ride normal, medium lines will ride long, and long lines will ride very long.

4-25 A, B, C, D, E, F, G, H. Most horse shows use the same basic pattern for every hunter section, varying the course for each class by merely changing the order in which the lines are ridden (A, B, C, D, E, F). The course can be made more interesting through the use of a single fence on a line (fence 1 in diagram G); starting between two fences in a line (fence 1 in diagram H); or using an in-and-out on course (fences 4 and 5 in diagram H). (The more typical setting of an in-and-out is as part of a three-fence line, in which the in-and-out is used at the end of the line.)

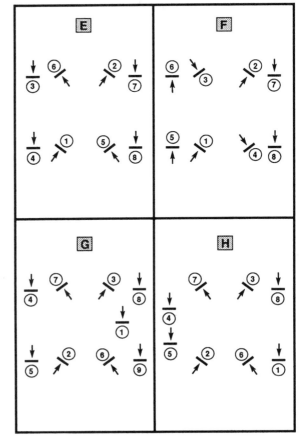

Setting Fences

Most hunter courses consist of two outside lines and two inside (diagonal) lines. Occasionally you will see a variation on these patterns through the addition of a single fence or the starting of the course over the second fence in a line (fig. 4-25 A, B, C, D, E, F, G, H).

To set a typical course of two outside and two inside lines, consider the length of the ring and plan for at least three straight strides to the first fence and following the last fence on each long side of a rectangular arena. In an oval ring, plan at least two straight strides preceding the first fence and two straight strides following the last fence on each long side of the arena (fig. 4-26 A & B). These arrangements give you time to adjust your horse's stride if you are approaching a bad take-off spot. (I prefer a rectangular arena to an oval one, not only because it is more useful for training horses and riders, but also because it gives the person setting the course more options and makes it easier to measure the arena.) When setting a diagonal line, leave at least four straight strides before the first fence in a rectangular arena and at least three straight strides in an oval arena, since the horse will have to regain

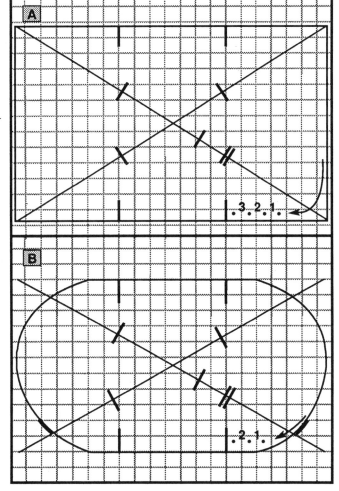

4-26 A & B. When setting hunter fences in a rectangular ring, allow for at least three straight strides preceding and following each outside line (A). In an oval arena, allow for at least two straight strides preceding and following each outside line (B).

more impulsion after the acute turn to a diagonal line than when approaching an outside line. (Nothing is psychologically worse for a rider than seeing that a striding adjustment is necessary and not having the time to make it!)

For horses, there are usually five or six strides between fences on an outside line in a hunter course set in an arena, unless an in-and-out is used, in which case the most typical striding is four strides to a one-stride in-and-out. Remember to account for the six-foot landing and six-foot take-off within the line when you are figuring the striding. For example, if you want the horse to take five strides between fences, measure six multiples of 12 feet, or 72 feet (fig. 4-27).

If the arena is at least half as wide as it is long, you can center the fences of each diagonal line on the imaginary lines from corner to corner. If the width is less than half of the length of the ring, it will be difficult, if not impossible, to set the diagonal lines, since they will crowd the outside lines (fig. 4-28 A, B, C, D).

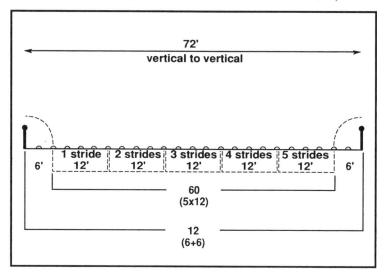

4-27. Remember to count the 6-foot landing and 6-foot take-off when figuring the distance between fences. For example, a five-stride distance for a horse would be 5 strides multiplied by 12 feet per stride (60 feet) plus a 6-foot landing and 6-foot take-off (12 feet), totaling 72 feet.

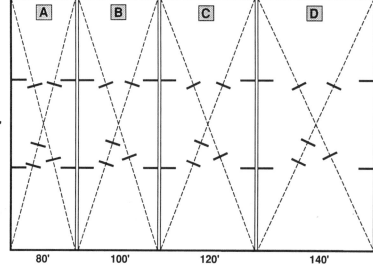

4-28 A, B, C, D. If the width of the ring is less than half the length, it will be difficult to set a good course. Notice how the fences become less crowded and the turns less acute as the width of the ring is increased.

When using an in-and-out, place it toward the end of the course, as the last segment in a line of fences. It will ride best if the "in" is a vertical and the "out" is an oxer. The vertical fence will invite the horse into the combination, and the oxer will help the horse maintain good form as it leaves the combination.

As for choosing types of fences for various locations, you can't go wrong with a brush box as your first fence. Generally, horses are most comfortable with substantially built obstacles in natural colors, such as brown or green. Bright colors and patterns tend to confuse horses visually, as do fences that allow daylight to poke through. Unfamiliar things (such as plastic flowers) or objects that move (such as a bucket in the pillar of a wishing well) will spook many horses.

Fences with shadowy places also make a horse hesitant to jump. I think this must be a combination of the visual problem that shadows present (since a horse's eye does not rapidly adjust to a decrease in light) and a natural instinct to avoid any shady crevice where an aggressive "critter" could be hiding.

The way you decide to place your fences, then, depends upon how difficult you want to make your schooling course. If you want a simple, inviting course, use quiet colors, solid construction, and definite ground lines to establish the bases of the fences. Place more challenging obstacles, such as the wishing well, at the end rather than the beginning of a line. Use the more difficult fences on lines coming toward the in-gate or out-gate, rather than going away from them. When setting fences for a hunter, try to make the course appealing to the horse, so that the animal will be encouraged to perform its best (Fig. 4-29).

When setting a practice equitation course, you can increase the difficulty of the fences by adding brightly colored rails, standards, or panels; by placing decorative objects around the fences; by setting spooky fences at the beginning of lines or on lines going away from the in-gate; by altering the distances between fences so that they are slightly longer or shorter than usual; or by lessening the number of poles on the face of an obstacle, making it airier and less inviting (fig. 4-30).

The point of practicing over equitation-type courses is to test your ability to apply your knowledge and physical skill to achieve a desired result. You don't want to overface yourself by setting a course that is too difficult any more than you want to overface your horse by setting jumps that are too wide or high or that require impossible striding adjustments. However, you do want to challenge yourself to think, just as a good course designer at a horse show would do. Take time, then, in working out your course plan, concentrating on testing the specific skills that will be required of you in the show ring. Nothing will give you more confidence at a horse show than having prepared yourself well at home.

We have looked at courses largely from the course designer's point of view so far, considering the elements that go into making a safe, yet challenging course. Now we will analyze courses from the rider's point of view, starting with the simplest course for a beginner equitation rider and moving on to the most advanced concepts tested in the Medal, Maclay, and USET Finals. Although I am not dealing specifically with jumpers in this book, I will discuss the major elements of course analysis and execution that pertain to jumpers, since the jumper division is really an extension of the equitation division.

A

C

B

D

4-29 A, B, C, D. Hunter Fences. The wall oxer has a dense composition, is painted a subdued brick color, has a definite groundline, and clearly shows a height difference between the front and back rails, making it an excellent hunter fence. Flowers are used discreetly at ground level to decorate the fence (A). The light-gray gate oxer is composed of rails and a small gate panel with a flower box at the groundline. This combination allows the course designer to lower the gate to the appropriate hunter pony heights when *necessary (B). White poles and standards help to define this dark-green roll-top fence. Although striped poles are prohibited in hunter classes, solid light-colored poles are acceptable, with white being the most frequently used color (C). The tan and dark-brown wall, set at a pony height, is inviting to the animal (D). Compare this plain fence with the less inviting stepped flower box in fig. 4-30 D.* Fences by Darren L. Frasier

A

C

B

D

4-30 A, B, C, D. Equitation Fences. *The vertical fence is composed of striped rails and striped panels shaped like sails, painted in green, yellow, red, orange, blue, and purple. The horse does not see the actual colors, but perceives the difference in coloration through the light and dark shades in the pattern, just as you do when viewing this black-and-white photo. The unusual shapes and colors would classify this as a novelty fence in an equitation class (A). The oxer is composed of striped rails and has a sparse interior. These two factors clearly make it an equitation or jumper fence (B). Tall arches in the wall give the fence an airy appearance and an indefinite groundline. As constructed, it would be appropriate for an equitation class. If a box were added at the foot of the wall on the near side of the fence, filling up most of the space in the arches, the fence could easily become a suitable hunter fence (C). The stepped flower boxes make this fence much busier than the simple wall placed between the same two standards in fig. 4-29 D. A flower-filled fence could be used in a hunter class, but it would be more appropriate for an equitation class, since banks of flowers are traditionally associated with the equitation and jumper divisions (D).* Fences by Darren L. Frasier

Basic Goals on Course

When your horse or pony is comfortable over cavalletti and gymnastics, you can move on to jumping segments of a basic hunter course. Break down the course into several elements: the initial circle, the first line, the second line, the third line, the fourth line, and the ending circle.

First, let's consider the purpose of the initial circle, how it should be performed in competition, and errors commonly made at this stage in the course. The purpose of the initial circle is to establish the proper pace for the entire course. When the circle is properly performed, you enter the ring and complete the first quarter of the circle at the posting trot. Then, you sit for a few steps to feel the sequence of your horse's footfalls and, once you sense that the horse is balanced and attentive, ask for the canter. Immediately after the horse has taken the proper lead, rise into two-point position. For the remainder of the circle, attempt to establish the proper pace. By the end of the circle, the horse should have the same pace it will have at the end of the course—no slower, no faster (fig. 4-31).

The circle gives you a chance to know your horse. A perceptive rider can sense a tense or tired animal and compensate for these problems on the approach to the first fence. As when working on the flat, you must be adaptable and deal with each problem as it arises, rather than permanently tagging your horse with a certain label, such as quick or dull, thinking that the horse never changes. The horse that was quick while schooling the course yesterday might now be tired and move reluctantly toward the fences. In contrast, the horse that is usually dull might react keenly to a billowing spectators' tent and suddenly be more alert in the show ring than it has ever been in its life!

The circle foretells much that will happen on course. For example, a horse that dwells as it passes the gate toward the end of the circle, is an animal that is "herdbound," preoccupied with staying near other horses. A herdbound animal works against the rider's efforts by concentrating on other horses rather than on the fences. It will usually be very bad

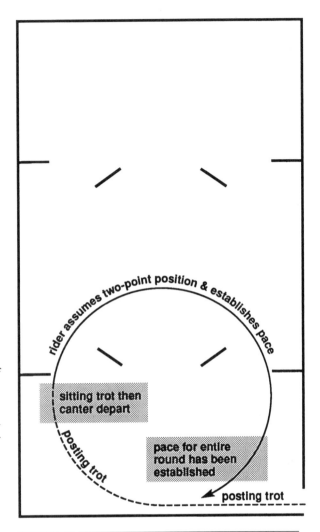

4-31. *The initial circle on course should give you enough space to reach the proper pace prior to the first line of fences. Begin with a posting trot the first quarter of the circle, then perform a sitting trot a few steps and ask for the canter depart. Immediately rise into two-point position and increase the horse's length of stride. By the end of the circle, you should have established the correct pace for the course. By performing the canter depart at the same place each time and striving to achieve the correct pace by the end of the circle, you give yourself restrictions which enable you to notice changes in the horse from one class to another.*

down the first line of the course, either chipping in at the first fence or refusing to jump altogether.

A horse that timidly shies from objects during the circle will often shorten its strides to each fence, run out, or stop at a fence. This is often the green horse, requiring a firm, but tactful, rider to get it through the course.

The overly bold animal that progressively lengthens its steps during the circle is the potential runaway. If you have not attended to this problem by bringing the horse down to a suitable pace before the circle ends, it is likely to leave out a stride within a line and jump dangerously, particularly when traveling toward the entrance or exit gates.

The circle is important, then, not only because it provides room to get the horse to its proper pace, but also because it allows time to evaluate your horse's general behavior and make the necessary adjustments to minimize potential problems. If your horse is dull, use the circle as a runway to lengthen the animal's stride and increase its pace. If it is quick, use the railing to slow the horse down, rather than rushing toward the first fence (fig. 4-32). You will find that the circle is often a more reliable indicator of how the horse will behave on a course than the earlier warm-up session in the schooling area, for an animal can be relaxed working alongside other horses when schooling, yet be panicked when asked to jump fences by itself.

It is the circle that frequently reveals a poor rider. He will often run his horse into the canter from the trot and pick up the wrong lead. If he is really bad, he won't realize his mistake and will approach the first fence on the incorrect lead rather than immediately bringing the horse back to the trot and correcting his error. A poor rider may also make a circle

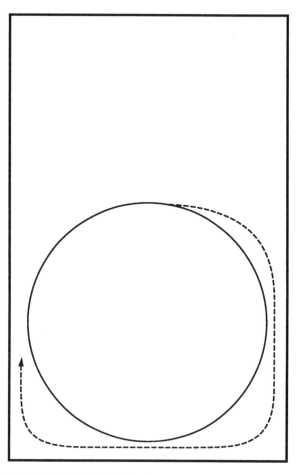

4-32. The solid line indicates the path that should be taken during the initial circle on a normal or dull horse. This path allows you to steadily increase the pace until the desired speed and length of stride have been reached. The dotted line indicates an alternate route that is useful for horses that start out too fast. Having completed the first half of the circle, you should realize if you are in trouble and steer the horse on a fairly square pattern, using the railing to confront the animal and help you slow it down.

that is too small, preventing the horse from reaching the proper pace or length of stride; or he may circle in the wrong direction to the first fence, which though completely illogical happens from time to time (fig. 4-33).

Since the main purpose of the circle is to set the proper pace for a course, you should not only use it when showing, but also when schooling your horse at home. The exception is when the approach to the first fence is so long that you can establish the correct pace without riding a circle (fig. 4-34 A & B).

Once the pace is set, concentrate on the first line of fences. In a typical hunter course, the first line starts as the horse crosses the centerline of the ring at the end of the circle and ends when the horse crosses the centerline on the opposite end of the ring (fig. 4-35). As a general principle, you should move the horse forward coming out of a turn, since a curve will tend to decrease the horse's pace, and should collect a horse going into a turn to balance it for the upcoming curve. From the centerline of the ring to the first fence, then, encourage the horse to move forward so that it can as closely as possible maintain the pace and length of stride established in the initial circle. After the last fence on the line, collect the horse in preparation for the upcoming corner (fig. 4-36).

Look at the first line of fences all the way from the centerline. This will give you plenty of time to decide what adjustment to the horse's stride is necessary to reach the proper spot to the first fence and will enable you to make the adjustment subtly. If you concentrate on the upcoming fence and don't allow your eyes to wander, you'll find a suitable take-off most of the time.

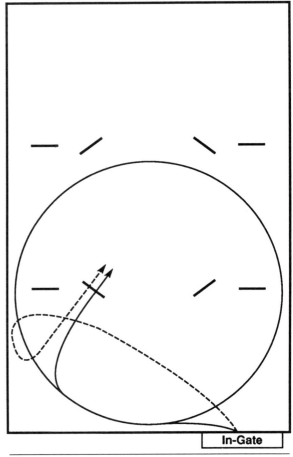

4-33. *The solid line shows the correct path to the first fence, which is a full circle followed by the approach to the fence. The dotted line shows a path that is used only by the most poorly educated rider.*

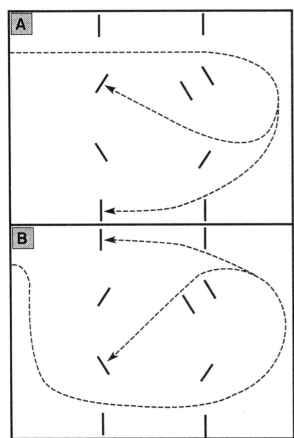

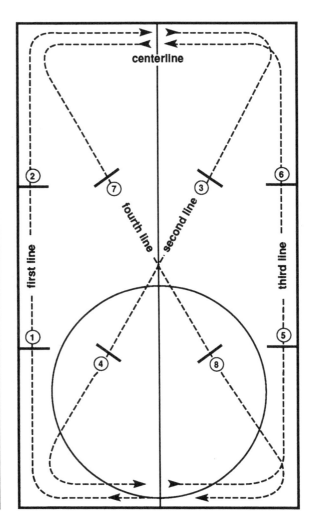

4-34 A & B. If the approach to the first fence allows plenty of room to establish pace, you do not need to circle. For example, starting between two fences on a line coming home, you could use a long clockwise (A) or counterclockwise (B) approach and leave the circle out altogether.

4-35. Think of a hunter course as four lines, with each beginning and ending at the centerline. (Note: When asked to "pull up on a line" following a fence, halt while in a straight line with the obstacle, rather than turning the corner.)

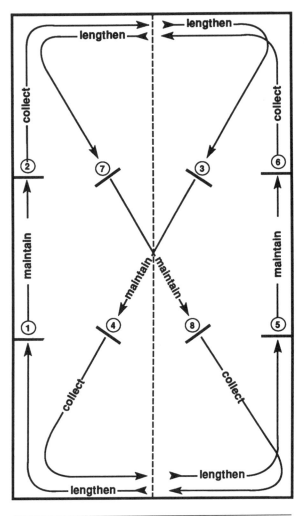

4-36. Press the horse forward from the centerline to prevent it from shortening its stride radically in the corner; maintain even strides between the fences; then collect the horse to shorten its stride, balancing it for the upcoming corner and, possibly, a change of lead.

You should visually line up the middle of the fences and keep your eyes riveted on that line no matter what happens. A bucking horse, an animal that is threatening to stop at a fence, or one that is "drifting" to the left or right on the approach to an obstacle are typical situations that can cause you to lose your focal point. If the horse is successful in distracting your attention either downward or to the side, you will not realize how far it is moving off of the proper line. When you finally look up, you might be unable to steer it over the fence (fig. 4-37 A & B). The proper response to a horse's bad behavior is to stare down the line of fences and drive your horse as straight as possible from the center of one obstacle to the center of the next, figuring out at each instant how to make corrections that will keep your horse straight and get it to a good take-off spot (fig. 4-38).

For the first line of fences, most people have to ride forward, pressing their horses into long strides not only to the first obstacle, but also between the first two fences. (The exception, of course, is when you are on a very long-strided horse.) Even if the first line is based on the same length of stride as the other lines, it will usually ride longer. There are two reasons for this. First, the initial fence is often set going away from both the in-gate and out-gate, so that the horse is not being drawn "home" toward the gates, which represent access to the companionship of other horses, as well as to a bath, food, and the comfort of a stall. Second, a horse is usually calmer prior to the first fence than it is after jumping several fences on the course. This holds true for even the most placid animal.

Knowing this, you should approach the first line by increasing the horse's length of stride out of the corner, seeking a bold, but reasonable, take-off spot to the first fence; then expect to ride strongly to the next fence, since in most cases this is necessary in order to reach the proper spot to the second fence on the first line. Once the horse has landed over the second fence, collect it, shortening its strides and balancing it for the upcoming turn.

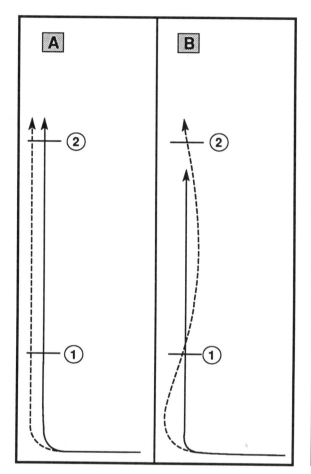

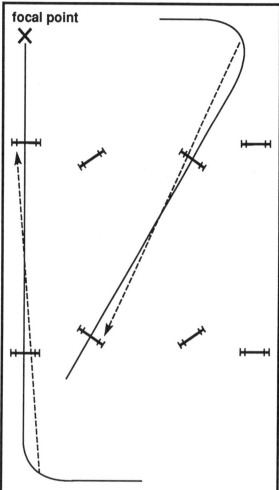

4-37 A & B. A rider distracted from focusing on the fences may slightly overshoot a line, so that he jumps it off center (A), or may overshoot the line so far that he ends up wavering between the fences (B).

4-38. To ride a line of fences properly, turn onto the line just as you see the far standard of the last fence on line come into view between the standards of the first fence on line. As you turn, look to the far end of the ring to sight a focal point that will help you steer the horse down the middle of the line of fences. Although the use of a focal point is demonstrated in the example of the outside line, it is even more important to have a focal point at the end of a diagonal line. A diagonal line, being off the rail and at the end of a more acute turn, is easier to overshoot.

A horse will land after the second fence with a great deal of impulsion and a stride that is longer than that established in the circle. Unchecked, it will become faster and longer in stride throughout the course, "running under the fence" at the end of each line or leaving out a stride and "diving" over the obstacles. Both of these are terrible errors, the second being very dangerous.

It is important, then, for you to collect the horse back to its initial length of stride at the end of each line. Teach the horse to expect collection at this point by schooling courses one line at a time and halting just before the turn at the end of each line (fig. 4-39). Once your horse understands that it must submit to your restricting aids, you can attempt to jump a line of fences and continue around the corner. If the horse lands on the counter lead after the last fence on the line, ask it to perform a flying change just before the upcoming turn.

Several exercises discussed earlier have prepared your horse for the flying change at the end of a line. First were the downward transitions on the flat. Later, flying changes were introduced during flatwork. Now, repeated halting serves to mark the place where the flying change should occur. If all of these exercises can be performed well by your horse, the flying change at the end of a line should be no problem.

The main error riders commit in attempting the flying change on course is turning the corner too soon, tracking a sloping turn that makes it very easy for the horse to remain on the counter lead. In contrast, a horse that is ridden directly toward the rail until the last couple of strides will be confronted by the rail and encouraged to make a decision about its lead (fig. 4-40). The deeper path to the rail also provides an extra stride or two during which you can think about the next line and correct any problems that might have arisen. For instance, if the horse is playing around or pulling a little, the extra strides make it easier to regain control before going forward to the next line.

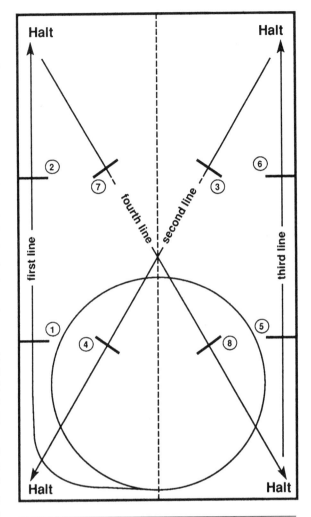

4-39. Halting at the end of each line promotes obedience in the horse. Approach the first line by circling, to reach a jumping pace. For the following lines, on a normal or dull animal you can circle at the ends of the ring preceding the approach to each line. If your horse is quick, pick up the canter at the place you halted and go directly to the next line, denying it the opportunity to gain too much speed.

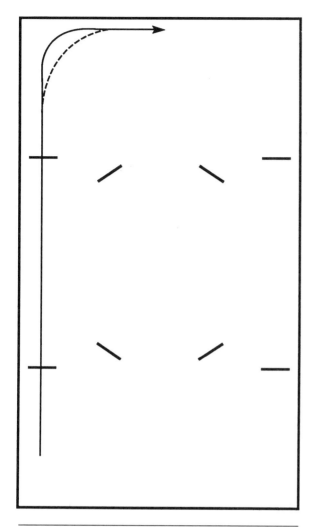

4-40. At the end of an arena, you will have a better chance of getting the flying change if you steer the horse on a fairly deep path through the corner (indicated by the solid line), rather than steering it on a path with a less acute curve (indicated by the dotted line). On the deeper path, the horse is confronted by the railing and must collect itself and make a decision about its lead. In contrast, the shallow path makes it just as convenient for the horse to remain on the counter lead as to perform a flying change.

I must stress again the importance of your eyes on course. If you will look in the direction of the upcoming turn while applying your outside leg for the flying change, the horse will clearly sense the direction you intend to go at the moment of the switch—that is, around the turn, not over the railing! The principle is similar to the situation of an automobile running off the road because the driver is sightseeing. When the driver looks to the right, everything in his body is subtly drawn in that direction. If he doesn't realize that the car is "following his eyes," he will inadvertently steer the vehicle off the road. While this works against a driver, it can work for a rider. A horse is not only affected by your intended aids, but also by delicate shifts in your weight. Therefore, when you look in the direction you are about to turn, the subtle movements of your body that occur at the same time will signal the horse that you want it to go in that direction. This does not mean that you should throw your weight to the inside of the turn, for this makes it more difficult for the horse to perform the flying change; but you should allow your natural reflexes to provide an additional aid as your body follows the direction in which you are looking.

Using your eyes well is critical when you are approaching a line of fences. By focusing down the entire line, rather than from one fence to another, you encourage straightness in your horse and make it much easier for the animal to get down the line *in the numbers*—that is, in the number of strides intended by the course designer. The straighter a horse is in a line of fences, the less footage the animal loses to sideways motion. Straightness, then, makes it possible for the horse to travel down the line in the proper striding without having excessive pace. In contrast, a horse that wanders off the correct line must increase its speed to lengthen its stride, so that it can make up for the footage lost in sideways motion (fig. 4-41 A & B).

A rider's eyes will often indicate his potential for success. If he homes in on the fences and doesn't let his horse or the surroundings distract him from his plan, he has a great chance for success. But if his eyes show no concentration, no sense of purpose, you can tell he is not going to do well.

The first line in the course ends as the horse crosses the centerline (see earlier fig. 4-35). From the last fence on the line until this point, collect the animal to control its pace and length of stride; make sure it is on the inside lead going into the turn; and bend it around the corner so that it will be balanced on the curve. When a horse is collected enough to go into a turn safely, it will be slightly below the length of stride appropriate between the fences. To get back to the desired length of stride, you must gradually increase the horse's impulsion as the animal comes out of the turn, so that it lengthens its stride incrementally. This is commonly referred to as "flowing out of the turn."

If you desperately drive your horse forward during the last two or three steps before the jumps, rather than encouraging it to lengthen gradually to the correct take-off spots, then your animal will become anxious. It may turn into a chronic rusher and dash to every fence, or it may begin to add an extra stride at the base of the fences rather than making the extraordinary effort to lengthen its stride within the short space. In fact, some horses will combine

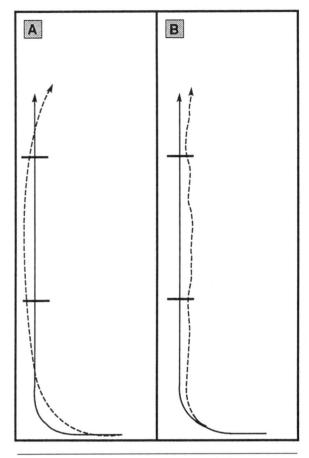

4-41 A & B. If you allow your horse to bulge (A) or waver (B) down a line, you will have to drive it between the fences at an overly fast pace to make up for the lost footage.

these errors of rushing to the fences, then adding an extra stride before take-off, when they don't trust their riders' commands.

To give your horse the best opportunity to jump safely and confidently, do not make radical adjustments to its stride, particularly just in front of the fences. Encourage it to maintain a steady tempo around the course, rather than allowing it to shorten its stride and slow down too much on the corners of the ring. Going into the corners, the horse should be collected just enough to ensure the change of leads and a safe turn. Any more collection than this works against the performance (fig. 4-42).

When spectators describe a horse on course as looking like a "machine," what they are noticing is the rider's ability to subtly collect and lengthen the stride, maintaining a steady tempo with little variation in pace. Everything looks smooth and flowing when the tempo is regular; and, when the pace is even, the take-off spots are more likely to be the same than when the horse is approaching certain obstacles slowly and others much faster.

For the second, third, and fourth lines, press the horse forward out of the corners, maintain a steady rhythm and length of stride between the fences, and collect when going into the corners. Usually, it will be easier to make the horse go forward to these lines than to the first line because it is more alert after jumping a couple of fences and has more natural impulsion, particularly when traveling toward the in-gate or out-gate. In fact, you may have to open your body angle a little and steady the horse as it travels home, in order to keep it from extending its stride too much.

When approaching a line that is set across the diagonal of the ring, you should look toward the first fence on the line earlier than when approaching a line set on the long side of the arena. The

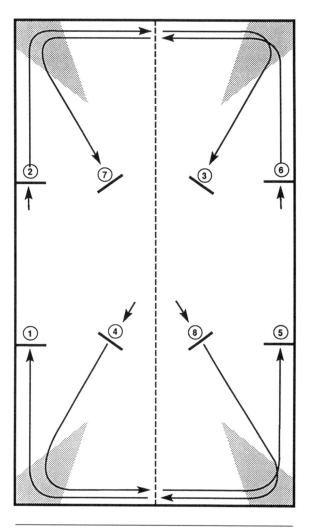

4-42. Horses lose impulsion in the corners of the arena (indicated by the gray-shaded areas). This is helpful when you are trying to collect an animal at the end of a line, but is a drawback when you try to increase impulsion on the approach to a new line. By pressing the horse forward from the centerline, you can prevent its impulsion from "dying." This will make it easier for you to find a good distance to the fences, as well as make the performance smoother.

reason for this is that diagonal lines are set closer to the centerline than are the outside lines, so that if you wait until you reach the centerline to look, you will tend to overshoot the diagonal. You should also increase the horse's impulsion sooner to a diagonal line because the turn to it is more acute than to an outside line, making it more difficult for the horse to reach the proper pace and length of stride before the first fence in the line. Look for the upcoming fence and begin to move your horse forward approximately two strides (24 feet) before the centerline, when approaching a diagonal line of fences (fig. 4-43).

Following the final line on course, make another large circle before you exit the arena. Use this circle to subtly correct your horse, so that it will be schooled for the next round. If the animal was a little quick on course, collect it and slow its rhythm during the final circle. If the horse was dull on course, firmly squeeze it forward with your legs to send a clear message that lagging is unacceptable. Either correction should be discreet. There is no point in jerking your horse or kicking it in the side out of anger. This behavior only demonstrates that abuse begins where talent and education end.

The final moments in the ring are very important. They give you the opportunity to show off, if, for example, you are riding a horse that moves very well in the hunter division or if you are a beautifully proportioned, correctly positioned rider in an equitation class. Nothing makes a judge feel better than to glance at a competitor on the final circle and think, "What a nice trip. That will be hard to beat." The judge is hoping for a clear winner, and it is up to you to prove that you are just that.

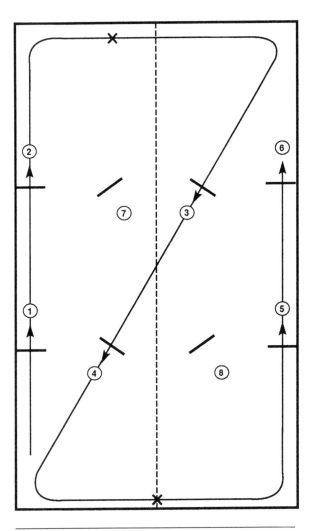

4-43. When approaching a diagonal line of fences, look toward the line when the horse is about two strides before the centerline of the ring. When approaching an outside line, look as the horse crosses the centerline. The point at which you should look at the upcoming line is indicated by the symbol "X."

5

Intermediate and Advanced Equitation Courses

You can change a basic hunter or equitation course into an intermediate or advanced equitation course through one or more of the following additions: (1) a line of fences that measures shorter or longer than the standard striding; (2) a combination, composed of two or more fences with only one or two strides between them; (3) a turn between fences (either a bending line or a roll-back turn); (4) a fence which must be jumped at an angle; (5) a narrow fence; (6) an end fence; (7) a long approach to a single fence; or (8) a novelty fence.

Isolated and Related Distances

By changing a course from measurements based solely on a 12-foot stride to measurements based on some 11-foot strides and some 13-foot strides, you can make a straightforward course very tough (fig. 5-1). For instance, in fig. 5-1, you could make four simply-arranged fences very difficult by alternating long and short strides. The setting of the first line of fences on 13-foot strides would require a tremendous amount of initial impulsion, not only because the distance is set long, but also because this is the first line on course, which typically rides longer, and the line is jumped traveling away from home. The distance between the first two fences on the second line, based on 11-foot strides, would require the horse to be collected, which would be especially difficult because the line is ridden coming toward home. The one-stride in-and-out, set at the end of

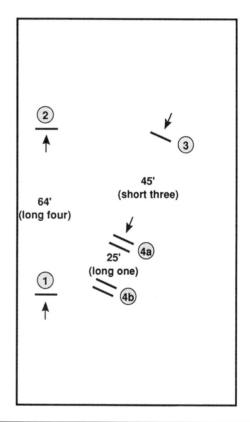

5-1. A change of only a few inches per stride can affect the way a course rides. For example, by combining short and long lines that have been altered from the standard striding by only one foot per stride, you could make a very simple course quite difficult. To negotiate the fences on the course in the diagram, a horse would have to have a tremendous amount of impulsion for the first line, collect greatly for the distance between fences 3 and 4a, then travel the one stride between fences 4a and 4b on a very long stride.

the second line, measures 25 feet and is composed of two oxers. The wide structure of the fences and the slightly long distance between them demands increased impulsion in a very short time to make the one stride following the collected strides preceding fence 4a. I am not suggesting that you actually set fences this way, for this is a radical example of changing measurements to increase the difficulty of a course. I am only using the example to show how changing just one foot in length per stride can greatly increase the difficulty of a course.

Usually at a horse show the course designer makes the first line of fences on an equitation course fairly easy by keeping it on a 12-foot stride, then varies the subsequent measurements according to the level of difficulty appropriate for the particular class. To make a course slightly difficult, he could change the footage about six inches to a foot per stride within a line that consists of only two fences. The distance between fences on a two-fence line is referred to as an *isolated distance*. If the riders are more advanced, the course designer might construct three fences on a line and use long-to-short distances or short-to-long distances to test the rider's ability to immediately adjust the animal's length of stride. These are referred to as *related distances*, since the distance between the first and second fences on the line affects the way the distance between the second and third fences can be ridden.

When riding through an *isolated long distance* —that is, a distance that measures longer than normal on a two-fence line—if you wait until you have jumped the first fence before lengthening the horse's stride, you will find it much more difficult to reach the proper take-off spot to the second fence than if you had prepared by lengthening before the first fence. For example, if there are three long strides between two fences, you should lengthen your horse's stride a little each step for about four to six strides before the first fence. This will set the horse on a sufficient length of step for it to make the long distance without having to run for it (fig. 5-2).

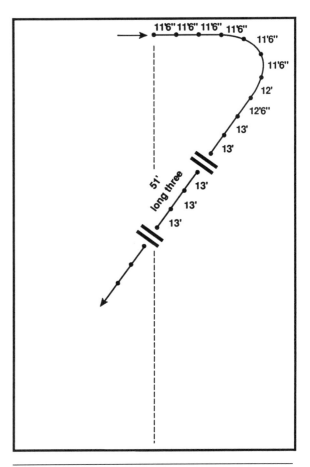

5-2. When approaching an isolated long distance, press the horse forward with your legs to prevent it from shortening its stride too much in the corner on the short side of the arena. Increase the length of stride until it is appropriate for the distance between the fences. Ideally, you should have the horse on the correct length of stride at least two strides before take-off. Once you have achieved the correct length of stride, maintain it each stride between the fences so that the line rides smoothly.

When approaching a long distance, don't wait to see a spot to the first fence before you make your move, but rather build impulsion early out of the corner so that the horse's lengthening of stride will help you find the long spot. I refer to this as "galloping into a spot," for when you keep increasing the impulsion and length of stride to a fence, an appropriately long take-off spot usually presents itself.

As the horse lengthens its stride, its energy flows more horizontally, requiring you to close your upper body forward in order to continue to be with the motion of the horse. It is important that you react to the lengthening with your upper body, rather than precede the lengthening by shifting your torso forward. If you lean ahead of the motion, trying to use your upper body as a driving aid, you will think your horse has begun to extend its stride, even if it has not. This is because you have moved your eyes forward, producing the same optical effect of covering more ground in a stride that would occur if you kept your upper body still and let your horse lengthen in response to your legs.

So don't be fooled into thinking your horse has lengthened, when all that has really happened is that you have moved your eyes forward. By staying with the motion and driving the animal with your legs, you can feel whether the horse surges forward in a true lengthening of stride or ignores your legs and stays the same.

Your hands should maintain a sensitive feel of the reins, so that as the horse begins to lengthen its stride and elongate its neck, you follow the motion of its head by moving your hands forward. If you try to lengthen the stride by suddenly offering slack in the reins, your horse will feel abandoned and may stop at the fence. On the other hand, if you do not ease off the horse's mouth at all, the animal won't be able to lengthen its stride sufficiently to cover the long distance and may have to add an extra step at the base of the fence in order to meet a safe take-off. The horse may even react to rigid hands by refusing to jump, fearing that it cannot keep its balance in the air without having the freedom of its neck. The hands, then, must provide enough contact to reassure the horse, but not so much as to restrict the motion of its head as it tries to lengthen its frame

and use its neck to balance itself in the air.

More difficult than an isolated long distance is a line in which the long distance is followed by a short distance. To ride related distances well, you must consider how the approach you make to the first distance in the line will affect the way the second distance rides. For example, if a line is composed of three long strides preceding three short strides — that is, the related distances form a *long-to-short line* — you should plan to lengthen the horse's stride and increase its impulsion more than normal on the approach to the first fence. This approach allows the horse to take strides decreasing in length on the approach to the second fence (fig. 5-3).

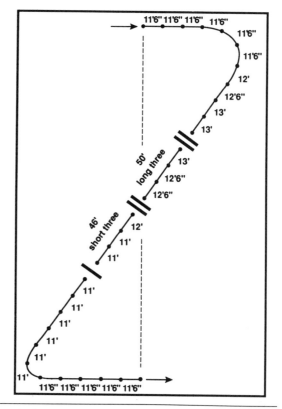

5-3. When approaching a long-to-short line, you must increase the horse's length of stride until you have slightly more than you need for the first distance. This way, you can collect the horse throughout the line.

By slightly collecting during the first three strides, you will be able to find a medium spot to the second fence and not land too far into the next, short line. Although you should not "drop back" in the air over the second fence by letting your seat hit the saddle before landing, you can open your upper body angle a little sooner than normal so that it subtly aids in restricting the length of the horse's landing. A slightly open upper-body angle between the second and third fences will also aid you in collecting the horse for the three short strides.

To understand how important it is to lengthen the stride before the first fence in a long-to-short line, consider what happens when you do not. If you find a medium spot to the first fence and have a medium length of stride, you must then drive the horse forward to the second fence in order to make up the footage of the long line. This causes the horse to land over the second fence with the impulsion building, rather than diminishing, making the following three short strides very difficult. In other words, instead of the horse smoothly collecting throughout the line, it goes from a medium stride on the approach, to a quick, lengthening stride between the first two fences, to an abrupt, collected stride between the second and third fence.

Now let's examine the opposite exercises from those discussed above. To ride an *isolated short distance*—that is, a distance which measures shorter than normal on a two-fence line—maintain a slightly collected stride on the approach to the first fence with a restricting hand and a strong de-

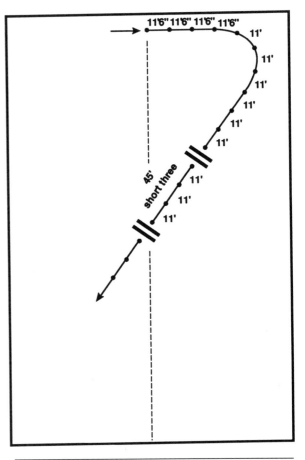

5-4. *Let the natural shortening of the horse's stride on a corner help you set up the horse for an isolated short distance. Be sure that the horse's stride is shortened through collection, rather than slowness, for the animal must have impulsion to make a good jumping effort.*

gree of impulsion with a supporting leg. Open your upper-body angle slightly from its normal two-point angulation so that it can subtly reinforce your hands. The more vertical upper body is in keeping with the increased vertical motion of the horse when it is traveling in a shorter frame and offers a position of readiness so that you can add the weight of your torso as a subtle restraining aid, in case you need a little more strength to collect your horse than your hands and arms alone can provide (fig. 5-4).

To ride a *short-to-long line* correctly, you must increase impulsion gradually through the line. It is important, then, to start with the horse collected on the approach to the first obstacle. The horse's natural inclination to "die in the corners" before approaching the lines will make it easy to shorten the stride; but you must make sure you maintain plenty of impulsion, rather than simply allowing the animal to slow down to decrease the length of stride. Otherwise, you will have to abruptly increase the pace, rather than smoothly extending the stride to successfully ride the line (fig. 5-5).

On the approach to the first fence, your upper-body angle should be open slightly more than the normal two-point position in order to reinforce your restricting aids. Then, in keeping with the forward shift of the horse's center of gravity as the animal changes from short to long strides, your upper body should close slightly forward between the second and third fences. To facilitate the horse's jumping effort, close your hip angle only enough to balance your upper body over your legs

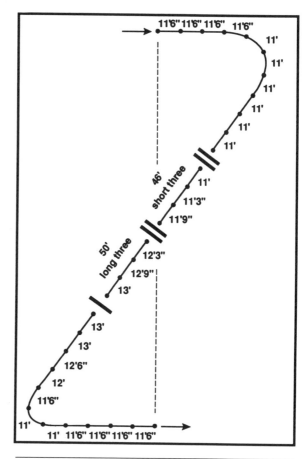

5-5. When riding a short-to-long line, keep a slightly open body angle and a restrictive hand to prevent the horse from overextending its stride in the short distance. Then, press with your legs and ease the tension on the reins for three long strides, closing your body angle forward as the horse incrementally lengthens its steps. Be prepared to collect your horse immediately upon landing, since the animal will be on a very long stride as it approaches the corner.

when the horse is in the longer frame—not so far forward that you add unnecessary weight to the horse's forehand.

Within a short-to-long line, many riders will land over the second fence, wait one stride to get reorganized, then desperately push the horse forward for the remaining strides before the third fence. This often results in the horse being unwilling to leave the ground from an overly long spot and adding an extra stride at the base of the third fence. If you press the horse forward every stride, you can make the long segment of the test both easier for the horse and smoother in overall appearance.

To be on the safe side in setting long-to-short or short-to-long practice exercises, lengthen or shorten the normal distance by 6 inches per stride for horses and 3 inches per stride for ponies. Remember that the 12-foot total of the take-off and landing distances should not be counted as a stride. For example, a long-to-short exercise for a horse, involving three long strides followed by three short strides, would measure 49 1/2 feet to 46 1/2 feet in a line of three vertical fences.

For horses only, you can increase the difficulty of the exercise by adding or deducting up to another 6 inches for every stride—that is, making the long three strides to short three strides measure a maximum of 51 feet to 45 feet. However, this may be dangerous for lower-level riders or unathletic horses. In fact, I wouldn't practice distance alterations with anyone who was not already riding very well over basic hunter and equitation courses.

Combinations

The addition of a combination is another means of making a course more difficult. Since the fences are placed so close to each other—only one or two strides apart—the horse must have quick reflexes and the rider must be able to adjust to the rapid shifting of the horse's center of gravity during the multiple jumping efforts. A talented, intermediate-level rider mounted on a horse of average ability should be able to stay with his horse's motion in a combination when the distances are set normally (for example, a 24-foot one-stride distance followed by a 36-foot two-stride distance for a horse). However, when a combination is set up to present a short-to-long distance (for example, a 23-foot one-stride distance followed by a 38-foot two-stride distance) or vice versa, the difficulty is greatly increased.

The principles of riding short-to-long or long-to-short distances in combinations are the same as for riding related distances with more strides between the fences. The only difference is that you have less time to correct an error. The placement of your horse at the proper take-off spots and your feel for the horse's impulsion and length of stride are critical when the fences are as close together as they are in combinations.

Turns

Hunter courses provide long, straight approaches to fences so that the horse has plenty of time to see an obstacle, reach the proper impulsion and length of stride, and balance itself for take-off. However, in equitation or jumper classes, turns often present problems for both horse and rider. It is sometimes unclear to the horse where the upcoming fence is, since the fences are not necessarily placed on the long sides of the arena or across the diagonals, but may be at other less familiar locations.

You must use your aids successfully to guide and balance the horse so that it will be both psychologically and physically prepared to jump. This will be difficult if you are weak in your position, since you will find it hard to keep your balance when turning the horse. If loss of balance results in your leaning on the hand toward the outside of the turn while you attempt to turn the horse with your inside hand, you will lose one side of your steering mechanism. When your outside hand becomes inactive, the horse drifts to the outside of the turn and overshoots the proper line to the upcoming fence. This usually results in a refusal, a run-out, or too deep a spot to the fence as the unbalanced animal adds an extra stride at take-off (fig. 5-6). To correct an outward drift, apply a strong outside leg and move both hands a little toward the inside of the turn, so that your inside hand is in a slight opening-rein position and your outside hand creates a neck rein. The pressure of the outside leg and neck rein "walls up," or contains, the energy that is escaping to the outside of the turn (fig. 5-7).

5-6. *The solid line between fences 2 and 3 shows the correct path between the fences. The dotted line indicates the path of a horse that has swung too wide on the turn, so that as it approaches the fence, an "open door" is created. From the diagram in the box, you can see how much more tempting it is for the horse to run out at the fence when there is an open door created by an oblique approach than when a fence is approached head on.*

5-7. *The rider is preventing the horse from overshooting the turn by applying her outside leg in a behind-the-girth position and shifting both of her hands slightly toward the inside of the turn.*

Another error that may occur during turns is the horse "cutting in" by leaning toward the inside of the turn and making a tighter turn than you desire, rather than fully using the available space. Cutting in causes loss of impulsion, provides less room for you to look for a take-off spot, and makes the horse unbalanced since most of its weight becomes tilted to the inside of the turn. To correct this problem, apply more inside leg to maintain the bend and restrict the horse from popping its shoulder inward. Also, move both hands slightly toward the outside of the turn, so that the outside hand acts as an opening rein to guide the horse and the inside hand works as a neck rein to push it away from the direction in which it wants to lean (fig. 5-8).

Horses tend to have too much impulsion going into a turn and too little coming out of one (fig. 5-9). To counteract these tendencies, land over the fence preceding the turn with your hands up and your body angle open slightly more than normal, rather than leaning forward onto your hands for support. This will enable you to begin collecting the horse on the first stride after landing. Once you reach the center of the turn, add leg pressure and drive the horse forward, increasing its impulsion and length of stride in time to have a good jumping effort over

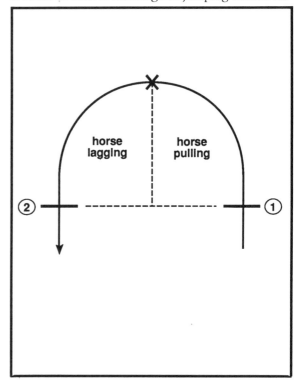

5-8. The rider is preventing the horse from cutting in on a turn by applying her inside leg at the girth and shifting both of her hands slightly toward the outside of the turn. She has also shifted the axis of her upper body slightly to the outside in order to use her weight as an aid.

5-9. When turning between fences, a horse will generally pull against the reins the first half of the turn, then lag the remaining half, reluctant to move forward from the rider's legs. This is most evident when the turn is very tight. To counteract this tendency, you must open your upper-body angle and collect the horse to the point marked "X"; then drive the horse forward with your legs to increase its impulsion and length of stride, closing your body angle again and easing the pressure of your hands as the horse's momentum becomes more horizontal.

the second fence. You must be insistent in lengthening the stride, since it is hard to press an animal forward coming out of a turn, particularly if the turn is short and acute (fig. 5-10).

The biggest mistake riders make on turns is not looking soon enough. On sweeping turns, look for the next fence as soon as you possibly can without having to look completely backward over your shoulder. On tight turns, look for the upcoming fence while you are in the air over the fence preceding the turn (fig. 5-11 A, B, C).

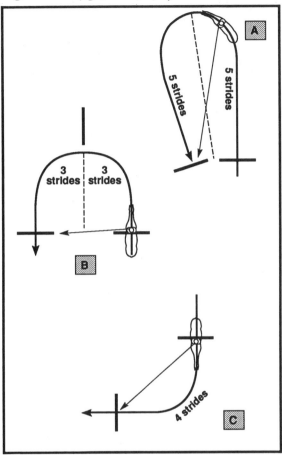

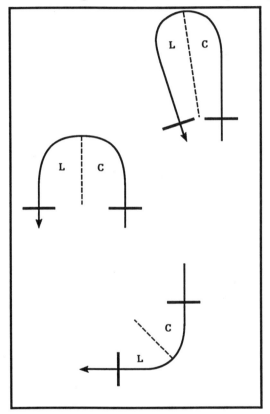

5-10. Horses will usually pull during the first half of a turn, then lag during the second half. To counteract this tendency, collect the horse as you move through the first half of the turn, as indicated by "C" in each of the examples. Once you reach the halfway mark, press the horse forward with your legs to lengthen its stride and increase its pace on the approach to the second fence, as indicted by "L" in the examples. By collecting, then lengthening, you will balance the horse going into the turn, then regain sufficient momentum.

5-11 A, B, C. In a long, roll-back turn, look to the upcoming fence as soon as you start to turn the corner. In the diagram, the rider is correctly looking sideways over his shoulder at the earliest point he can reasonably see the fence (A). On a tight roll-back turn, you cannot afford to lose sight of the second fence for even a moment. In the diagram, the rider is correctly spotting the second fence while he is in midair over the first fence. He should maintain this focal point throughout the turn to make sure he does not overshoot the fence (B). A right-angle turn is less difficult than a roll-back turn, but still requires concentration on your focal point, especially when the turn consists of only a few strides, as in the diagram (C).

5-12. The rider is looking in the air for the upcoming fence, which is located next to the one the horse is jumping and is only six strides away on a tight roll-back turn. By applying pressure with her left leg and shifting both hands toward the right, she causes the horse to land on the right lead, as indicated by the right foreleg stretching out farthest in the air as the horse begins to land.

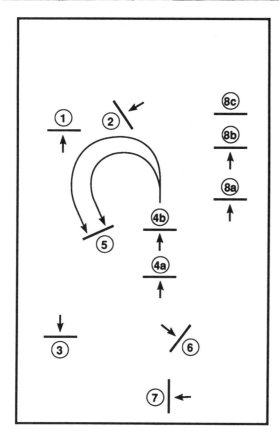

5-13. The solid lines between fences 4b and 5 indicate the shortest and longest paths you could reasonably take in an equitation class. By turning on these lines or anywhere between them, you can use the path of the turn, as well as adjustments to the horse's length of stride, to help you meet a suitable take-off spot to fence 5.

Once you have looked for the upcoming fence, do not look away from it. Keeping your eyes fixed on the obstacle will allow you to see a take-off spot while you are turning (fig. 5-12). The curve presents not only the options of collection or extension, but also of cutting or widening the turn in order to reach a good take-off spot, actually making it easier to see a spot from a turn than when approaching from a straightaway. If you keep your eyes fixed on the upcoming fence, you can make the necessary adjustments to the horses's length of stride and path to the fence to meet a perfect spot (fig. 5-13).

Jumping on an Angle

When you are jumping a fence on an angle, your hands and legs should form a narrow corridor that prevents the horse from drifting on the approach to the fence or in midair. Form this corridor by maintaining pressure against the horse with both legs and placing your hands a little closer to each other than normal as you approach the fence (fig. 5-14).

Eyes are essential to your success in jumping fences at an angle. If you find a focal point on the far side of the obstacle and ride straight toward it, your horse will have a clear sense of direction. But if your eyes wander, the horse will begin to wander also, unsure of where it is meant to go (fig. 5-15 A & B).

Jumping on an angle is usually reserved for advanced equitation courses and jumper classes (often as an option in "jump-off" rounds in which the speed with which the course is negotiated is a deciding factor for final placement). It is a test of your control of the horse and requires you to have a keen sense of the animal's balance as you approach the fence. You must maintain steady contact with the horse's mouth on the approach, during take-off, and in the air. Otherwise, the animal will find it easy to run out at the obstacle.

It's best to find a medium take-off spot to a fence that will be jumped at an angle because a deep spot can easily cause a knockdown, while a long spot encourages a run-out. The balance of the horse on the approach is just as important as the take-off spot. Horses tend to shift their weight away from a fence when approaching it at an angle, probably due to their confusion about whether they are being asked to jump it or simply gallop past it. When this happens, you must counteract the tendency by using a firm hand and leg on the side of the horse that is away from the fence and, if needed, using an opening rein on the side nearest the fence (fig. 5-16).

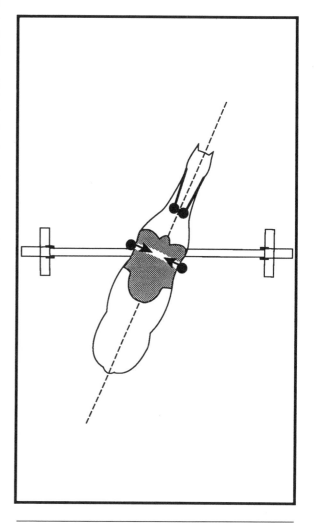

5-14. The diagram shows the horse jumping a fence on an angle. When approaching the fence, concentrate on a focal point on the far side of the obstacle, as indicated by the dotted line. Use supporting legs and closely positioned hands to form a narrow corridor that holds the horse in a straight line on the approach to the fence, in midair, and all the way to your focal point.

Narrow Fence and End Fence

The *narrow fence*, with its face measuring between six and eight feet in width, is commonly used in equitation finals (fig. 5-17). To ride well over a narrow obstacle, you must be able to steer your horse perfectly straight through the center. If the animal drifts to either side, a run-out can easily occur.

The most difficult setting of a narrow obstacle is as an *end fence* — that is, a fence at one end of the ring that is set perpendicular to the short side of the arena. Typically, it is placed away from the railing to present a steering problem. This requires you to

5-15 A & B. To jump a fence at an angle within a row of fences, line up the obstacles and ride straight between them (A). Be sure to let your focal point extend far enough that the line you plan to ride will not cause you to run into other fences after you have jumped the difficult angle fence (B). Notice in figure B that the rider has used some markers to help him stay on a good line to the angle fence. When walking the course, he planned to turn onto the line at the trash can (indicated by the circle outside the ring) and to focus on the concession booth (indicated by the rectangle at the top of the diagram). These mental notes about the path he needed to take helped him to correctly jump line B and avoid running into the first fence on line A.

5-16. If your horse begins to drift away from an angle fence, shift both hands toward the fence and press with your leg that is away from the fence, to hold the horse onto the proper line.

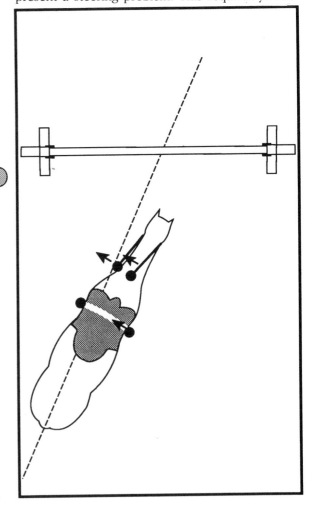

collect your horse after the preceding obstacle and turn toward the upcoming narrow fence without falling on your hands for support, for if your hands drop, you are sure to overshoot the curving line. Your eyes must be active in locating and maintaining the bending line so that you will realize immediately if your horse is cutting inward or drifting outward on the curve. Many refusals in the equitation finals have occurred at a narrow fence set at the end of the arena, since the fence is placed where a horse least expects to find it and the tight turn that precedes it doesn't allow a margin for error (fig. 5-18).

A Long Gallop to a Single Fence

A long gallop to a single fence may also present a problem. Often, the rider lengthens the stride cor-

rectly coming out of the corner, but rather than maintaining the proper length of stride once the horse reaches it, he allows the animal to keep on extending. As a result, the rider sees a take-off spot that is much too long and places the horse so far from the obstacle that it either dives over the fence or loses heart at the last moment and chips in.

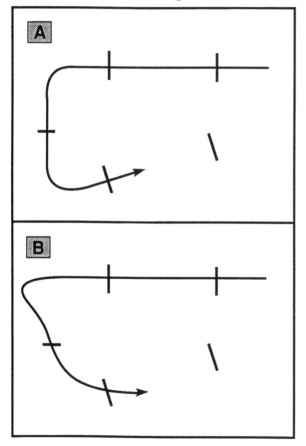

5-17. This simply constructed, six-foot-wide obstacle makes an excellent narrow fence for schooling. Constructed without wings, it forces the rider to develop accurate steering. The fence is so narrow that it is not necessary to paint stripes on the rails as a guide down the center.

5-18 A & B. A narrow fence set at the end of the arena and away from the rail presents a steering problem for the rider. You can avoid overshooting the line by looking for the fence while in midair over the preceding obstacle. You must also keep your hands up as you land, so that you will be able to turn the horse immediately and accurately toward the narrow fence (A). By overshooting the line to an end fence, you create problems at the next set of fences. Although the rider has been able to jump the narrow fence and the one that follows, his horse is not lined up to jump the second fence on the diagonal line and is headed for a run-out (B).

To prevent this mistake, lengthen the stride as usual coming out of the corner of the ring, but concentrate on maintaining the length of stride you have achieved after the first four straight strides, rather than letting the horse lengthen for the next five or six strides before the fence (fig. 5-19).

Novelty Fences

Novelty fences are obstacles that look strange because they are made of unusual materials or are oddly shaped. For example, if a beer company is sponsoring a Grand Prix at a horse show, one of the fences you might see in the equitation as well as jumper classes is a large rubber beer bottle, lying on its side to form the length of the fence. Technically, this is not a difficult fence; but it may present a psychological problem for the horse or rider because it looks odd.

Sometimes a novelty fence has moving parts that will spook an animal, such as objects that move in the wind. Others may be designed in such a way that the horse has to jump through an arch, which more often than not is ignored by the horse and intimidates the rider. You should be aware of potential problems when approaching a fence that is out of the horse's realm of experience; but don't become so preoccupied with a novelty fence that you have a hangup about it, for this will prevent you from concentrating on other important elements while on course.

Summary

You can be successful in low-level hunter and equitation competition, where the distances are conservative and the fences low, by maintaining a steady pace throughout the course and finding good spots to all your fences. As you progress competitively, however, you will find it necessary to be able to alter your horse's length of stride through changing its frame during the course. This allows you to negotiate more difficult distances while maintaining a steady tempo that makes your round beautiful both visually and audibly.

When faced with the most difficult equitation or jumper courses, you must be capable of analyzing the technical difficulties of the course, not only as singular problems, but also as interrelated tests. By analyzing how preceding or following lines affect the way a particular fence should be ridden, you can devise an overall plan that will work smoothly, rather than one that will result in riding from one fence to another with no apparent continuity. It is the rider who has the mental capacity to devise a good plan, the technical ability to ride out that plan, and the artistry to perform difficult tests with fluidity that will rise above the others in paramount competitions.

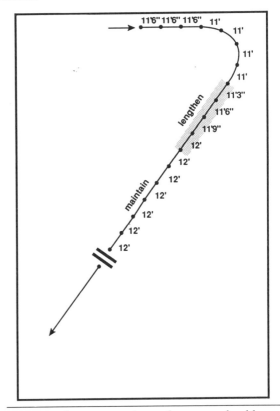

5-19. On a long approach to a fence, you should incrementally lengthen the horse's stride for about four strides out of the corner, as normal; but do not allow the horse to continue to extend its stride beyond that point. Instead, maintain a medium length of stride for the remainder of the approach to the fence. This will help you find a medium take-off spot.

6

Solving Typical Problems

Rider Problems

Developing a Better Eye

Difficulty in determining what adjustments must be made to place the horse properly for take-off is known as a *bad eye*. Two things have struck me about riders with this problem. First, they usually look too late at the upcoming fence, leaving themselves little time to make a decision and adjust the horse's stride. Second, they usually have a poor sense of rhythm, which is evident not only as they approach the fences, but also when they work on the flat. They find it difficult to feel the tempo of the horse's footfalls at the different gaits, even at the slowest gait, the walk. (Not surprisingly, they usually have little, if any, musical ability.)

As discussed earlier, on course the rider's eyes should: (1) look toward an outside line of fences as the horse crosses the centerline; and (2) look toward a diagonal line of fences about two strides before the centerline. Your eyes should never lose sight of the focal point at the end of a line of fences. When you look to determine what adjustments must be made to meet a good take-off spot, you should still be aware of your focal point through use of your peripheral vision. By looking soon enough and not allowing your eyes to wander for even a moment, you will notice that your success rate in meeting good spots will greatly increase.

The reason for maintaining a steady tempo on course is to prevent the horse from having to change its pace drastically at the last moment to reach the correct take-off spot. Typically, the problem of erratic pace arises when a rider allows his

horse to slow down when passing the in-gate. He must then drive the animal forward too forcefully a few strides before the upcoming fence to have enough momentum and length of stride to travel between the fences in the correct number of strides. To prevent this error, concentrate on maintaining even strides throughout the course, particularly when you are traveling past the in-gate or out-gate. This will make it much easier for the horse to meet the fences properly.

To improve your ability to dictate a steady tempo to the horse, practice humming a three-beat song or simply thinking a steady rhythm, such as "dah, dah, dum...dah, dah, dum...," throughout the course. An instructor can help you develop a stronger sense of rhythm by steadily beating out the downbeat for each stride—that is, the third beat, in which the horse's leading leg strikes—using a riding crop against a jump standard. Another option is to obtain a battery-operated metronome and use it with a megaphone or microphone to project the appropriate tempo. The metronome is particularly practical because it provides a continuous beat that can be adjusted to suit your horse's ideal rhythm.

Some riders have trouble finding a good distance because their horses are moving slightly slower than the appropriate pace throughout the entire course. If your stirrups are too long, you will be particularly prone to this problem. I think the reason is that long stirrups cause your seat to be closer to the saddle, so you subconsciously slow the horse down to create a smoother ride. If the stirrups are the correct length for jumping (resting at the middle of your ankle bones when your feet are dropped out of the stirrups and your legs are relaxed) then you will not be uncomfortable at a hand-gallop and will therefore be more likely to maintain the proper pace (fig. 6-1 A & B). (When I'm very tired and start missing spots to fences, I take my stirrups up an extra notch to further distance myself from the horse's motion, so that I will be encouraged to hand gallop rather than drop to a slower canter tempo to the obstacles.)

The following ground pole exercise, which represents one line of fences, will help you learn to sustain the correct pace on course and develop a better eye. It allows you to simulate jumping a line of fences without having to stress the horse physically with the much greater effort of taking off and landing over larger obstacles. In a rectangular arena,

measure 24 feet from the railing at the end of the line and place a ground pole there; this will be pole number 4 and will represent the place at which the horse should change leads after it jumps a line of fences. Then place three more poles in line with pole 4, leaving spaces of 57′, 60′, and 57′ between them for horses; 54′, 57′, and 54′ for large ponies; 51′, 54′, and 51′ for medium ponies; and 48′, 51′, and 48′ for small ponies. These are all 4-stride dis-

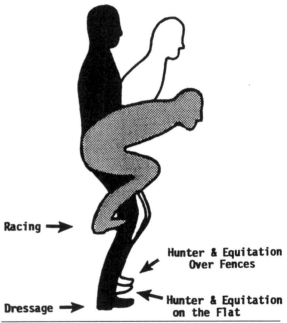

6-1 B. The black image shows the position of a dressage rider. His stirrup rests just below the anklebone, but his leg falls far down the side of the horse because the front of the flap of a dressage saddle is shaped more vertically than the flap of a hunter seat saddle. The dressage saddle is cut to promote deepness of the rider's seat and to enable the rider to keep his upper body balanced as precisely as possible over the horse's center of gravity. As pace increases, it is necessary for the stirrup iron to be raised, as indicated by the white and gray images. The white image shows the leg position of a hunter seat rider, whose knee rests farther forward than the dressage rider and whose stirrup length is shorter for jumping fences than for working on the flat. The shortest length of stirrup is used for racing, which is indicated by the gray image. The shorter the stirrup, the less the rider's weight encumbers the horse.

6-1 A. When the stirrup is at the correct length for jumping, the bottom of the iron hits the middle of the rider's anklebone as the leg hangs relaxed along the horse's side.

tances between poles.

The distance between the first and second pole represents the approach to a line of fences; the distance between the second and third pole represents the footage between a line of two fences; and the distance between the third and fourth pole represents the space in which you must collect your horse, balancing it for the upcoming turn (fig. 6-2 A, B, C).

To practice establishing and maintaining the proper pace on course, build the horse's impulsion and increase its length of stride around the end of the ring, approaching the line of poles at a pace you believe to be correct. Try to negotiate the space between poles 1 and 2 and between poles 2 and 3 in four strides each. On most horses, you will have to progressively lengthen the horse's steps between poles 1 and 2 to cover this distance in four strides, since the horse is coming out of a corner which restricts not only its pace, but also its length of stride. However, you should be able to cover the distance between poles 2 and 3 in four even strides, since the horse should have reached the proper length of stride just before jumping pole 2. Following pole 3, perform a downward transition, halting in front of pole 4. After halting for 4 to 6 seconds, walk the horse over the pole.

Now analyze each segment of your performance. If your horse added a stride between the first and second pole, the pace to the first obstacle (represented by pole 2) was too slow. If the horse left out a

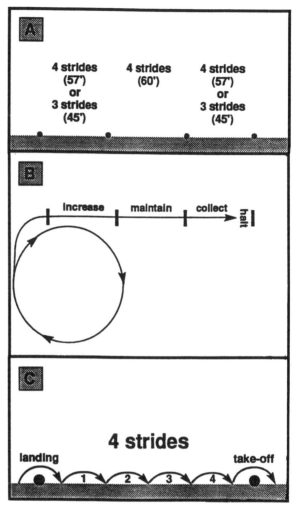

6-2 A, B, C. You can simulate a line of fences by setting four poles on the ground, with the space between the first and second pole representing the approach to the first fence, the space between the second and third pole representing the distance between two fences, and the space between the third and fourth pole representing the area in which you must collect your horse before the corner. The diagram shows the distances for horses, using either four strides between each set of poles in a large ring, or three strides for the first and third distance in a smaller ring (A). To practice riding a line, start with a large circle that will enable you to reach the correct pace for the course. Increase the horse's length of stride between the first and second pole to make up for the natural shortening of stride that takes place as the horse goes around the corner following the circle. You should achieve the correct length of stride before you jump the second pole, then maintain it between poles 2 and 3. Following pole 3, collect the horse and halt for 4 to 6 seconds in front of pole 4. Finally, walk the horse over pole 4. If the animal is slow to respond in the downward transition and ends up straddling the fourth pole at the halt, do not back up over the pole, since this could damage the fetlocks. Instead, halt the proper length of time, then walk the horse forward (B). The horse should take four even strides between the poles which represent the fences (C). However, if your horse is consistently too strong to the fourth pole, you can approach the second pole with more momentum so that you can collect between poles 2 and 3, making the halt in front of pole 4 easier.

stride between the first and second pole, or took half a step on the near side of the second pole and half a step on the far side (representing a crash), then the pace to the first obstacle (pole 2) was too fast.

The same holds true for the distance between poles 2 and 3. If the horse added a stride, it did not have enough pace; and if the horse left out a stride or straddled the rail, then the pace was too great. Finally, consider the horse's willingness to stop at the fourth pole. If the horse pulled on the reins and crossed the pole, then you know it would be unwilling to collect its frame and lighten its forehand for a change of lead.

Practice smoothly negotiating the three poles and halting before the fourth. When you are able to do this exercise well, continue galloping over the fourth pole, asking the horse to switch leads as it crosses this pole, if it is traveling on the counter lead. Use an outside leg at a behind-the-girth position to signal the horse to change leads while in the moment of suspension above the pole.

If your ring is too short to set the poles four strides apart, delete one stride between poles 1 and 2 and poles 3 and 4, so that the approach and departure will call for three strides, instead of four. The measurements would then be 45', 60', and 45' for horses; 43', 57', and 43' for large ponies; 40'6", 54', and 40'6" for medium ponies; and 38', 51', and 38' for small ponies. This tighter setting of the distances is harder to negotiate because it requires abrupt adjustments of the horse's stride, particularly during the last strides before the halt. It also causes more trauma to the horse's legs leading into the halt, which is the main reason that I prefer the four-stride setting.

The next step is to raise poles 2 and 3 so that you can practice seeing distances to actual fences, with the approach and departure still marked by poles 1 and 4. (Set the fences three feet high for horses and six inches below the normal fence heights for ponies. Use additional poles to fill in the spaces underneath poles 2 and 3 so that these fences are not too airy.) During this exercise, the horse's arc should be even—that is, the animal should leave the ground

and land equidistant from the center of each obstacle—and the strides between the fences should be of equal length. If you have difficulty finding a good take-off to the two fences, draw lines in the dirt six feet away from the near side of them to help you concentrate on placing your horse's front feet on these lines. Of course, white lines made with lime would be even easier for you to see, but sometimes a horse will spook at something unfamiliar on the ground, which can be dangerous at the point of take-off. If you decide to mark the take-off with a bright substance, practice over very small obstacles first.

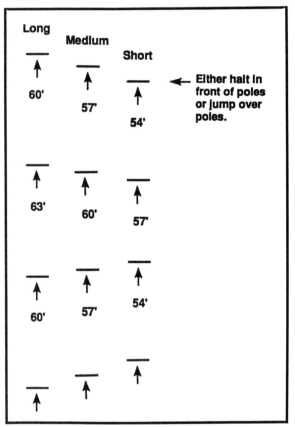

6-3. By setting three lines of varying lengths side by side, you can compare the feeling of riding to long, medium, and short lines. The distances listed are for horses, with the striding between each set of poles being four strides.

When training your eye, it is beneficial to set three separate lines of fences—normal, short, and long—with the same number of strides between them, so that they can be used for comparison (fig. 6-3). To set the short and long lines, subtract six inches to a foot per stride for the short line and add six inches to a foot per stride for the long line, still allowing for a six-foot landing and take-off at each obstacle. Concentrate on pace and evenness of stride, rather than worry about the take-off spot. By keeping the horse collected on the approaching strides to the short-distance line, and by galloping forward on lengthened strides to the long-distance line, you can greatly increase your chances of finding a suitable take-off spot to the first fences in each line.

Finding the Right Spot to the First Fence

A common problem among hunter seat riders is finding a bad spot to the first fence in a class. It usually results from the rider coming out of his initial circle at too dull a pace, so that he looks at the first fence only to see a deep distance or a distance that is much too long for the amount of impulsion his horse has. This leaves him with two choices: (1) place the horse at the deep spot, then struggle to lengthen the horse's strides to the second fence; or (2) try to jump from the long spot out of too little impulsion, in which case the horse will either make a dangerously weak attempt or will chip in, adding an extra stride at the base of the fence.

Often, when a rider meets a bad spot to the first fence in a couple of classes, he becomes so preoccupied with that fence that he spends the rest of the show worrying about it. If you have this problem, concentrate on using the time you have during the initial circle to steadily increase the horse's pace. Look at the first line as you cross the centerline of the ring and keep your eyes riveted on it while driving the horse forward through the corner, preventing it from shortening its stride. Try to "override" the approach to the first line a little by having more impulsion than you think you need. By doing this, you will have about the right amount to the

first fence and will find a better spot.

Strengthening the Rider's Position

You must be physically fit in order to remain glued to your horse at all times. Fitness can prevent such accidents as being slung into the fence if your horse stops, or sliding off if it spooks to one side. Ideally, you would like to be so fit and well-coordinated that the only way you would hit the ground is if your horse fell, too.

To help reach this level of fitness, you should practice the following exercises: (1) maintaining two-point position at the trot with stirrups; (2) sitting the trot without stirrups; and (3) posting the trot without stirrups.

Work done in two-point position strengthens the front and inner part of your thighs, so that you'll soon become fit enough to hold yourself out of the saddle over a fence, rather than weakly dropping your seat onto the horse's back. Two-point work also strengthens your lower leg, making your calves steadier against the horse's sides and creating more weight in your heels.

To perform this exercise, first shorten the stirrups to your jumping length. Then pick up the trot and work around the ring in two-point position, with your heels pressed downward, your calves snugly held on the horse's sides, and your knees and thighs supporting the weight of your upper body. You can grab a bit of mane in one hand to stabilize your upper body, but do not lean on your hands (fig. 6-4).

It is essential for beginning riders to practice two-point position daily, since this will provide the security they need to jump safely. It is also a good exercise for an intermediate or advanced rider, particularly one who has just one horse a day to ride. Two-point position will help upper-level riders achieve and retain the degree of fitness they need to ride over complicated courses.

The second strengthening exercise is sitting the trot without stirrups. It helps you learn to sit comfortably and securely and to remain in the center of

6-4. *The rider is practicing in two-point position at the trot to improve her strength and balance. She holds a bit of mane in her inside hand to stabilize her upper body, while using her outside hand to steer the horse. Normally, holding the horse to the rail with the outside hand, instead of an inside indirect rein, is incorrect; but in this particular exercise, it is acceptable because it enables the rider to maintain her balance at this bumpy gait so that she can concentrate on improving her leg.*

the horse. To prepare, drop your stirrups, pull the buckle on each stirrup down about six or eight inches, then cross the stirrup leathers over the horse's withers. If you turn the top strap of the leather upside down before you cross it, your inner thigh won't be resting on a lump that could bruise you (fig. 6-5).

Your crotch should stay as close to the pommel as possible during this exercise, so that you are forked into the saddle with a secure thigh and knee position. (If you begin to slip backwards, grasp the pommel with one hand and adjust your position by pulling yourself forward.) Your calves should rest snugly against the animal's sides, and the toes of your boots should be tipped upward as though you still had your feet in the stirrups. When working without stirrups at the sitting trot, then, your leg position should be exactly the same as it was when you had stirrups.

The third exercise, which is more strenuous than sitting the trot without stirrups, is posting without them. This strengthens your thighs and calves, stabilizes your knee position, and helps your upper body find its center of gravity over your legs. As discussed earlier in the description of AHSA Test 8,

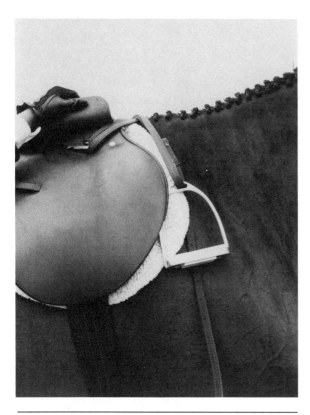

6-5. To cross your stirrup correctly, pull the buckle down six or eight inches, turn the top leather upside down to prevent a lump beneath your thigh, then pull the bottom leather upside down, dropping the stirrup over the other side of the horse.

your leg position at the posting trot without stirrups should be the same as with stirrups, except that you can carry your knee slightly higher to make up for the lack of support from your irons.

Between every three- to five-minute session of work without stirrups, you can take a break, walking the horse on a long rein and hanging your legs loosely along the horse's sides to stretch and relax the muscles so that they will not cramp. It is virtually impossible for most riders to keep posting without stirrups for even three minutes when they first begin this exercise. In fact, many cannot make more than one circuit of the arena before they feel exhausted. This exercise is very taxing; it is best practiced correctly for short intervals, rather than incorrectly for extended periods of time.

At this point a fourth set of exercises should be mentioned. Although they do not increase your strength, they help you learn how to stay on the horse through balance rather than through gripping. These exercises entail your being longed without stirrups or reins by an instructor, so that you can concentrate on your body rather than on controlling the horse. To prepare, set the horse up as described in the longeing section in Chapter 2, except for the stirrups and reins. Remove the stirrups entirely and knot the reins around a clump of mane or around the part of a martingale that rests just in front of the withers.

When being longed, try to feel your center of gravity at the various gaits and keep it as closely aligned to the horse's center of gravity as possible. If you slip backward in the saddle, grab the pommel with your outside hand and the cantle with your inside hand and adjust your seat to the front of the saddle. By remaining close to the pommel and keeping your weight equally distributed on each side of the animal's body, you will be able to sit comfortably at every gait.

Your leg should remain in a normal riding position while you perform the various suppling exercises with your upper body. The exercises are designed to reduce tension in your body, help you develop better balance, and raise your level of confidence (fig. 6-6 A, B, C, D, E, F, G, H, I, J).

A

B

C

D

E

6-6 A, B, C, D, E, F, G, H, I, J. Grasping the pommel with her outside hand and the cantle with her inside hand, the rider adjusts her seat by pulling herself to the front of the saddle (A). Longeing with hands on the hips helps the rider feel her center of gravity and prevents her from hanging on the horse's mouth for support, as riders holding reins sometimes do (B). The rider starts with her arms outstretched at shoulder level, then turns to the left and right to reduce upper-body stiffness and increase her confidence on horseback (C & D). Rotating her arm in a clockwise motion, the rider feels her weight sink deeply into the horse as the arm moves back and downward. This exercise shows the rider how a relaxed, deep seat feels. You can rotate one arm, then the other, using the hand on the opposing arm to grasp the pommel and

F

G

H

I

hold you steadily near the front of the saddle (E, F, G,
H). Touching your toe with the opposing hand is
another exercise that reduces upper-body tension.
Although this is intended to be performed on both
sides of the horse, you will find it much easier to do it
to the inside of the circle than the outside, since
centrifugal force pulls you toward the outside of the
figure. As you bend in each direction, you will feel
yourself moving away from the horse's center of
gravity, then back over it again as you rise to the
original, erect position (I). Raising your knees above
the pommel will encourage you to find the horse's
center of gravity and stay on through balance, since
you are no longer able to hold on by gripping with
your legs. When doing this exercise, hold the pommel
with your outside hand (J).

J

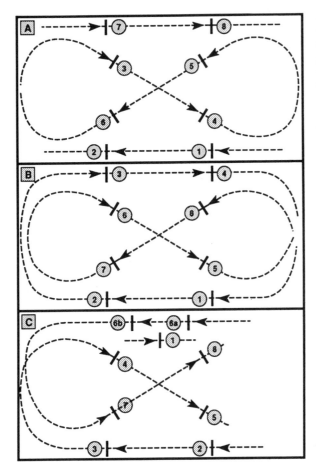

6-7 A, B, C. Memorize the first course as an outside line, the pattern of the number 8, and another outside line (A). The second course is once around, followed by an 8 (B). The third course is a single fence and two half-turns (C).

6-7 D. This equitation course can be easily memorized as a half-turn followed by a half-turn in reverse.

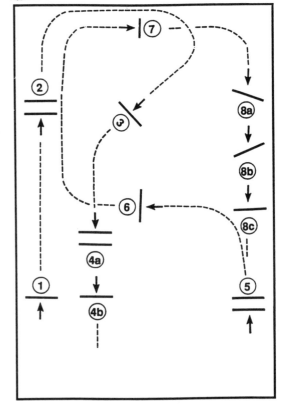

Memorizing a Course

It has always been easier for me to remember shapes than numbers. For this reason, I have never thought of a course as fence 1, fence 2, fence 3, etc., but have always memorized the shapes of the lines.

To do this, separate the segments into outside lines, inside lines, half-turns, half-turns in reverse, circles, figure eights, and so on. For instance, think about the course in fig. 6-7 A as an outside line, a path describing the number eight, and an outside line. In fig. 6-7 B, memorize a circle (once around) and an eight. For the course in fig. 6-7 C, visualize a single fence, then a half-turn to a half-turn. In equitation classes, it is particularly helpful to think of the segments as shapes, since the courses are usually more complicated than the those found in hunter classes. For example, fig. 6-7 D would be a half-turn to a half-turn in reverse.

Memorize your course as early as you can and be sure to walk it before you ride it. When walking between the fences, pay attention to your approaches to the lines and decide at what point you should look at the upcoming line. Work this strategy into your plan, so that your eyes will automatically turn toward the line when you get to certain points on course.

Discuss the course with your coach or, if he is not available, go over it several times in your mind, until you are sure you know where to go. Finally, think about your plan just before you enter the ring, so that it is fresh in your mind.

Controlling Nervousness

Relaxation Exercises Off the Horse

It is important to control nervousness both before and during competition, for if you allow yourself to become too anxious, you will physically and mentally exhaust yourself, your confidence level will sink, and you'll become your own worst enemy. Overly nervous competitors are affected by environmental changes sooner and more radically than calm competitors. The combination of chilly weather and nervousness can lead to muscle injury, since both conditions tend to draw your body into a stiff knot that fights, rather than follows, the horse's motion. Stretching exercises are useful anytime, but are particularly important on cool days.

Try to stretch in a warm place, before you put on your boots. Sitting on the floor with your legs spread, drop your upper body forward and let it hang for ten counts, so that your weight alone stretches your back and the backs of your thighs (fig. 6-8 A).

Then, move your arms toward your right foot and hold this position for ten counts, to stretch the left leg and the left side of the torso (fig. 6-8 B). Do the same to the left, to stretch your right leg and right side of your upper body (fig. 6-8 C).

Next, put the soles of your feet together and drop your upper body forward for ten counts (fig. 6-9 A). Then straighten your back and raise it slowly, stopping when it is about 20 degrees in front of an imaginary vertical line extending upward from your hip (fig. 6-9 B & C). As soon as you reach this angle, again relax the upper body by collapsing forward. Repeat this exercise ten times to stretch the back muscles and those in the inner thighs.

To relax your neck muscles, slowly roll your head in a circular motion in one direction for three revolutions, then in the other direction for three revolutions (fig. 6-10 A, B, C).

Stand and extend your arms outward from your sides. Turn in one direction (first count), then in the other direction (second count) for ten counts (fig. 6-11 A, B, C). This relaxes the muscles in your torso.

Finally, placing one hand on your hip, lift the other hand upward to stretch the muscles on your side (first count). Reverse the hand positions and repeat (second count). These positions should be alternated with each count, until you reach ten (fig. 6-12 A & B).

Now you are ready to finish dressing and go to the show. These exercises are not a must as a daily routine, but can be helpful when your anxiety level is high.

A

6-8 A, B, C. To begin the limbering exercises, sit on the floor with your legs spread, then drop your torso forward (A). Move your hands toward your right foot and stretch forward (B), then move them toward your left foot and do the same (C).

B

C

A

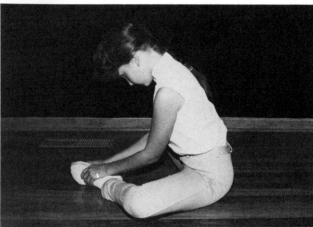

6-9 A, B, C. Begin with the soles of your feet together and your torso dropped forward (A). Straighten your back slowly (B) until your upper body is inclined forward at a 20-degree angle (C), then collapse your torso forward again.

B

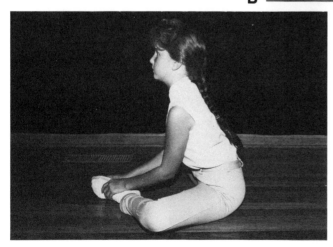

C

A

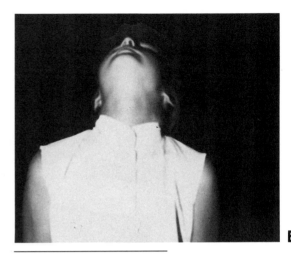

B

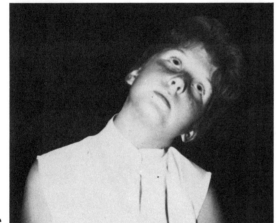

C

6-10 A, B, C. Begin with your head hanging forward, then roll it to one side (A), back (B), to the other side (C), and down again to relax the muscles in your neck and shoulders.

11A

6-11 A, B, C. Face forward with your arms extended straight from your shoulders (A), then, with your feet in place, turn right (B) and left (C) to stretch and relax the muscles in your torso.

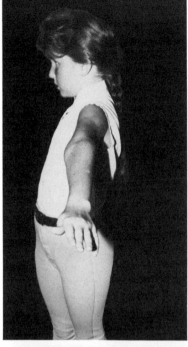

6-12 A & B. Stretch the sides of your body by alternately extending your right arm (A) and left arm (B).

A

B

Relaxation Techniques On the Horse

Nervousness may cause you to clench your hands into fists, resulting in "fixed hands" that cannot sensitively feel the horse's mouth. Fixed hands make it difficult to gauge the horse's length of stride and, consequently, lessen your ability to find good spots to the fences. Although hand muscles are warmed up in the morning through normal activity such as getting dressed, eating breakfast and possibly braiding or tacking the horse, nervousness just before the class may cause them to stiffen. To counteract this, put both reins in one hand and shake out the free hand, then swap the reins to the other hand and do the same (fig. 6-13).

Another major area of tension is the stomach. If you hold your stomach in, you will find it impossible to sit on the horse comfortably, since your contracted abdominal muscles will pull you upward, away from the horse's back. Even worse is a tense stomach combined with tense thighs, because the pinching of the thighs makes the upward pull even greater.

If you are unable to sit a trot comfortably, most likely your stomach and thighs are tense. To solve this problem, take a deep breath and let the air out slowly, allowing your abdominal muscles to relax. Don't try to hold your stomach in when you ride, but let it hang out in front of you. Let your buttocks and thighs relax also, so that they sink into the saddle. If you cannot feel your seat bones resting on the saddle, you know the muscles in your buttocks are tense.

Now check your calves to make sure you didn't relaxed these muscles when you relaxed the muscles just above. Every part of your body from the waist down should be exerting downward pressure, with the stomach, buttocks, and thighs providing passive weight and the calves and heels providing active weight. The knee simply acts as a hinge, remaining close to the saddle to offer stability, but not pinching to hold you on.

If you're still having difficulty sitting the trot, try the same exercise without stirrups. The lack of stirrup support will make it easier for you to sink your hips deeper into the saddle. Once you are comfort-

able riding the sitting trot without stirrups, try it with stirrups once again.

Straighten your back so that your spine, working as a solid unit rather than a series of flexible discs, can be used to reinforce your hands and arms. In trying to keep the back straight, you may tend to get stiff. To counteract this, concentrate on relaxing the muscles in the back, allowing them to drop downward. The straightness of your spine, then, enables you to be effective and elegant, while relaxed back muscles allow you to follow the horse's motion and not look stiff (fig. 6-14).

Your shoulders should be spread and dropped downward, anchoring your arms at the widest part of your back, so that the shoulders offer a strong

6-13. The rider shakes her hand to relax the muscles in it. It is helpful to shake each hand just before you go into a class.

6-14. At the sitting trot, the rider's upper body is correct with the back stretched upward, but the shoulders dropped low rather than held up tensely near her neck.

link between your back and hands. Nervous riders often draw their shoulders upward toward their necks. If this happens, try to relax the muscles leading from your neck to your shoulders by dropping and separating your shoulders. The shoulders should maintain this position, or even a lower one if the horse begins to pull, since by pressing downward with your shoulders and flexing the muscles in your back you can put yourself in a position of greater power. Draw your head and neck upward, following the line of the spine, so that they work in concert with your back.

The divisions of the body, then, are: everything below the waist dropped downward; the spinal column stacked upward with the surrounding muscles relaxed; the shoulders spread wide and dropped downward; and the head and neck following the upward line of the spine.

If you feel yourself getting nervous, check for tension points and try to relax the muscles that are taut. Applying the techniques described above will alleviate the detrimental responses of your body to anxiety and give you a sense of control of the situation.

Additional Concerns

Many other problems can be brought on by nervousness, such as poor appetite, nausea, sleeplessness, chills, and restricted breathing. To deal with loss of appetite, stick as closely as possible to your normal eating schedule. When mealtime arrives, eat something even if you don't feel hungry. Weakness brought on by lack of food only adds to the problem of nervousness, making it more difficult for you to think clearly and perform well physically. (Be sure to eat breakfast. Remember, an early class provides the same number of points toward a championship as a later class, so you need to be prepared to compete first thing in the morning.)

The typical horse show fare of hamburgers and hot dogs is hard to digest and tends to aggravate an already nervous stomach. Although a busy show schedule often makes it difficult to leave the grounds for lunch, try to locate a nearby restaurant that serves food that is not so greasy. If you have severe stomach problems, it may be worthwhile to bring food to the show. Some suitable items for lunch or snacks are: bread, turkey, chicken, tuna fish, peanut butter, pasta, potatoes, pretzels, and honey graham crackers. Fruit is also suitable, as long as you're not prone to diarrhea when you're nervous, in which case bananas are one of the few fruits you'll be able to handle. As a general rule, starches (such as bread, pretzels, and potatoes) are a better source of energy for a competitor than short-term sugars (such as candy and soft drinks). The high energy level provided by short-term sugars is quickly followed by a radical drop, which can make a nervous person feel nauseous.

It is also important to be careful about what you drink. Coffee and soft drinks are easy to come by at horse shows and are often drunk in excess. The caffeine they contain will not only make you more keyed up than normal during the day, but may also affect your ability to sleep at night. Water or Gatorade are better alternatives. Milk and orange juice are also acceptable choices that can usually be found on show grounds.

If sleeplessness is a problem, again try to stick to a normal schedule, preparing for bed at your usual time even if you are not sleepy. A long, warm shower will help you relax, and thoughtful preparation for the next day will alleviate some of your anxiety. For example, set an alarm clock as well as leaving a wake-up call so that you know you have a backup; and be sure to have your riding clothes laid out to prevent wasting time searching for anything in the morning. If you are already nervous, nothing will undo you more than having to thrash through a suitcase for an odd bit of clothing.

It helps to have a checklist for clothing and equipment. This way, you won't assume you have everything ready only to find out the next morning that you don't. (Also, keep extras of important items stored in a trunk on the show grounds so that they will always be near you, rather than in the car of someone who just went back to the hotel!)

If you suffer from chills under pressure, wear something under your shirt that is warm but thin, such as a tight-fitting cashmere pullover sweater. This will keep you from shivering and allow you to drop your shoulders into their correct position, rather than raise them up toward your neck as a chilled person is prone to do.

Some nervous riders subconsciously hold their breath as they enter a ring and may not take another until late in the course. You may not even realize that you do this, but may find yourself weak and breathless at the course's end and think it is simply due to physical exertion. If you find that restricted breathing is a problem, train yourself to take a deep breath as you finish the introductory circle on course. You should also use selected check points for breathing, for instance, the centerline at each end of the ring.

Often, nervousness is related to a preoccupation with another person's opinion of you. It's hard enough to try to please yourself. Don't add to your anxiety by worrying about the opinion of your coach, friends, parents, or anyone else. Just do the best you can and forget about what others might think.

Most good riders are less nervous in the show ring than they were before the class, for their concentration on the task at hand allows them to ignore the concerns that caused their nervousness initially. Especially in higher levels of competition, concentration becomes a major factor in success. As the courses become more complex, a rider has less time to make decisions. Knowing that a moment's lapse can cost him the class, a good competitor will channel his nervousness into total concentration. He does this by consciously shutting out distracting noises or movements, so that all he thinks about are the requirements of the class.

A good competitor will often stare into the arena, seemingly transfixed upon the course as he waits at the in-gate for his turn to compete. In his mind, there is just the course, the horse, and himself. He may be as nervous as the other riders, or possibly more nervous; but he uses the intensity of his emotions to help him focus solely on the course.

Don't ever think that you are alone in your anxious state. The only people who aren't nervous about competition are those who don't really care whether they win or lose. I have yet to see a big winner who had an "I don't care" attitude, so consider yourself among the potential greats if you get the jitters before a class.

Horse Problems

Flying Changes

As discussed earlier, you can set a series of four poles on the ground to simulate a line of fences, with the fourth pole representing the point at which the horse should change leads (see fig. 6-2 A, B, C). As the horse's legs cross over the fourth pole, they will be approximately four inches farther off the ground than when galloping between the poles. This additional elevation gives the animal more time to switch the sequence of its feet than when you ask for a change of leads without using the pole.

Ask for a change of leads by applying pressure with your outside leg over the fourth pole, but only if the horse is on the counter (outside) lead following the third pole. It is very important to feel which

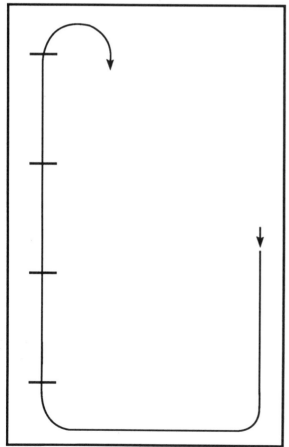

lead the horse is on, for the animal will react angrily if you keep asking for a change of lead when it is already on the correct one. On course, there are usually not many strides between the final fence on a line and the corner, so you must make an immediate decision concerning the necessity of a lead change. Being able to feel the lead your horse is on is just a matter of practice: try to feel which you are on, then glance to see if you are right. After awhile, you will feel whether you are right or wrong and will not have to look anymore.

If applying your outside leg over the fourth pole does not produce the correct lead, the next time you go through the exercise, circle the horse toward the inside of the arena as you cross the fourth pole. The turn will encourage the horse to change leads in order to catch its balance. You may have to practice turning over the final pole several times to teach the horse the correct response to your outside leg aid (fig. 6-15 A).

6-15 A & B. If the horse is reluctant to switch leads over the fourth pole, turn the animal toward the desired lead as you jump the pole. This will not only reinforce your aids, but also encourage the horse to switch leads to catch its balance (A). If you raise a pole on one side, you will encourage the horse to take the opposite lead. For example, by raising a pole on the left side, you would encourage the animal to land on the right lead, since the horse would shift the axis of its body slightly to the right in keeping with the angle of the rail. This, in combination with the extra elevation the pole provides, enables the horse to easily switch to the desired lead (B).

If this is not enough to help you get the change, raise the fourth pole on the side toward the railing to encourage the animal onto the correct lead. For example, if you want the horse to take the right lead, raise the left side of the pole to about 2 feet high and let the right side of the pole rest on the ground. This will cause the horse to tilt the axis of its body slightly to the right in the air and will encourage it to land on the right lead (fig. 6-15 B).

In some cases, the horse will still remain on the outside lead, and you must construct an X fence to provide additional elevation to accomplish the switch (fig. 6-16). Once the horse has the correct idea at the X and changes leads in the air, you can work through the previous exercises—first, a pole raised on one side, then a pole on the ground—until you are finally able to accomplish the lead change with no pole at all.

When schooling, if you have to rely on one of the three pole variations to help the horse achieve a flying change, don't be discouraged. Repetition of the exercises will teach the horse to correctly respond to your aids and give it practice coordinating its feet, so that it will be able to memorize the feeling of the lead change. It is only a matter of time before it will respond to your signals with accuracy and confidence, without the aid of any poles.

You can set an entire course of poles on the ground until you and the horse have mastered stride regulation and flying changes of lead in both directions, switching from the left to the right lead and vice versa. Then, build obstacles at the second and third poles on each line, still using the introductory pole to help rate the horse and the final pole to aid with the flying changes. Make sure the arena is big enough so that you don't run into a pole from one line while approaching a pole on another line (fig. 6-17 A & B).

The horse may begin to anticipate your leg aid by becoming too quick to the poles used for lead changes. In this case, go back to the original exercise of halting before the fourth pole on each line. After the halt, ask the horse to walk across the pole, pick up the canter, and proceed to the next line.

If you have a horse that anticipates the lead change by diving toward the turn, striped poles will help you solve the problem. Paint your schooling poles so that approximately a two-foot band of white is in the center of each pole (fig. 6-18). After you line up the poles for this exercise, make sure you ride to the center of each pole. This will make it obvious to you if the horse is beginning to drift while moving down the line. Halt the horse in front of the center of the last pole on each line until the animal realizes it won't be allowed to anticipate the direction of the turn. Once the horse is obediently following a straight path to the final pole, start the exercise from the beginning and jump the fourth pole, switching leads while in the air.

By encouraging elevation through collection and balance through straightness, you will find that most horses respond positively to the aid for the flying change. Of course, your outside leg must be applied at the appropriate time, as the horse's feet are coming off the ground for the split second of suspension that occurs just after the leading leg strikes. If your leg is applied at the wrong moment, the horse will not switch leads.

6-16. If more elevation is needed, you can use an X-fence to help the horse change leads.

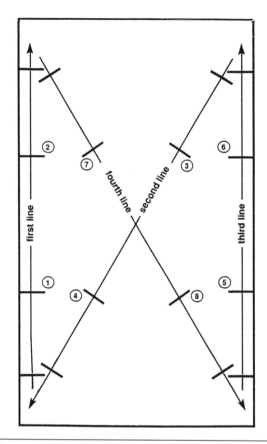

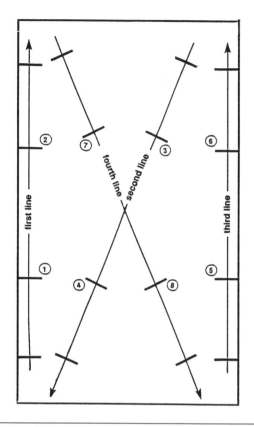

6-17 A. *If you are not careful, the ground poles you set will interfere with the approach to or departure from other lines.*

6-17 B. *If your ring is wide enough, you will be able to angle the diagonal lines toward the short side of the arena. This will prevent the ground poles from obstructing the paths to other lines.*

6-18. *I use striped rails and cross-footed standards, all made of lightweight and durable cedar, as schooling obstacles. (By placing ground poles several strides in front of or behind the line of fences pictured above, you can give the rider visual guidelines to follow so that he won't cut corners on the line.) I also use the Helvetia jump cup, which is made of rubber and has rustproof pins. I have had the set of jumps and jump cups shown in this picture for 10 years, which attests to their longevity.*

When the horse is comfortable changing leads over poles in both directions, remove the lead-change poles one by one, starting with the pole over which the horse is the most confident. (You can leave the ground poles leading into each line to help you practice placing your horse correctly at the first fence on a line; or you can remove these poles, too, and practice riding a normal course.) If the lead-change problem crops up again, reset the final pole on the lines where needed.

Rushing Fences

A horse that rushes fences is not an animal that "loves to jump," as uneducated riders often remark, but rather is the horse that is anxious about jumping. Once a horse has learned to rush, it is difficult to break the habit. It may take many hours and much patience to develop trust between the horse and rider again. In fact, it is best to remove an inexperienced rider from a rusher and place him on a horse that is very dull, requiring little hand pressure and steady leg pressure, so that the rider can learn the correct use of his aids. Conversely, it is wise to put a well-educated, patient rider on the rusher, so that the horse can be properly retrained.

There are several exercises used to teach a horse not to rush, all of them based on the idea of denying it the chance to run to the fences. In the first exercise, approach a fence at a trot or canter and pull up in front of the obstacle, making the horse stand for a few seconds. The downward transition should be as smooth as possible; but if the horse is running to the fence, use a pulley rein rather than let it ignore the aids and jump the obstacle.

If the horse is frantic and cannot approach the jump at the canter without wanting to accelerate tremendously, try approaching the obstacle at a posting trot. You may even have to approach it at the walk if the rushing is completely beyond control. A walk fence should be set quite low to make the jumping effort easy from the slow pace—about a foot high for horses and nine inches or less for ponies. The idea is to regulate pace on the approach, promote discipline through denial (that is,

make the horse stop, rather than allow it to run at the fence), and develop trust, so that the animal will confidently obey your commands.

It is interesting to watch different riders attempt to retrain horses that rush. The impatient, uneducated rider will pull the horse up harshly before the fences and back it up rapidly, using only his hands. All this does is make the horse more anxious. In contrast, a good rider will take care to quell the animal's fear. He will be firm, but not abrupt, in using his aids. If he backs the horse, he will be tactful with his hands and legs, using only the amount of pressure necessary. He will also be very careful in applying his aids after the halt, using minimum leg pressure to resume forward motion. At first his horse may overreact even to the slightest use of the aids; but after a few times the animal will learn there is nothing to fear and may even heave a large sigh of relief as it realizes the rider is not its foe.

Backing is useful in retraining a rusher because it requires greater obedience in the horse than the halt alone. An anxious horse is still thinking "forward," and only a mental change in direction will enable it to move backward. After you halt, ease the pressure on the reins to reward the horse for stopping. Then, add enough pressure on the reins to restrict the horse from moving forward as you apply your leg aid for backing up.

You may experience a brief deadlock in which the horse does not respond at all to your legs when you try to back. Attuned to the idea of running forward, it may refuse to think about moving in the other direction. The lack of response to the leg requires the slight persuasion of a spur or stick to reinforce the initial leg aid. You may ask, "Why would you use a spur or a stick on a rusher?" The answer is that you are seeking obedience in the horse. In the correct sequence of aids, the leg is followed by the spur, then the stick (it is leg, then stick, if you are not wearing spurs). It doesn't matter in which direction you are going, if the horse doesn't respond to your legs, reinforce them with the use of a spur or stick. The message to the horse is that you are willing to increase your aids until it reacts in the manner you desire.

Besides restricting a rusher by halting or backing, you can use a circle to teach obedience. As you approach the fence, try to regulate the pace of the horse. If it begins to speed up, circle before the obstacle, denying it the opportunity to rush toward the fence. Complete the circle and make a second approach, again trying to regulate the pace. If the horse tries to rush a second time, circle once again. Continue this pattern until it responds by sustaining an even pace all the way to the fence.

Personally, I prefer halting at an obstacle, or halting and backing, rather than circling on the approach. While circling is a means of disciplining the horse and regulating its pace, I would rather stop in front of the fence and literally show the animal there is nothing to fear. I want the horse to put its head down and sniff the obstacle. This gives me the opportunity to reassure it with a pat on the neck.

The nonchalance of the rider should calm the horse and help it begin to look at the obstacles. A scared horse never really looks at the fences. It doesn't try to gauge itself for a safe, comfortable jumping effort, but flies over the obstacles as though its tail were on fire. For this reason, I think it is important for a rusher to learn to look and to be rewarded for doing so with a calming and reassuring pat.

In general, when dealing with a nervous horse, try to instill a sense of calmness in the animal by emphasizing the relaxation of your aids, especially your hands. Instead of grabbing at the horse's mouth when the animal gets quick, maintain rein contact as lightly as possible. This sends the subtle message, "I am not afraid, so there is no reason for you to be afraid." You can halt, back, or circle the horse to control it if it continues to rush; but it is never appropriate to incessantly hang on its mouth, since this perpetuates the animal's hysteria and deadens the feeling in its mouth.

It is difficult to maintain leg pressure on a tense horse without the horse interpreting it as a driving aid. To develop a steady, yet sensitive leg, think of your calves as a clamp with a slight but consistent pressure. If you concentrate on hugging the horse's sides lightly with your legs and never succumb to removing them entirely when the horse is tense, it will learn not only to accept the legs, but also to expect their support. The steadiness of the legs will then be comforting to the animal, and the horse will worry when this security blanket is taken away, rather than when it is on. As the horse increasingly accepts the pressure of the legs, you will be able to add more pressure, until you reach the point where you can manipulate your horse mainly through your legs, with the hands acting only to balance the animal and help the legs in steering.

Disobediences (Refusals)

A horse usually stops at fences for one of the following reasons: (1) the rider places the horse too deep to or too far from the obstacle for the horse to jump it comfortably; (2) the footing is slippery or deep, making the horse doubt that it can clear the obstacle; (3) the horse is steered to the fence poorly, so that it sees the obstacle too late to set itself up properly or is so off-balance that it is unable to jump; (4) the horse is frightened by a fence that has patterns on it that are visually confusing; (5) parts of the obstacle or of nearby objects or surroundings are mobile or noisy; (6) the fence is too big for the horse to believe it can jump it; or (7) the pain of an unsoundness overrides the horse's fear of being punished for refusing.

You can control many of a horse's reasons for stopping at a fence. Practicing over ground poles and obstacles will help you develop better pace regulation, placement of the horse, and steering. Exposing the horse to many showgrounds will decrease the animal's chances of overreacting to spooky fences or surroundings. (Some riders pay stabling fees for their green horses and ride them around several different showgrounds to familiarize them with the atmosphere before the animals are ever entered in competition. Most riders, however, let their horses become accustomed to new environments through exposure during competition.) Placing the horse in the proper division for its abilities will preclude it from being overfaced by large fences; and proper veterinary treatment and rest will solve many kinds of unsoundness.

Bad footing continues to be a problem at some shows. You must use good judgement in determining when the poor quality of the footing is affecting your horse's performance, for you cannot develop absolute obedience in a horse if your demands are unreasonable. By asking the horse to jump in threatening conditions, you may cause a crash and undo the many hours you have spent building its trust.

It's a long road to accurate riding, and on the way you'll make some mistakes that will leave you sitting on a horse on the near side of an obstacle wondering what to do now that it has refused the fence. First of all, think of the correction for a refusal as a matter of opposites. You want to do exactly the opposite of what the horse wants to do. For instance, if the horse refuses the fence by running out to the left, turn it back to the right as a correction. Then, make the animal stand in front of the fence to receive its punishment. Conversely, if the horse tries to run out to the right, turn it back to the left, again making it stand in front of the fence to be punished.

Whether the horse tries to run out at the fence or simply stops directly in front of it, the issue is the animal's lack of obedience in going forward over the obstacle. For this reason, once you have the horse standing squarely in front of the fence, punish its source of forward momentum, which is the rear part of its body, with your stick in the area just behind your calf (fig. 6-19). If the horse stopped straight, you can punish it on either side; but if it veered when stopping, apply the stick on the side to which the animal tried to escape.

By being prompt with your correction, you won't have to exert a tremendous amount of physical force. You are not trying to inflict pain, but rather just enough discomfort so that the horse would rather jump the obstacle on the next approach than be punished again with the stick.

You should always carry a stick when jumping, so that it can be used immediately. If you have to hunt for one when a problem arises, the horse may have forgotten what it did wrong by the time you apply it, so that the punishment is seemingly unrelated to the initial problem.

Riders will sometimes say, "I don't carry a stick because my horse is scared of it." The solution is to always carry a stick, so that the animal learns to regard it as standard equipment. Carry it on the flat, as well as over fences, until the horse is comfortable with its presence. Any horse that convinces you that you shouldn't carry a stick is controlling you. Remember, you are the brains, the horse is the brawn. Any other relationship is dangerous.

Always remember to ease off the mouth when the horse leaves the ground to jump, for if your hands are hard and restricting, you will encourage it to

6-19. *The correct punishment for a refusal is applied on the side to which the horse tried to escape. For example, this horse would be receiving punishment for having run out toward its right side. Before you apply the stick on the horse's barrel, make sure the animal is facing the fence so that it clearly connects the punishment to lack of forward movement over a particular obstacle.*

refuse fences. Especially when it has stopped and you are approaching the obstacle for the second time, emphasize your driving aids—legs and seat, too, if necessary—and relax your hands as much as possible, keeping just enough tension on the reins to steer the horse. Your objective is to make going forward much easier than stopping.

You may not be able to keep a very light hand on a horse that wants to run out. In fact, you may have to use a great deal of hand pressure to hold it into the fence as it tries to veer in one direction. If this is the case, be sure to release as it leaves the ground, offering more than enough slack in the reins over the fence so that it will realize that forward is the most comfortable direction.

If you ride the horse accurately to take-off spots, but it tries to refuse fences, ask a veterinarian to check for unsoundness. Lameness in a leg or foot, sore back muscles, or a spinal problem are typical unsoundnesses that will cause a horse to stop.

Cutting Corners

Several problems are created when a horse cuts the corners of the ring on course. First, the horse's weight is distributed too heavily toward the inside of the turn, so that the animal is unbalanced on its approach to the upcoming line. Second, this habit is usually accompanied by the horse being bent in the wrong direction, so that its vision is jeopardized. Third, by cutting corners, the horse leaves the rider with fewer strides in which to make adjustments following and leading into lines of fences.

The main thing to remember in solving this problem is to push the horse to the rail with an inside leg and an inside indirect rein, rather than pulling it to the rail with an outside hand. The following exercises will help you correct a horse that cuts corners. First, pick up a canter and rise into two-point position, then try to canter the correct path around the short side of the arena. Concentrate on keeping the horse bent correctly. If it tries to throw its shoulder to the inside of the ring, sit and perform a downward transition to the walk; then push the animal away from the center of the ring with pressure from your inside leg. Your hands, which should maintain an inside indirect rein, can aid your inside leg by shifting slightly toward the outside of the ring. This causes the inside rein to act as a neck rein and the outside rein as a leading rein.

If the horse still tries to lean to the inside, practice a leg-yield, requiring it to cross its inside feet over its outside feet, so that it displaces its weight to the outside of the figure. You can use an opening outside rein to give the animal a clearer sense of the direction in which you want it to move. If the horse does not respond sufficiently, switch both reins to your outside hand and use your stick behind your inside leg to reinforce your leg aid. When the horse responds correctly by displacing its body toward the outside of the figure, reward it with a long rein and a one-minute free walk to let the exercise sink in.

Then gather your reins and pick up a posting trot. Try to keep the animal bent in the proper direction around the short side of the arena. If it attempts to throw its shoulder to the inside, walk again and go through the procedure described above. When the horse is trotting around the end of the ring without trying to lean inward, pick up a canter and practice going around the short side with your body in three-point position. If the horse throws its shoulder to the inside again, walk and go through the procedure suggested above. Once the canter work in three-point position is correct, rise into two-point position and approach the short side of the arena, going back to the procedure at the walk if necessary.

Finally, try galloping around the ring in two-point position, keeping the horse to the rail with an inside indirect rein and inside leg. (Your outside leg should be supportive enough to prevent the horse from switching to the counter lead.) You can also attempt a course of fences to see if your flatwork has solved the problem. Remember that the greater the pace, the more the horse will be at the advantage. Therefore, if the problem starts again, go back to the walk and perform the necessary exercises to correct the horse at the point at which it begins to cut the corner.

Anxiety at Shows

There is no quick way to cure a horse's anxiety, but there are methods to minimize the problem. It helps to ship the horse to shows early, so that the animal has at least a full day in the new surroundings prior to competition. Take it out to graze near the show rings and familiarize it with any objects that might later present a problem, such as a barrier made of plastic string lined with hanging flags. Let the horse look, listen, and smell its environment.

If your animal is very nervous at the new location, don't try to walk it by hand. First, longe it on a large circle for about twenty minutes, changing direction every five minutes. After longeing, give the horse a bath (provided the weather is warm) and let it cool out and calm down. Once it is dry, return it to the stall so that it can drink water and urinate. Remember, it is easy to become so obsessed with working a horse down that you don't allow for its basic physical needs.

Give the horse about an hour's break. (This might be a good time for you to get a bite to eat so that hunger won't affect your mental attitude toward the horse. It is vital that you approach the nervous horse patiently if you are to improve its state of mind.) Then, tack up and ride for about 30 minutes. If the horse still seems tense, you can ride for up to another 30 minutes; but do not ride longer than an hour during any single session.

Avoid movements that are not easily within the horse's level of education. By sticking to familiar tasks, you will promote confidence and relaxation. Also, take frequent breaks and try to let the horse move on a long rein at the walk, showing that you are relaxed in the new surroundings. Of course, you don't want to take this so far that your horse catches you napping and suddenly dashes off to the hinterlands, leaving you behind on the ground! But trust your horse as much as you reasonably can.

If the animal is still nervous after an hour of riding, cool it down again and let it rest in the stall awhile. Then do another session later in the day. Be sure to provide plenty of water and hay between these sessions.

Next morning, take the horse out of the stall, and if it seems reasonably relaxed ride it awhile. (If, however, the animal is still very tense, longe it first.) Do about ten minutes of flatwork, then gallop the horse for about three minutes to see if it becomes excited from the increased pace. Testing the horse at pace is the best way of determining its anxiety level. If the animal is quiet, cool it down and put it in the stall until you need to prepare for the first class. If the horse becomes keyed up during the gallop, continue to gallop in three-minute sessions, with a few minutes of break time between, until the horse becomes more relaxed. (If you cannot control the animal at the gallop, return it to the longe line, again alternating directions every few minutes.)

You must find that fine line between reducing the horse's anxiety and working the animal to the bone. If your horse calms down, but in the process becomes lame, colicky, or tied up, then the work obviously hasn't done much good. Short, multiple riding sessions will give you the opportunity to gauge its energy level correctly, whereas the flow of adrenalin caused by a lengthy, emotional work session will often disguise an animal's exhaustion. Through regular breaks, you give the horse a chance to realize how tired it is, as well as give yourself the chance to evaluate precisely when the horse's spent energy has produced the calmness you desire. Following the correct preparation for the first day of showing, the anxiety level of the horse will remain the same or decrease throughout the show as it becomes tired and more familiar with the surroundings.

Various Problems Solved with Poles

When a horse consistently wants to pick up the wrong lead, you can use a ground pole to correct the problem. For example, when traveling clockwise, if the horse tries to pick up the left lead instead of the right, place a ground pole at the point at which the horse must turn as it moves from the long side of the arena into the corner. Trot the horse toward the pole, then use your normal aids for the canter just as it reaches the pole, so that it canters rather than trots over it. The combination of the pole's placement just in front of the turn and the extra elevation provided by the pole helps the horse to get the correct lead (fig. 6-20 A, B, C).

A

B

C

6-20 A, B, C. *When using a pole to get the correct lead while traveling clockwise, approach the pole at a sitting trot (A), apply the aids for the right lead as the horse hops the pole (B), then bend the animal around the short turn (C). Notice that the rider has shifted her upper body forward into modified three-point position as the horse jumps the rail. This relieves some of her weight from its back, but still provides close contact immediately following landing.*

If the horse does not respond properly and continues to pick up the counter lead, try turning the animal toward the inside of the arena while in mid-air over the pole. Apply your outside leg, the same as for the normal canter depart, and shift both of your hands slightly toward the inside of the arena so that the inside hand acts as a leading rein and the outside hand as a neck rein.

If this does not result in the horse picking up the correct lead, build an X fence at the site of the ground pole to provide additional elevation. Then approach the fence at a sitting trot, rising into two-point position as the horse leaves the ground and using the aids described above to ask the horse to take the correct lead while it is in midair.

Once the horse is picking up the proper lead consistently as it lands over the X, reset the ground pole and try again. When this is successful, remove the ground pole and attempt to pick up the proper lead at the same point, just prior to the turn. Go back to the previous exercises if the horse still needs the help of the pole or X. Eventually, it will develop the coordination to pick up the correct lead from your aids alone.

Another use for poles is to correct a horse that lands in a cross-canter sequence after a fence. This rare habit can be corrected by setting a pole 12 feet from the middle of an obstacle on the landing side (fig. 6-21). The location of the pole allows the horse to land normally, then requires it to hop the pole during the first stride after the fence. Once the animal has practiced this exercise several times, it will learn the proper coordination for landing on a normal lead and will not continue to land cross-cantering when the pole is removed.

6-21. A pole placed 12 feet from the middle of an obstacle on the far side will correct a horse that wants to land cross-cantering.

Poles can also be used to teach a horse to land on a particular lead after a fence (fig. 6-22 A & B). To set up this exercise, place a small fence (about 1 to 2 feet high) at a 45-degree angle from the railing of the arena. Approach the fence on a counter canter so that the horse must change leads in the air to land on the proper lead. (As the animal jumps the obstacle, it will shift its weight away from the railing to avoid running into it. This will help you get it to land on the proper lead.) Apply your outside leg and shift your hands toward the inside of the arena while the horse is in midair to signal it to land on the inside lead. If you look toward the inside of the arena in midair and ride your horse on a curve that direction as it lands, you will increase the chances of landing on the proper lead.

6-22 A & B. Setting a small obstacle at a 45-degree angle from the railing can help you teach a horse to land on a particular lead. Approach the obstacle at the counter canter (A), then ask for the lead change while you are in the air (B). To switch from the right to left lead, as pictured, you would apply your right leg and shift both hands slightly to the left. Your eyes should also look in the upcoming direction of travel to encourage the horse onto the proper lead. The rider is using a short release to firmly control the change in the sequence of the horse's feet in mid-air. Once the horse understands what it must do, the rider should use her hands more subtly to affect the change, as in fig. 5-12.

Poles can also be used before, between, or after fences to make a horse seek the ground with its head and neck and slow its pace. Ground poles are particularly beneficial when placed between elements of a gymnastic. For a horse, set the regulating poles 12 feet from the middle of the fence on the near or far side of the obstacle to slow the horse on the approach or landing, respectively. You can use regulating poles on both sides of obstacles to generally slow a horse's pace through a gymnastic; but to use them safely, you must ride very well. Either single or multiple regulating poles are not advisable for riders who do not have a good eye for a fence or for those atop frantic horses (fig. 6-23).

6-23. A ground pole placed twelve feet from the middle of an obstacle can be used for a variety of purposes. A pole preceding a fence helps to slow a horse down on the approach; a pole between two fences not only slows a horse down, but also makes the horse land and take off at established points; and a pole placed behind a fence prevents the horse from landing too far from the fence and discourages it from running.

7

Showing

Top Priority Items

Although there are many items which are necessary for showing, the most important ones are your horse, horse trailer, saddle, and boots. Of foremost importance is the horse.

The Horse

When looking for a show horse, first consider the job that the animal will be required to do. For example, a Junior Hunter must be able to clear 3'6" in good form and have a long enough stride to extend beyond twelve feet when necessary at bigger horse shows. If a horse will be used for advanced equitation classes, such as the USET Class, then it must be capable of jumping fences set at 3'9" with 5' spreads.

Not only must you consider whether or not the horse can do the tasks that will be asked of it, but also how well the animal can perform them. If you are trying to win in A-rated classes, your hunter must be a good mover as well as a good athlete over fences. Your first considerations, then, center on the horse's talent.

It is best to have a horse that comfortably travels on a twelve-foot stride, but can readily shorten or lengthen its stride by a foot when called upon to do so. Horses that have a much longer natural stride may appear dull as they lope around the course. If the horse is very tall and long-strided, it may also be lazy with its legs in the air, since a very tall horse, measuring 17.2 hands for example, will not have to make as big a jumping effort as a normal-sized horse measuring about 16 hands.

However, the horse with an excessive length of stride is generally preferable to the very short-strided horse, since anything is better than a horse of limited ability struggling to get through a course in the normal number of strides. Rushing to make the distances, a short-strided horse looks dangerous, giving both the judge and spectators the uncomfortable feeling that if the rider missed a spot, he would end up in the hospital.

This is not to say you must give up on all short-strided horses. They have their place as beginner mounts and may even be sufficient for the Children's Hunter classes in certain areas of the country. If the stride is not too inhibited, a very good rider who maintains the horse's impulsion on corners and finds excellent spots to the fences may transform a slightly short-strided horse into a brilliant performer. This is the rare exception, however. Too often, parents of junior riders expect their children to work miracles to make up for a horse's inadequacies, such as the tremendous drawback of an overly short stride. This unrealistic expectation can lead to frustration and disappointment for the child, or even worse, to a serious accident.

Next, consider the rider's build in relation to the horse's. A short or very thin rider will look better on a normal to slightly narrow-bodied horse than on a wide-barreled, coarse animal and will usually be more physically capable of controlling the delicately built horse. In contrast, a tall or slightly overweight rider should avoid a finely built animal, since it will emphasize the rider's size. Instead, large riders should seek medium to heavyweight hunters.

Short riders often have problems finding the right horse because when a proportional match in size is achieved, the horse is too small to cover the distances or jump the bigger fences well. In this case, a narrow-bodied horse of medium size (about 16 hands) is the best option, since it would allow the rider's leg to drop downward and appear as long as it possibly could, rather than sticking out as it would on a wider horse.

Ideally, when the rider's foot is in the stirrup, the heel should rest just above the bottom of the horse's belly so that the animal's coat forms a backdrop. If the rider's feet hang below the horse's belly when the stirrups are adjusted correctly, then the rider is too tall for the horse. Also, when the horse jumps, the rider's face should be over or slightly ahead of the dip just in front of the withers. If the torso of the rider is so long that when his body is positioned correctly his face is over the middle of the horse's neck in midair, then the horse's neck is too short for the length of the rider's upper body, which generally means that the animal is too small for the rider.

Equally important as the physical match between horse and rider is the temperamental match between the two. While their physical builds should be similar, a temperamental match is often best achieved by pairing dissimilar personalities. A tense rider will usually do better on a dull horse, while an overly relaxed rider will fare better on a slightly keen animal. Of course, when you have a physically relaxed, but mentally alert rider, which is the ideal, the best pairing is on a horse with exactly the same qualities.

The Trailer

Once you have chosen the right horse for the job, it is important to transport it to and from competitions safely. If you are pulling your own trailer, it must be big enough to house the animal comfortably. Many horses will panic if they bang their heads on a low ceiling and will try to exit the vehicle, even if it is moving.

It is also harder to load a horse into a small trailer because it will resist when it senses that the space is too tight. Do not buy a trailer that sports a fancy dressing room or extra storage space while neglecting the needs of the horse. The horse must: (1) have enough room to stand comfortably and spread its legs to balance during travel; (2) have ventilation on hot days, with the vent positioned so that hay doesn't fly into its eyes; (3) have easy access to water and extra hay during periodic stops on long trips; and (4) be easily reached by a person in case of an emergency. (I prefer to have a space in the front of the trailer that you can stand in when you stop to check the horse. This provides a good view of the horse's legs and makes its possible to reach the front of the animal as well as the back.)

A two-horse trailer is preferable to a one-horse trailer, even if you only have one animal to haul. The extra space can be used to carry trunks or feed and is available in case you decide to transport someone else's animal to defray your own expenses. When using a two-horse trailer for a single animal, load it on the left side so that its weight is toward the middle of the road rather than the shoulder.

Also, be sure to buy a trailer with a ramp. It is often hard to get a horse to load, even without asking it to hop into a trailer or back out off a ledge. Without a ramp, the risk of injury is high.

Both the trailer and the vehicle you pull it with should have a low center of gravity. This makes them steadier and less likely to tip over on sharp curves. A sway bar, which can be purchased and attached at most dealers of recreational vehicles, will help stabilize the trailer.

The trailer must also be equipped with chains to hold it to the frame (not the bumper) of the vehicle in case the trailer hitch disengages during travel. The ball of the hitch should be well greased, and the lock hammered shut when you attach it, rather than closed by the strength of your hands alone.

Check all lights before you start driving, including the running lights, which are used in inclement weather or for night travel. Also, be sure to check the air in all of the tires and have a spare in case of a flat.

The Saddle

Your saddle is another very important piece of equipment. If it fits you poorly, it will make it impossible to have the correct position on a horse and will negatively affect your balance and your ability to apply your aids properly.

If a saddle fits well, you are able to sit comfortably just behind the pommel without feeling that the seat is sloping down behind you, drawing you backwards as your horse moves. You should be able to maintain steady knee contact near the front of the saddle flap while resting your calf against the horse's flesh.

I recommend the Hermès saddle (pronounced "air-mays") to hunter seat riders who are able to afford one. Crosby saddles, which cost less than half the price of an Hermès, are also popular on horse-show circuits. Although it is an expensive piece of equipment, a good saddle is well worth the investment. One that is properly handled and cleaned will be useful for many years.

While on the topic of saddles, I should also mention the importance of a properly fitting girth. When the girth is drawn tight, the buckles should be half-way up the underflaps of the saddle so that there is extra room on both sides of the horse to draw the girth farther up or let it down. I prefer a leather girth that is contoured to fit the horse's body by curving in behind each of the front legs and that has elastic on one end. These are usually advertised as "chafeless" girths. The elastic should be on the near side of the horse, and all adjustments to the girth should be made on this side. The only reason you originally fit the girth on the far side to be at the middle of the underflap is so that you can adjust it if the horse becomes a little fatter or thinner.

Your saddle is a major investment and should be treated as such. Clean it following each time you ride, using a bar of glycerine soap, a natural sponge, and a minimal amount of water. It is wise to stamp your initials into the top side of the underflap, in case of theft. If you have any doubts about its safety at a show, take your saddle back to your hotel room at night. A sweep of saddles at large horse shows has happened a number of times.

Store the saddle on a saddle rack or, when one is not available, lay it so that the weight rests on the pommel. If you put your saddle on a flat surface in the same position as it goes on the horse's back, you can spring the tree and permanently ruin it (fig. 7-1).

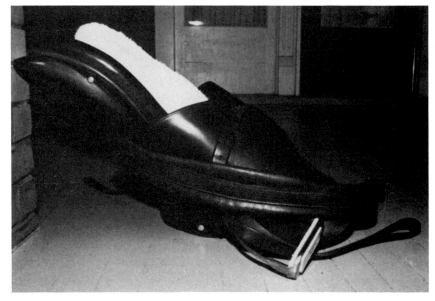

7-1. By resting this saddle on its pommel, the rider has prevented springing its tree. It would have been wiser, however, if the saddle pad had been used as a cushion between the cantle and the brick pillar, since a rough surface could easily scratch the leather.

Boots

Boots are also an important investment for a show rider. Poorly fitting boots signal the judge that the competitor is either uneducated or sloppy. The first thing a judge looks at in an equitation class is the rider's lower leg, since this is the base upon which everything else depends. If your boots are too short or are not tight enough around your calves, your leg will not have the long, neat appearance that is necessary to make a good impression.

Custom-made boots will ensure that you get the best look and fit. They can be measured by a competent person at a tack store and ordered from a boot-maker. (My favorite is the Vogel Boot Company in New York City.) Another option is to buy ready-made boots, which are available in both the dress boot style and the field boot, which laces up at the arch. Although traditional field boots are made in brown leather, the black field boots have become acceptable in recent years to accommodate people struggling to find affordable black boots that fit their arches. If you fit either style well, I would suggest buying black dress boots. They give a neater appearance and are traditionally correct.

Boots are an investment that will last a long time, assuming you have stopped growing. By keeping them clean and resoling them occasionally, you can use them for many years. The only thing that may be a problem is shrinkage following a drenching rain. To prevent this with custom-made boots, you can purchase custom-made boot trees that will fit tightly and keep them from shrinking as they dry. Of course, these trees are also used daily to hold the shape of the boots whenever you are not wearing them, so that they will not sag around the ankles when you ride.

Clean your boots with glycerine soap, but never oil them, for once they have been oiled they can't be brought again to a high shine. It is best to have them polished at a shoe repair store. Professional polish is tough and holds up better than ordinary polish.

Warming Up For A Class

When you're warming up for a class, you want to simulate the upcoming conditions as much as possible. If you are going to ride in an under saddle class, then you should walk, trot, and canter your horse in the schooling arena in the same frame and with the same pace at each gait that you will be using in the class.

If you find your horse is too strong or too dull, now is the time to correct these errors, while you are still out of the judge's view. You may want to switch bits — say, from a snaffle to a pelham — if your horse is too strong, or add spurs if an additional driving aid is needed. The time you spend in warm-up, then, should not be just to loosen the horse up for the class, but to correct any last-minute problems.

When you're going to show over fences, begin by warming up on the flat for a short time — less than ten minutes, unless the animal is excited and needs to be worked longer. Start the jumping portion of your warm-up by trotting the horse over a small X (about a foot off the ground at the center for horses and even lower for ponies), then halt at the end of the line.

After trotting back and forth over the X two or three times, change its construction to a vertical fence, set about six inches lower than the height of the fences in the upcoming hunter or equitation class. Hand gallop the horse around the schooling arena once to wake it up a bit, then approach the fence, seeking a medium take-off spot from a medium pace. After the jump, halt at the end of the line. If your horse is excited and wants to rush the fence, turn the animal around and jump the fence off a short approach. If the horse is dull and doesn't want to reach the proper pace, make a large circle at the hand gallop and approach the fence again, being prepared to use your stick if the animal tries to slow down.

Once the horse is jumping the vertical well at the low height, raise the fence three inches and jump it once or twice at the new height. Then raise it another three inches, so that it is at the height at which the horse will be shown. When you have jumped the vertical one or two times at this height, you can change the fence to an oxer to encourage good form in the air. You may even want to raise the uppermost poles of each element of the oxer one notch higher than the height of the fences in the class to make the horse pay attention. (Although a square oxer will not be found in hunter classes, you can use it for warming up both hunters and equitation horses. It makes a horse try harder to clear the fence than does an ascending oxer and thus "tunes" the horse.)

Consider the type of course you'll be jumping and prepare during your warm-up for the specific tests on course. For example, if a hunter course is set with long strides between the fences, practice riding up to pace by galloping around the arena then approaching the warm-up fence with long, bold strides. If an equitation course contains a tight turn, a fence to be jumped at an angle, or some other test that is difficult, then simulate it in your warm-up. (Difficult tests should be practiced over fences set no higher than the normal height for the class, since a higher fence will encourage the horse to stop.)

If your horse tends to spook at colorful or unusual objects in a ring, you can prepare by placing a wool cooler or towel over a vertical fence to make the animal hesitant to approach it in practice. If the horse tries to slow down or stop at the fence, punish it with the stick so that it knows it must go forward. Once you have cleared the obstacle, take the cooler or towel away and jump the fence again. In this way, the horse will not end the practice being anxious, but will clearly get the message that it must go forward.

When you have finished schooling, you should feel completely prepared to ride the course ahead. The schooling area is not a place for you to try new tests which you haven't taken the time to practice at home. Instead, it should be used as a last-minute preparation, to ready yourself and your horse to perform well in the upcoming class.

Make sure you have enough time to think about

the course before you enter the ring. Mount early enough so that you can school and still have one or two horses waiting ahead of you when you get to the in-gate. If there is a delay and you cannot compete soon after warming up, take the horse to an area where you can gallop just before you go in, so that it won't be dull from waiting.

Monitoring Horse and Rider

A horse show should not be viewed as a single competition spanning several days, but rather as a number of different competitive situations. Typically, horse and rider begin with a high level of excitement caused by the new surroundings, the bustle of people and animals, and the anticipation of winning a ribbon. This usually lasts throughout the first day of a multiday show and may even extend into the second day, if the number of classes ridden the first day were few.

By the third day, however, the horse and rider are tired. Gone is the earlier elation, replaced either by a nice sense of "things are going well" or the opposite feeling that "my horse is going terribly; I can't see my spots to the fences; the judge doesn't place me even when I think my horse has gone well," and so forth.

Going into the final days of the show, everyone is really tired. The riders who continue to win are those who are able to stay mentally sharp for each class, even though they are physically tired.

The changes in the horse and rider that occur from day to day are the result of many subtle changes that take place from class to class. Generally, in the first class the horses are "backed off" at the fences, warily approaching the unfamiliar obstacles. Frequently riders do not compensate for this, and they "underride" to the fences, not using enough leg to create sufficient pace and impulsion for the course.

By the second class, everyone is awake. Those who didn't ride well in the first class are kicking themselves and closely watching the round of the horse that won class one. In general, it will take a better performance to win the second class than it did the first, for everyone's competitive spirits have been aroused. The next few classes will be very competitive, particularly if they come before lunch. By noontime, the heat and the lure of food distract many competitors. After lunch, there is usually a post-meal lag as riders struggle to fight the drowsiness brought on by digestion. As for those who skipped lunch, they are feeling the effects of the lack of food.

By the end of day one, both horse and rider are tired, as well as the grooms and coaches who are just coming down from the emotional high of setting up their stable area and schooling for the first day of the show. As day two starts, the horses will be calmer, as will the riders. This is usually a good competitive day, but riders will begin to notice that it takes more leg to get their horses up to pace than it did the day before. From day three on, it is a matter of maintenance of the horse's and rider's energy levels, as well as of the horse's soundness. The big winners are the competitors who best minimize the aspects of nervousness leading into the show and who sustain an appropriate level of energy throughout the final days.

At a one- or two-day show, you and your horse will experience the same changes mentioned above, but they will occur in a much shorter time frame. If you're smart, you will be aware of the pitfalls of showing and will avoid becoming overly tired, hungry, cold, wet, or sunburned. You'll protect yourself so that your mind and body can produce peak performances for as long as possible.

Each time you mount for a class, think about the changes that have occurred in the horse since the previous performance. For example, if your horse was taken back to the barn for a break between classes, what went on during the break? Even if you have a groom, you should know the answer to this question, not only from asking the groom, but also from checking on the horse periodically. Did the horse have plenty of water and hay during the break? Was there enough ventilation in the stall to be comfortable on a hot day, or was there sufficient protection from the wind on a cold day? Breaks between classes are opportunities for the animal to relax. If your horse is so uncomfortable that it is denied this respite, there is a good chance it will not be willing or able to perform its best in the next class.

If the time between classes is so short that the horse must be kept near the ring, make sure its needs are not neglected. On a hot day, keep the animal in the shade whenever possible and have water available in a nearby bucket. On a cold day, keep a wool cooler at ringside. It will allow perspiration to pass through the fabric and bead up on top of the blanket, while the fibers next to the horse remain relatively dry, keeping the animal warm.

As for maintaining your own energy level, on hot days it helps to have something to drink in an ice chest at ringside, saving numerous trips to the concession stand. A folding chair to rest on between classes is also helpful. The ultimate energy-saver is a small motor scooter or a golf cart to spare you from endless walks to and from the barn. In general, avoid fatigue as much as possible throughout the show. The most important classes are usually held toward the end, and you don't want to run out of steam then.

Personal Evaluation

Resources: Coaches, Judges, Books

Too often, riders pick a coach based on convenience or personality rather than on knowledge. However, you cannot get an accurate evaluation from a person who is not well-educated in the sport, so be sure to choose based on that person's record as a coach. If he has also been a successful rider, that is another point in his favor; but in choosing, it is better to have a very good teacher who was not a very good rider than a very good rider who cannot teach what he knows. Of course, the best combination is a coach who has proven his capabilities in both areas.

Once you have a capable teacher, do exactly what he tells you to do. If you are always straying off in your own direction, ignoring the suggestions of your coach, then you might as well not have one. He should have an overview of the sport and be able to steer you toward reasonable goals. His evaluation should be the most meaningful because he sees you ride regularly and knows whether you are progressing, regressing, or standing still.

Another great help in personal evaluation is the judge. (First, you must receive permission through the steward to speak to the judge.) Most judges don't mind answering questions from a competitor, as long as the rider doesn't have an aggressive or defensive attitude. To find out specifically why you were penalized, ask the judge to critique you from the score cards. For him to do this, you must know the number of each class you would like to have critiqued, as well as the number you wore in the class.

Good judges keep an accurate record for every class over fences. (Normally, judges don't keep detailed notes for flat classes in either the equitation or hunter divisions.) The judge will have a mark for each fence on course and may have some written comments as well. The comments of a well-respected judge should be about the same as what your coach told you when you left the ring after each class. Consequently, if you've talked to several good judges and they all have similar comments, but your coach's comments are quite different, then you're working with the wrong coach.

Finally, books can be helpful references for self-evaluation. The best for equitation is George Morris' *Hunter Seat Equitation*, which offers numerous photographs and diagrams to support a clear and concise text. You might also find my first book, *Judging Hunters and Hunter Seat Equitation*, to be useful, for it enables riders to identify their errors and determine the impact of each upon placement in competition.

In locating other useful books, my advice is to choose according to the author's reputation as a rider or coach. The more you read, the more opportunity you will have to find a system, or parts of several systems, that will help you reach your riding goals. I find this preferable to adhering to any single method out of ignorance of other approaches.

Setting An Attainable Goal

Besides evaluating yourself and your horse on a daily basis, try to formulate some long-term goals. Of course, they cannot be determined until you have had a certain amount of experience. Your basics must be strong — that is, heels down, lower legs secure, your upper body balanced over your legs, and your hands sensitive to the horse's mouth. You must also be jumping small courses, demonstrating your ability to determine the proper take-off spot to the fences. Once you have reached this point, you are ready to sit down with your coach — and, in the case of a junior rider, your parents — to discuss long-term goals.

If a child is well-proportioned for riding, has several years still ahead in the junior division, and shows a good eye for fences, then the coach should be thinking about the Medal, Maclay, and USET Finals. The family's finances will come into play as a show schedule is devised. Although you can save money by stabling your horse at home, shipping the animal yourself, and doing your own grooming at shows, it is difficult to be highly competitive if you are exhausted from doing the chores as well as the riding. You'll have a better chance if you have a loyal relative or friend who is willing to get up before dawn to feed and braid your horse, as well as help out in other ways for the duration the show.

It is important to set attainable goals. Riders who do not have a good physique for the sport, those who are mounted on inadequate horses, or those who can't afford to show regularly are setting themselves up for disappointment if they set goals that are too high, such as winning one of the Finals. Parents can get caught up in a bad situation as well by making financial commitments they cannot reasonably meet. You must be realistic about the rider's and horse's ability and about the available financial backing. Otherwise, what was intended to be a fun and exciting experience will be tainted by frustration and financial woes.

Winning

Riders who have the best competitive records over long periods of time rely on hard work and serious analysis of their riding experiences to keep them ahead of other competitors. If you devote your time to practice as you should, then your confidence level will rise along with your skill. Instead of looking at a test and thinking, "Can I do this?," you will be so well prepared that your only concern will be to ride to the best of your ability and excel at that which you have practiced many times before.

A systematic approach to riding will help you most when you are under the stress of an unusual situation, such as competing in bad weather, riding an unfamiliar horse, or showing indoors, where schooling is often limited in both time and space. These are the kinds of situations that end in defeat for the seat-of-the-pants rider, for difficult situations demand more technical skill, which is gained only through a dedicated approach to the sport.

If possible, surround yourself with people who are committed to your success — an attentive coach, a reliable groom, and even supportive friends or relatives. Your dedication should inspire the people you work with and fuel their desire for your success. When a rider wins at the highest levels of competition, you will usually find he or she has a wonderful support team.

Concentrate on excellence in your daily work, rather than focusing mainly upon the goal of winning. Continuous progress means you have the possibility of being truly great in your sport, while ribbons and trophies can be gained simply when you are better than the rest of your local competitors, who may not ride particularly well. Of course, we're all happy when we get a ribbon, but the thrill of winning may cloud the priority of improving your skill.

Most importantly, put winning in perspective, not only for the sense of fulfillment that a sound personal philosophy can provide, but also for the betterment of the sport. Too often we focus solely on talent and ambition while overlooking other important aspects of people's characters. If we as a society turn away from the concept of good sportsmanship and place all our emphasis on winning, we will demean the most important and inspiring qualities of mankind. Talent and ambition are an exciting combination, no doubt; but it is dedication, emotional stability, and a gracious acceptance of defeat, as well as victory, that are the marks of a true winner.

GLOSSARY

ahead of the motion   An overly forward position of the rider's upper body at a particular gait.

(AHSA) American Horse Shows Association   The governing body that oversees recognized competitions in America and serves as the National Equestrian Federation of the United States for worldwide competitions.

aids   The rider's means of communication with his horse. "Natural aids" include the rider's legs, hands, weight, and voice. "Artificial aids" include crop, spurs, bit, martingale, and any other type of equipment that reinforces the rider's body commands.

at the girth   The position of the rider's leg in which the calf rests just behind the back of the girth.

backing   The horse walking backwards for several steps; also known as "backing up" or "reining back."

bascule   The extension of a horse's head and neck outward and downward to counterbalance its hindquarters over a fence.

behind the girth   The position of the rider's leg in which the calf is about four inches behind the back edge of the girth.

behind the motion   An overly vertical position of the rider's upper body at a particular gait.

bending   Positioning the horse's body so that it is curved to the left or right.

bounces   A series of small fences with no strides between them.

built up in front   This term describes a horse whose forehand is slightly taller than its haunches and/or whose neck attaches high upon its shoulder.

cavalletti   Closely-spaced poles on the ground which are used to regulate the horse's rhythm and length of step.

centerline   An imaginary line extending down the length of the arena and bisecting the ring.

chipping in   The horse adding an extra step at the base of the fence just prior to take-off.

cooler   A wool blanket used to cover a horse on a chilly day. When the cooler is used following work, the horse's sweat passes through the fibers and beads up on the top of the blanket, leaving dry fibers next to the animal's body to keep it warm.

combination   Two or more fences with distances between each pair of fences being 39'5" or less when measured from the base of an obstacle on the landing side to the base of the next obstacle on the take-off side. A "double combination," also known as an "in-and-out," is made up of two fences; a "triple combination" is made up of three obstacles; and a "multiple combination" contains more than three obstacles.

counter canter   A schooling and competition movement in which the horse canters on a turn in one direction while traveling on the lead to the outside of the turn. For example, the horse canters clockwise while traveling on the left lead.

cutting in   A horse leaning its shoulder toward the inside of a turn so that it makes a turn that is tighter than the rider desires.

daisy cutting   The movement of the horse's feet close to the ground as the animal swings its legs forward correctly.

dictate the rhythm   To use the rider's aids to create and maintain a particular tempo of the horse's footfalls.

disobedience The refusal of a horse to jump a fence.

distance The footage between two fences. A "long distance" measures longer than the standard striding between fences, while a "short distance" measures less than standard striding. A long-to-short distance is the combination of the two measurements with the long distance coming first in the line. A short-to-long distance is the combination of the two measurements with the short distance coming first in the line.

diving over a fence A form fault in which the horse stretches its front legs forward as it clears the rails, rather than tucking its legs neatly in front of its chest. This error usually results when a rider places his horse at a take-off spot that is much too far from the fence.

drifting The movement of the horse to the left or right, either while working on the flat or while jumping over a fence.

dropping back The rider allowing the angle of his hip to open too early over a fence so that his buttocks hit the saddle while the horse is still airborne.

dull horse An animal that requires a great deal of pressure from the rider's legs before it reacts with a forward response.

engaged hocks A movement of the horse's hind legs in which the hock joint has a circular motion and stays well underneath the horse for most of the cycle. When a horse "loses engagement," the hock joint has a flat motion causing the joint to be behind the horse much of the time.

equitation division A category of classes at horse shows in which the rider's ability alone is judged. Hunter seat equitation riders compete either over fences or on the flat and are judged on their position and their ability to produce an accurate performance on their horses.

falling out of frame An abrupt change from the horse being balanced and collected to being unbalanced and strung out.

feeling good The horse being full of energy and often wanting to run or buck.

fences Obstacles over which a horse jumps in schooling or competition. They are also referred to as "jumps."

flatwork Exercise of the horse that does not involve jumping fences.

flying change A complete alteration of sequence in the order of the horse's footfalls at the canter, hand-gallop, or gallop without a break in gait. The horse begins on one sequence or "lead" and, in a moment of suspension of all four feet, switches to the other lead.

forehand The horse's front end, including its forelegs, shoulders, neck, and head.

form The style in which a horse jumps a fence. When a horse jumps in "good form," its topline forms a convex curve and the horse is said to be "using itself" over the fence. When the topline is level, the horse is "jumping flat"; and when the topline forms a concave curve, the horse is "jumping inverted."

frame The degree of collection of the horse as determined by the animal's length of body and step, elevation of its forehand, and engagement of its haunches.

gaits The various sequences of foot movements of the horse. The walk is a four-beat gait; the trot is a two-beat gait; the canter and hand-gallop are three-beat gaits; and the gallop is a four-beat gait.

good eye The rider's ability to accurately determine what corrections must be made to the horse's stride in order to reach the correct take-off spot at each fence.

green horse This term loosely refers to any inexperienced horse. Technically, however, a "green horse" is a horse of any age in its first or second year of showing at Regular Member competitions of the AHSA or the Canadian Equestrian Federation in any classes that require horses to jump 3'6" or higher. When shown in a Green section, a horse in its first year of showing must show as a First Year Green horse and a horse in its second year of showing must show as a Second Year Green horse.

ground pole   A jump pole that has been placed on the ground.

gymnastics   Closely-set fences designed to improve a horse's athletic abilities.

half-halt   A technique in which the rider's hands and legs are coordinated so that they cause the horse to collect slightly and move with less weight on its forehand.

hands   An increment of four inches used in measuring horses and ponies. The measurements are taken from the ground to the animal's withers with a special measuring stick during official measuring sessions at AHSA recognized horse shows. In the Junior Hunter Division (for riders under 18 years of age), the horses are often divided into "sections" based on height. Horses that are 16 hands or over are placed in the Large Junior Hunter section; while horses measuring less than 16 hands compete in the Small Junior Hunter section. Hunter Pony sections are also determined by height.

haunches   The horse's hind legs and hips.

herdbound   The horse's desire to stay near other horses, rather than work alone.

home   The in-gate or out-gate of a show arena, which remind the horse of going back to the barn.

hot horse   An animal with an overly sensitive, nervous temperament.

hunter division   A category of classes at horse shows in which the performance of the animal is judged, with scoring based upon the horse's jumping style and way of moving.

impulsion   The force a horse uses as it pushes off the ground each step.

isolated distance   The distance between fences on a two fence line. (See *related distances.*)

jumper division   A category of classes at horse shows in which the animals' faults over fences are scored with a designated number of points for each particular error. In jumper classes, the fences are brightly colored and are high enough to challenge the horses to clear them. The object of most jumper classes is to test the horses' ability to jump the fences without any errors within a given amount of time. In the case of ties, the time taken to complete a course is usually a factor in placement of the animals.

jump off   A round of competition following the initial round in a jumper class.

junior rider   An individual who has not reached his 18th birthday as of December 1st of the current competition year.

knockdown   The lowering of the height of a fence through contact with any part of the horse or rider.

lateral movements   Exercises which promote suppleness of the horse from side to side.

lead   The sequence of the horse's feet at the canter, hand-gallop, or gallop. When traveling on the left lead, the horse's left foreleg is the last leg to strike in the sequence; when traveling on the right lead, the horse's right foreleg is the last to strike.

line   A segment of a course of fences. The term "line" refers to: (1) fences set either on a long side of the arena (an "outside line") or across the diagonal of the arena (an "inside line" or "diagonal line"); or (2) fences set on either a straightaway ("straight line") or a curve ("bending line").

longeing   Exercising a horse in a circle on a long line held by a person at the center of the circle.

Maclay Finals   The Alfred B. Maclay Finals (also known as the ASPCA Finals) is a national equitation championship class that has been held annually at New York's Madison Square Garden for many years. Recently, the site of the competition was changed to The Meadowlands arena in New Jersey.

mechanics of jumping   Standardized procedures that result in the rider's or horse's correct performance over a fence. "Mechanics" refers to learned techniques, as opposed to "feel," which refers to innate ability.

Medal Finals   The AHSA Medal Finals is an annual equitation competition held in Harrisburg, Pennsylvania. This prestigious class determines the AHSA's national equitation champion each year.

numbers   The correct number of strides to be taken between two fences. Usually referred to as "the numbers."

overfacing the horse   Asking the animal to do something it is either emotionally or physically incapable of doing. This usually refers to asking the horse to jump a course that is too complicated or which has fences that are high enough to discourage the horse at its particular level of training.

oxer   A fence that is constructed on two vertical planes. An "ascending oxer" is composed of a slightly lower element on the near side of the oxer than on the far side (usually about a three- to six-inch difference). A "square oxer" consists of a near and a far element that are equal in height.

pace   The speed at which the horse is traveling.

poll   The point directly between the horse's ears.

pony   An animal measuring 14.2 hands or less. To compete in the Large Pony Hunter section, an animal must not exceed 14.2 hands; to compete in the Medium Pony Hunter section, an animal must not exceed 13.2 hands; and to compete in the Small Pony Hunter section, an animal must not exceed 12.2 hands.

popping the shoulder   The horse's shoulder falling to the outside or inside of the uniform curve of a bend.

posting trot   The rhythmic rising and sitting of the rider as the horse performs the trot. The rider should rise when the horse's outside foreleg (toward the rail of the arena) goes forward; he should sit when it moves backward and strikes the ground.

puller   A horse that constantly tugs on the reins.

punishment and reward   Punishment is the application of the rider's natural or artificial aids; reward is the cessation of the rider's aids.

quick horse   An animal that overreacts to the rider's aids by rushing forward.

recognized competitions   All competitions which are under the auspices of the American Horse Shows Association.

related distances   The measurements between fences on a line composed of three or more elements. The way the distance rides between the first two fences will affect the way the distance or distances can be ridden between the remaining fences.

rhythm   The recurring pattern of the horse's footfalls, such as a 3-beat cadence of the footfalls at the canter; or the repeated accent on a particular beat, such as the canter having an accented third beat (dah, dah, *dum*).

rub   The horse touching a fence with its legs while in the air, without lowering the height of the obstacle.

running into the canter   The horse increasing the speed of its trot until it has to canter.

running out at a fence   An error in which a horse avoids jumping an obstacle by veering away from or passing it.

running under a fence   The horse taking short, quick, additional steps just before take-off.

rusher   A horse that anxiously hurries to a fence, rather than waiting for the rider's commands.

school horse   An animal used for training students at a riding academy.

schooling   The horse and rider practicing either on the flat or over fences.

side reins   Longeing equipment made of leather and elastic, which attaches between the horse's bit and girth on both sides of the animal.

standard   The part of a fence which is used to support the poles and, in the case of a "wing standard," to give extra width to the obstacle. The poles, or "rails," rest in cups which are attached to the standard.

stick   A riding whip, crop, or bat.

stride   Each full sequence of the horse's footfalls at the canter, hand-gallop, or gallop. The sequence begins with a hind foot, followed by a diagonal pair of feet striking together (except at the gallop, in which they strike separately). Finally, the remaining forefoot strikes, completing the stride.

strong horse   An animal that pulls hard on the reins, usually in an effort to increase its pace.

strung out   A method of traveling in which the horse's frame is overly long and the animal moves with sloppy motions.

take-off spot   The place at which the horse leaves the ground to jump a fence. When the horse leaves the ground too far from the obstacle, it has left from a "long spot." When the horse leaves the ground too close to the obstacle, it has left from a "short spot" or "deep spot."

tempo   The frequency of the horse's footfalls.

three-point position   The rider's body making contact with the horse at three places: his two legs and his seat.

throwing a horse on the lead   The rider making a horse pick up a particular lead by slinging his upper body in the direction of the desired lead.

timing   The rider's ability to place his horse correctly for take-off at a fence.

topline   The uppermost parts of the horse's body, all the way from the top of its head (poll) to the top of its tail (dock).

transitions   The periods of change between one gait and another. When changing from a slower to a faster gait, the horse performs an "upward transition." When changing from a faster to a slower gait, the animal performs a "downward transition."

triple bar   A fence composed of three planes with gradually ascending heights from the near to the far side.

two-point position   The rider's buttocks raised out of the saddle so that only his two legs make contact with the horse.

under saddle classes   Hunter classes in which the horse competes on the flat only. The animal must be shown at the walk, trot, and canter both directions in the arena. Sometimes the judge will also ask competitors to show at the hand-gallop. The animal is judged on its way of moving and its manners.

upper body   The rider's parts above his buttocks.

USET Finals   The United States Equestrian Team Finals are split into East Coast and West Coast competitions. These equitation finals are intended to encourage young riders capable of successfully showing jumpers. The courses are more difficult than those of regular horsemanship classes and are constructed similar to jumper courses.

verticals   Fences that are built straight up-and-down, on a single plane.

wall up the horse's energy   To restrict a horse's drifting to the outside of a turn through the use of the rider's legs, hands, and weight.

withers   The boney ridge above the horse's shoulders.

with the motion   The correct inclination of the rider's upper body at a particular gait, allowing the rider to remain balanced on his horse while the animal is in motion.

work-off   A test which takes place after the first round of competition. It usually consists of individual testing of a few riders who are being considered for top placings.

X fence   A small obstacle composed of two crossed rails that form the shape of the letter X.

INDEX

Reader's Notes

Reader's Notes

Reader's Notes

Reader's Notes

Reader's Notes